W9-CKI-935

Notre Dame's
Era Of Ara

NOTRE DAME'S
ERA OF ARA

by

Tom Pagna With Bob Best

THE STRODE PUBLISHERS, INC.
HUNTSVILLE, ALABAMA 35802

Copyright 1976 By
Tom Pagna And Bob Best
All Rights In This Book
Reserved Including The Right
To Reproduce This Book Or Parts
Thereof In Any Form—Printed In U.S.A.
Library Of Congress Catalog Number 76-24238
Standard Book Number 87397-104-3

I dedicate this book to the people that caused my life to be full of love, purpose and meaning. It is to my mother Rose and father Tony, to my sister Terry, brothers Sam and Joe, to my wife Shirley and daughters Sandy and Susan. It is to all the remarkable men who played and worked with Ara and of course to Ara and his family.

Tom

To Jo, who showed me how and when to gamble. To my Mom and Dad, who taught me everything else. And mostly to Letty, who gave me the encouragement to attempt this book and pointed me in the right direction along the way.

Bob

Fame is a vapor

Popularity an accident

Riches take wings

Those that cheer you today

Will curse you tomorrow

One thing endures . . . character.

Horace Greeley
(on his deathbed)

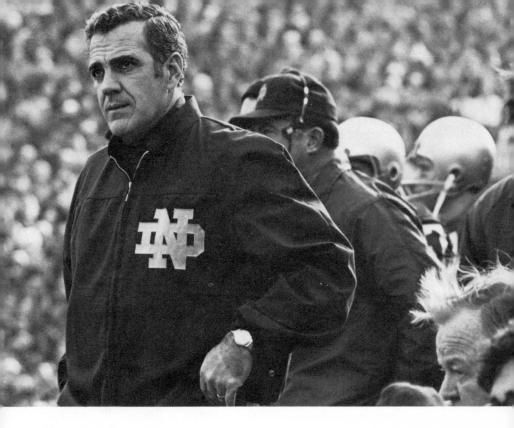

Contents

All Photographs Courtesy Of Notre Dame Sports Information, Cleveland Browns Publicity Department, Northwestern Sports Information, Jim Hunt, Brother Charles McBride, Robert Hammond, Jr., Miami Sports Information, Malcolm W. Emmons, Joe Raymond, Bill Ray (*Life* Magazine), Notre Dame Publication Department, Bill Maguire, Robert P. Hartman, James Drake, Bruce Harlan, Southern Cal Sports Information, Zenon Bidzinski, John Dlugolecki.

Foreword

By Ara Parseghian

Whoever it was that coined the phrase, "Era of Ara," I admit to a feeling of mixed emotions. It does allow a light humorous pride to reflect against a slight embarrassment. In honesty, it is being human enough to enjoy the high praise meant, and more human in realizing that it is not totally deserved.

Aside from the play on words, it does identify a phase of time in collegiate sport and, in particular, football at Notre Dame.

That era represented 11 seasons, over 100 games and slightly more than 500 players and coaches involved in something that will live in our minds and hearts for the rest of our lives.

It would be vain to think that just I or my players and coaches lived this drama, or that only at Notre Dame could this take place. It happens on every practice field and stadium at all levels of athletic competition.

These unique team experiences are part of the lure of athletics for all those who choose to make it such a major part of their lives. We already accept that the interest and adrenalin, the tears and the grief, are not just restricted to the players. Thousands of spectators cheer and despair, follow and report, on behalf of "their team." It is an identity, a link, something to get excited about and pull for, that adds purpose to their lives.

What goes into one player or one team in one season, how the many seasons unfold into a player or coach's career, how the graduated players weave their athletic lives into the fabric of their whole lives, is more than a book. It is a history that each person lives and writes daily.

The moments of splendor, the ruthlessness of injury, the private inner sanctum of one's naked feeling exposed in loss or victory, the *humor* and tragedy of men at play and work can never be captured totally in words or pictures. Books can only hint, recall or reflect upon the most candid events.

Bob Best and Tom Pagna have indeed succeeded in this. When I consider what a monumental task it was to record those years and relate the pulse and feelings of players, their exploits and humilities in a different manner than you can read in any box score or in a scandal sheet expose, I am amazed, totally amazed!

I know that such an endeavor has to be massive. As I read it I was filled with a sense that they had mercy on a scowling, growling tyrant and made him appear a little too bright, saintly, clever and all knowing. Lord forgive them their exaggerations, and then forgive me for enjoying them so much.

Aside from my appearance as a flawless judge of men who makes Machiavellian moves and who is a creative, energetic, organized wizard, they articulate something significant.

Tom Pagna and Bob Best have woven a string of seasons and players into a saga that depicts people as life dictates we live it. They don't resort to high sounding intellectualism or make believe sensationalism. They hold true as reporters but step even higher as storytellers, unfolding a decade of time that witnessed more world and social change than happened in the whole preceding century. Subtle reading of the book brings alive a depth of what transpired not just on the field of sport, but within the greater scope of a nation, a world.

I've watched Tom Pagna grow from boyhood days and as a player on my first 1950 frosh football team at Miami of Ohio. I always kidded Tom about his sensitivity and about being an emotional Italian. It doesn't surprise me that with his rare view-point from the inside he would write such a volume. Off and on he has worked on this manuscript since 1964. Publishing it wasn't his objective at the outset. Frankly, the volumes he originally composed gave every name, statistic, personality trait, injury and highlight in such detail few publishers would undertake such an encyclopedia of information.

Size alone frightened off the most brilliant of editors, not sure a market for idealism would ever exist again.

It was a rare crossing with a loyal Notre Dame graduate who possessed the youth and energy, who was close enough to understand the emotionalism of our program and yet not too close to be able to edit it into candid readability.

Bob Best, an assistant to Roger Valdiserri, Notre Dame's Sports Information chief, is the catalyst editor who formed such a publication.

Obviously, after hours of interviewing sessions and examining the Pagna manuscript, their cooperation has produced the *Era of Ara* book.

I'm sure no writer could be as close to the subject as Tom Pagna. He was instrumental in many major decisions, he knew our inner workings, our total program, and his imagination often contributed to what we did.

Tom passed up many opportunities to move on from Notre Dame to head college coaching positions or to the professional leagues. His reasons for staying were quite simple—he dearly loves Notre Dame and what it stands for. This capacity overshadowed any need to be recognized as "Head Coach." Tom has been invited to speak at nearly every major football clinic, and in the world of college football Tom was already recognized.

Tom Pagna resigned from Notre Dame football shortly after I did. Notre Dame's choice of a new coach other than one of my own staff prompted that action on Tom's part. It saddens me that the coaching profession will lose such a talented man, my first pupil, but there are other ways to score touchdowns. Tom will ride it out with a chuckle and tear, a comic-tragic facet of his personality as he states flippantly, "Just think of the thousands of people who don't know there is a Rockne-Lombardi-Parseghian floating around in one body...mine!"

To Bob Best and to Tom Pagna and to the world of Notre Dame people, to all those who love sport, to the marvelous young men who were a part of that era, to their mothers and fathers, to my family and my own mother and father, I wish to say a heart-felt thank you. The effort alone is a compliment that far exceeds what most men are fortunate enough to receive. That this book is done through the eyes of one of my own coaches and refined by another Notre Dame man who was both a student and later an athletic administrator during my tenure, is another accolade.

Lastly, this book is good and vibrant, it is candid and warm, it says things about people! It speaks of emotion and depth and effort and sacrifice. It breathes life to a word that has served as mortar in my own foundation. It speaks of *loyalty*.

If not another soul enjoys the book, the players, parents, fans, haters and lovers of Notre Dame can at least reflect that it was done as a tribute to all those who lived during those wonderful and exciting days. Truly this book is not the catchy phrase "Era of Ara," it is the "Era of People."

May you always be champions where it counts, in your hearts!

Ara Parseghian

Adversity Elicits Talent

Millions of football fans *lived* the 1975 Orange Bowl Game on New Year's night. There were those who thought Alabama could overcome a 13-3 halftime deficit and capture the National Championship. But many of the spectators were pulling for the underdog, Notre Dame—or more particularly, for its coach, Ara Parseghian. He had become the latest Notre Dame football legend, and this was his last game with the Fighting Irish.

Tucked away from all this speculation in a crowded, humid locker room under the Orange Bowl Stadium stands, Parseghian was preparing his Notre Dame team for the second half with Alabama. Only those of us who had known him for years could read the full emotion in his voice.

"Win this game. LET'S SHOW THEM WHY WE'RE NOTRE DAME AND THE TRADITION WE HAVE," Ara shouted, interrupting the previously subdued tones in the locker room and alerting the players it was time to get ready for action.

"The last time we went out in the second half we got ourselves in trouble," he continued, reminding them of the Southern Cal game a month earlier when they led 24-6 at the half, only to suffer the most embarrassing defeat of his career, 55-24. "This is our chance to redeem ourselves, to go out there and beat...this football team."

His voice grew with each phrase, screaming to capacity his final words of encouragement. The players listened as never before. They knew it would be their last chance to play for him.

13

Ara spoke with inspiration extraordinary even for him.

"This will be the last time I walk out of this locker room at halftime and I WANT THIS WIN. I WANT IT FOR NOTRE DAME. LET'S GET OUT THERE."

As the players headed out of the room I heard Ara holler, "Pagna! Tom, where are you? Is the offensive unit ready?" I quickly assured him we were set, and only then did it begin to dawn on me that this might be the last time I would ever work with Ara. At least I had the chance to spend 25 years learning and growing with him.

The first time I ever saw Ara Raoul Parseghian I knew there was something special about him. I was watching a basketball game and was immediately captivated by this stocky left-hander playing for Miami of Ohio. He could dribble your eyes out and put the ball up with either hand. Everything about him was distinctive—the heavy eyebrows, the piercing stare, the husky physique and especially the name *Ara Parseghian*. That was not like Joe Jones. It had a ring to it. "Ara" was a common name in his father's native Armenia, but I had never known an Ara before. The name stuck, and I began to follow his career.

In 1948, months after I had seen Ara as a basketball star with Miami University, he was a rookie running back with the Cleveland Browns of the newly-formed All-American Football League. Ara left Miami early to play for the Browns, after being named the Redskins' most valuable player the previous season and chosen captain-elect for the upcoming year. But he saw an opportunity to earn financial security for himself and his wife-to-be, Katie, by playing for Cleveland and completing his degree in the off-season.

The Browns were scheduled to play an exhibition game in the Rubber Bowl in Akron, Ohio, my hometown and also Ara's. Paul Brown was the coach, and he had quite a list of players: Otto Graham, Marion Motley, Lou Groza, Dante Lavelli, Max Speedie and Ara Parseghian. Naturally Ara was hot copy in his hometown paper, and when I read he was on the team I had to see that game.

I kept my binoculars on Ara the entire time. He was much shorter than the other players, but he pass-protected like

Ara (seated) with his brother Jerry.

14

nobody I had ever seen. Everything was "pocket passing" in those days, and Otto Graham was the last word in quarterbacking. Occasionally Graham would throw a short pass to Ara. After one reception Ara bulldozed his way for about 15 yards, dragging defenders with him. That was the kind of thing I had hoped to see. I felt confident Ara would have a great career.

But his first year of play was his last complete one. At the start of his second season a hip injury ruined his chance for stardom and affected his life for years. The problem was frayed cartilage at the joint of his hip. Ara was in pain, but the injury didn't show in x-rays. The team doctors informed Paul Brown they could find nothing wrong. That crushed Ara. To any athlete the worst hurt is to know you are injured and have your coaches think you are dogging it.

Further examination bore out his complaint. Through the years the hip continued to bother him, giving him a periodic reminder of the painful experience.

The abrupt ending of his pro career left Ara with little to fall back on. He had some job offers unrelated to sports and was considering them when the athletic director at Miami, John Brickles, contacted him. He invited Ara to earn his master's degree while coaching the freshman football team under head coach Woody Hayes. Ara accepted, and his coaching career was under way. One year later he took over the head job when Hayes went to Ohio State. In five years at Miami, Ara was 39-6-1. He moved to Northwestern in 1956 for a 36-35-1 mark and then to Notre Dame in 1964 where he was 95-17-4 during the 11 years that marked his *era*.

I watched Ara from the vantage point of a player, a subordinate and a friend during most of those years. And I saw him develop. When he was a young man he was robust, had a great sense of humor, an enormous appetite and a feigned ego. Winning came easy for Ara at Miami and allowed him to experiment with innovative coaching.

Little did he realize when he went to Northwestern that the football team was a "have not" in the Big 10. Northwestern did not get as many quality athletes as the other schools in the conference. Ara's charisma helped the first season, but only

Ara was also a leader with the Navy.

16

enough for a 4-4-1 record. That was fantastic compared to the next year when the Wildcats went 0-9.

That effected a major change in Ara's character. It was the first time in his life he had lost. He had been a star in all sports in high school; he was captain and Little All-American in college; he played for a World Championship team in the pros; he had an undefeated season as a freshman coach and then established one of the best won-lost marks in Miami history when he took over the top job. He had never known loss. And it was not just *a* loss, but *0-9*. It made him introspective.

I saw Ara after that season. He looked much thinner, his pants were actually baggy. That cock-of-the-walk personality that could lick the world was toned down. He was not as outgoing and effervescent. He was suffering the deep personal hurt of failure. But he did not give up. He kept questioning himself to discover where he had gone wrong. "Did I organize them? Did they have the right equipment? Were we out-hustled or out-smarted? Did we work hard enough?"

Ara found a quotation then that he kept with him thereafter. "Adversity has the effect of eliciting talent, that under more prosperous circumstances would have lain dormant." The adversity elicited the talent in Ara. It changed him into a more mature, searching, determined coach. His record the next year was 5-4, and he continued to improve from then on.

Still, it wasn't until we moved to Notre Dame that Ara reached his potential. At Northwestern a strong intellectual atmosphere had prevailed, and the players were the only students who felt deeply about athletics. Ara was ecstatic about the enthusiasm the Notre Dame students showed. Two, three, four thousand people would jam the sidelines for our spring drills. That brought out the showman in Ara. He always called for some razzle-dazzle play to end practice and excite the crowd. He reacted to the importance football seemed to play at the school. It gave him a full purpose.

Ara's attitude had become totally positive at Notre Dame. He had come to realize that at Northwestern, no matter how well-prepared or how well-conditioned his teams were, the lack of depth would always be a limiting factor. But in our early staff meetings at Notre Dame he told us, "If we're organized I think we can win five games, because we are much deeper

18

than at Northwestern. If we do a super job we could win seven. And with a little luck we might even go 10-0." He came close to being exactly right.

In 1966 we played the original "Game of the Century" against Michigan State when we were ranked 1-2 in the nation. The outcome of that game echoed through the rest of Ara's coaching days. Every football fan associates that 10-10 tie with Ara, though tying certainly was not his objective. God knows what a competitor he is, and a guy like that would never be satisfied with a stalemate. All anyone has to do is examine the circumstances closely to see that Ara's reasoning was valid.

We had fought hard from a 10-0 deficit to tie the score in the second half. We did it without four of our key starters. With five minutes to go, our place kicker, Joe Azzaro, narrowly missed a field goal that would have put us ahead.

We got the ball back on our own 30-yard line with three minutes left and a 12-mile-per-hour wind blowing into us. Michigan State went into a prevent defense, guarding against any long pass attempts while conceding the short ones. Playing with several substitutes against an outstanding Spartan defense, Ara did not want to do anything foolish. So he called for three straight rushing plays. That left us a yard short of a first down. Ara decided to go for it. Had we failed, MSU would have had the ball 39 yards from a winning score with time to accomplish it. Coley O'Brien, our substitute quarterback, made the first down. Ara then signalled him to pass. He dropped back, and before he could even look for a receiver, Bubba Smith, MSU's great defensive end, smothered him for a loss. With time enough for just one more play and the Spartans waiting for us to try the bomb, Ara told O'Brien to carry the ball. That's the way the game ended.

But because several national sportswriters who had no stake in the game wanted to see wreckless abandon at the finish, they accused Ara of playing for a tie. Enemies of Notre Dame and Ara picked up that chant, and it lingered. It hurt him, but he refused to whine about it. He felt badly for his assistant coaches and the players because he didn't want them belittled. His only comment to us was, "Time will vindicate us." He was right, and it did not take long. The next week we *were* vindicated when we clobbered Southern Cal and were awarded the

Ara (number 70) thought he "still had a lot of playing years left."

National Championship. Still, many of the great decisions Ara made after that were overshadowed by the memory of the Michigan State game.

The aftermath of that great game made him a little leery of the press. He stressed with the players, "When the press walks into this locker room, I don't ever want you to criticize our opponent, I don't want you to alibi, I don't want you to show any emotion or temperament other than those of young gentlemen." He was careful to follow the same rules himself.

In the late sixties during the period of student unrest, Ara was affected by the times. We talked about the situation often in staff meetings. Ara told us, "We may very well be the last bastion of discipline left in the United States. The military doesn't have it the way it used to, schools, churches and families don't have it. Athletics might be the only thing left where a young man, for two hours or so a day, yields himself to

us because he wants to be a part of a team. We tell him to discipline himself so that he loses himself for something bigger—the team. In that way he will actually become a better person."

The times also made Ara more tolerant. He developed a saying, "Give me a reason I can hang my hat on and I'll accept any logical suggestion." Long hair was one of his first big tests. After the period when hair length was just a badge, we had to consider it as a legitimate fashion. "Just because a player's hair sticks out of his helmet and our fans joke that he looks like a girl, that's no reason," Ara said. "I don't like it myself, but I can't defend that logic." So we eventually permitted longer hair. But facial hair could be a hindrance if a player got cut and needed stitches. Ara could hang his hat on that, and moustaches were out.

Ara campaigned from the time we came to Notre Dame for our team to be able to attend postseason bowls. He knew it would allow us to play one more game against a top-ranked team and help us advance in the polls. Notre Dame administrators objected to it because it would stretch the season a month longer and interfere with the players' main objective—an education. A change in the academic calendar weakened that argument, and the University officials began to consider the bowls' monetary rewards. In 1969 the policy was amended, and we accepted an invitation to the Cotton Bowl on New Year's Day in 1970. We returned there the following year and had an opportunity to go to the Gator Bowl the next season.

As usual Ara left it up to the team to make the decision. He never wanted to force a team to go, but he could not understand why players would ever turn down such an opportunity. He should have sensed opposition to this game, though. It was that kind of a team, and the times were full of unrest. We weren't explosive offensively. We had to struggle for every yard in 1971. Because of that we had to work the team harder than usual. The players had their fill of football at the end of the season, so the last thing they wanted was another month of practices. Especially when the game wasn't in one of the four major bowls.

Ara got the team together and outlined the proposal. Ara explained to the players we would practice just once a day and they would have the rest of the time to themselves. He said he would try to get them cars, but in some matters his hands were tied.

The players asked about other rewards. "Do we get spending money? Can I bring a girlfriend? Do I have to go straight home or can I have a plane ticket anywhere? I want to go home for Christmas, so can I fly down and meet you? Do we get our names on our jerseys?" They thought it was the horn of plenty. Ara tried to throw it open to them in a mature fashion, and they took advantage of the situation.

The coaching staff left the room so the players could discuss and then vote on the issue. A few of the seniors spoke out against the bowl. One questioned the promises Ara had made. Another said no matter how the vote turned out he would not play in the game. The vote was close, but such influence was enough to defeat the proposal.

Ara was crushed when he heard what went on. "There'll

come a time when those guys will regret not taking this opportunity," Ara predicted. Many of the players later wrote and apologized to him. But this was the first time he had experienced rebellion from his team.

Ara spent as much time as possible with his family. I have always been impressed with the closeness of that group. That is why one of the most drastic changes in his life took place in 1967 when he discovered that his oldest daughter, Karan, had multiple sclerosis.

Ara and I were showering one day after the other coaches had gone. We were talking about Karan. I could see he was more concerned about her than usual. I shocked him when I asked "How long have you known she had multiple sclerosis?" He looked at me and turned pale. He mumbled, "Just recently," and did not say another thing the rest of the afternoon.

The next morning he called me into his office. He shut the door, walked behind his desk and gave me a look that told me I was in trouble. His ire must have been building all night. "How the hell did you know about Karan?" he hollered. "Karan doesn't even know. My secretary is the only one besides Katie and the doctor and if she told you I'll fire her right now. The doctor isn't even certain it is MS and I don't want Karan to hear it from someone else. We'll have to break it to her, but I've been troubled in my own mind how to do it."

I chose my words carefully in response. "Ara," I began, "stop and think about it. Our lives have been intertwined for a long while now. I feel the same empathy for your family as I do for my own. I babysat for your sister who has MS. Katie's brother died from it. I have a friend who has it so I know the symptoms. I saw Karan dragging her leg and I just assumed she had it."

He apologized for snapping at me. He slumped to his desk, put his head in his hands and fought back the tears as he told me all about it. After countless tests verified the suspicions over the next several months, Karan's doctor broke it to her. Helping her adjust to that reality was the most difficult thing Ara ever had to do.

Like any other obstacle, as soon as he found out what it was, he made up his mind to go out and conquer it. He learned all he could about multiple sclerosis. He talked to doctors, he

23

With the Cleveland Browns.

24

got medical journals—any way he could get information, he got it. Money was the bottom line to all the research. So he threw himself into a money-raising campaign that continues today. He got upset when he found out how much some professional fund-raisers lopped off the top. He knew he could raise money and he did. He even paid many of his expenses to make appearances for MS. God only knows how much he's raised or the time he has spent. But he felt if his efforts improved the lives of all those who suffered from the disease, it would be time well spent.

He developed a special speech. "In football the offensive players drive for 10 yards and make a first down. They might not have scored yet, but they got the first down. So they try to get another one. Along the way they might have a penalty that will set them back. But they just have to make up that yardage. And if they make enough first downs, eventually they'll take the ball over for a touchdown. The same thing is true in the research for a cure to multiple sclerosis. With enough small discoveries, someday scientists might find the answer."

Football provided him a good vehicle for accomplishment of this MS work. But it was at this time that the pressure of his job began to mount. This latest concern, student and team unrest of the late sixties, the constant demands on his time and his desire to win, all started to wear on him.

Resignation had been on Ara's mind after we won the National Championship in 1973. He asked himself where he was going and what more he could accomplish. He always told the players that achieving success is not nearly as difficult as maintaining it, and the same was true in his life. He had been a head coach for 23 years, longer than most men in the field. But to walk away from the Notre Dame job is not easy.

The 1974 season brought further heartaches. Six players were suspended during the summer for violations of dormitory rules, several top players were injured seriously in freak summer accidents, an even larger number were hurt early in fall practice, there were rumors of team dissension, there were more close games than usual and then the disheartening loss to Southern Cal.

Ara privately had made up his mind to resign after we rallied late in the 1974 Navy game to win. He said he felt the pressure during that game more than at any other time.

Contrary to what many people think, the stunning loss to Southern Cal almost altered his plans. Ara considered returning so he could go out a winner. Because his original decision had not been hastily made he admitted to himself that one game should not affect it.

Fortunately we won the Orange Bowl game. Ara never did ask the players to dedicate it to him, but all of them did anyway. The millions of fans who watched with excitement saw Ara beat the number-one ranked team and deprive it of the National Championship. It was the last time Notre Dame would see him overcome adversity.

Tom Pagna and Ara. "Ara," I began, "stop and think about it. Our lives have been intertwined for a long while now."

The Path To Notre Dame

Coaching is the last frontier for a benevolent dictator. It is also a battle of wits and personalities. Woody Hayes and Ara are both strong in these characteristics, and as a result there were periodic clashes between the two men when Ara became the freshman coach under Woody at Miami.

Woody could observe that Ara was a natural leader. As head coach he often benefitted from Ara's innovation. But he liked the idea of teasing Ara at every opportunity. "Hey, Ara, run out and get us a cup of coffee," he would say. Ara was only 27 then but worldly wise. He had been a successful athlete at all levels, a leader in the Navy, and he was married. When Woody taunted him, Ara flamed and let it show. That only made Woody dig all the more.

That set the stage for several disagreements. One of them involved me. I graduated at mid-semester from Springfield Township High School, but the job market was tight in 1950. So I passed the time by playing basketball in an industrial league. On the recommendation of one of my high school coaches, who was a Miami alumnus, Ara came to see one of our games in January. Part of his new job was recruiting, and Akron being his hometown, it was one of his main responsibilities.

After the game he invited me to go out for ice cream. Ara had no idea what a thrill that would be for me. He didn't realize the respect I had for him or how closely I had followed his career. That night I studied him and was captivated by his appearance. His shoulders were wide and fully filled his con-

*Ara, wearing his Cleveland Browns' warm-up jacket, overcame
the obstacles and led his Miami freshman team to a 4-0 record.*

servative blue suit. Every step was marked with confidence. There was an electricity about him. When he talked he hung his head slightly as though it was too heavy for the rest of his body. Then he would look up at an angle. I was even more impressed with him in person than I had been with my previous distant contact. No doubt other young players with dreams of pro ball were, too.

I was amused at the amount of ice cream he could eat. He ordered us the largest sundaes the restaurant served. I barely managed to finish mine. Ara ate a second. He could handle his weight in ice cream.

We started talking about that night's game. Ara stunned me by saying, "I don't know what kind of basketball player you're supposed to be, but I think you're going to be a good football player. Why don't you come to Miami?"

So off I went to Oxford, Ohio, for a visit. After I got there I had to wonder how welcome I really was. Woody looked me over and told Ara I was too small to play football. But Ara insisted I weighed 185 pounds, plenty big enough for a half-back. Woody retorted, "What the hell does he have in his pockets, cement blocks?" They put me on a scale, and I weighed 190.

Despite that scene I had made up my mind to go to Miami. They wanted me to start at mid-semester, but I explained to Ara that would be impossible. My family needed help financially, and I was going to have to work until September. Ara understood and told me he would try to help me through a Miami alumnus.

He got me a job at the Goodyear Tire plant in Akron. By this time some of the schools that had earlier recruited me found out that I hadn't enrolled at Miami, and one in particular tried to get me to reconsider. They offered me clothing and cash allowances that would have appealed to any kid. But I couldn't have done that to Ara. He was the main link in my decision, and I identified with him. I felt we had a lot in common.

I enrolled at Miami in the fall and went out for football along with 24 other guys. Ara was the freshman coach—it was his first team. He had only part-time graduate assistants to help him so he wound up coaching the offense, defense and kicking

30

game himself. Even though it was just a freshman team, Ara took it seriously. It bothered him when he had to make us available to prepare the varsity. At Woody's direction we had to stop what we were doing and work with the upperclassmen.

Despite the obstacles, Ara managed to train us. We had a four-game schedule, and the first was the hardest. There was a lot of emotion behind it. Sid Gillman was the head coach at Cincinnati, but he had been at Miami in that capacity a few years earlier. Ara had played for him. There were deep feelings between Gillman and Hayes. They were both great competitors, and they expected the intensity of the rivalry to filter down to the frosh.

Ara warned us it would be like that. But he asked us to stick together, to play as a team. That request started something that remained with every Ara Parseghian-coached team. He asked us to touch one another and join with him in prayer. "I know we're all not of the same religious persuasion," he said. "I think the Lord's Prayer ought to cover everyone." As we prayed and were reaching out for each other, we felt tremendous unity. It really had an effect as we ran out to the field.

Miraculously we won the game playing in their stadium and with that kind of rivalry. It was only because of our preparation. Even in the short time Ara had to work with us he had us as well prepared as our varsity. He proved that an organized coach can overcome any obstacle. We knew exactly what we had to do. He said all the things we needed to hear before the game and at halftime.

It's funny, I loved Miami and I always will. But whenever I suited up, I was playing for Ara Parseghian, not Miami. And my teammates admitted the same thing. Ara seemed to affect people that way.

After the Cincinnati game Ara was elated. He charged into the locker room proud as he could be. He took time to approach each one of us and congratulate us. I was soaked with sweat like the other players when he came to me and put his forehead near mine. He smiled and said simply, "Thanks."

The next day the local paper had words of praise for Ara and several of our players. It said that Ara merited watching after his performance against the Bearcats. This was the first notice to the public of what I sensed from the start and would

31

become more convinced of as I learned more about him—Ara
Parseghian was something special.

I wasn't able to practice for our third game after separating
my shoulder in our win over Xavier. My mom was coming for
this home game with Ohio University, and I wanted to play. Ara
gave me a test before the game. He grabbed my wrist and told
me to apply pressure. I tried but could not do it. He let me suit
up but said I would not play. Late in the game we were well
ahead, and I begged him to let me in. I reminded him that my
mother was in the stands and this would be her only chance to
see me. He eyed me disgustedly. "I'm sure your mother would
rather look at your back on the bench than see you carried off
the field on a stretcher. You're not ready to play, and I'm not
going to risk it!"

Dayton was our final game, and Ara asked me to go with
him to scout the Flyers against Toledo. He wanted to talk to
the Toledo coach after the game to find out what he could

*Ara's 1955 Miami staff (left to right): Woodrow Wills, John
Pont, Ara, Doc Urich, Paul Shoults, and Bruce Beatty.*

about Dayton. We waited for the stadium to empty. The lights were still on as we slowly headed for the field. We hadn't walked far when all of a sudden Ara kicked hard at the turf. "Son of a bitch," he blurted. "I've still got a lot of good playing years left in me."

I was startled, but I understood his feelings. He had no way of knowing then what his future held. The only thing he knew for sure was that playing football could have made him financially secure and he enjoyed doing it. Now that was behind him—imposed by injury. When he walked onto the Toledo field, all the memories of past stardom seemed to come back. The pain didn't subside until he became a varsity coach. Then he had a position of prestige and destiny, and he was able to compete vicariously through his players.

We went on to beat Dayton, and Ara earned his perfect season. That winter Hayes was offered the head job at Ohio State, known then as the "Graveyard of Coaches." Woody took most of his assistants with him. Ara knew he was in contention for the Miami job, but I'm not so sure he would've worked for Woody again anyway. John Brickles did not hesitate to name Ara the successor. Ara was flattered, and he had every right to be. Before his 28th birthday he was named head coach of a tradition-rich football program after serving only one season as an assistant.

But Ara's first team was a different group. Many of the players had just been to a bowl game, and they weren't especially hungry. He did have a fairly experienced backfield with John Pont at halfback and Boxcar Bailey at fullback. I was the other running back. Bailey was the greatest athlete I've ever seen, but he did present problems.

Ara's first varsity game was against Wichita State. We were to play in Kansas, and when we got to our hotel I noticed a delay as we walked through the lobby to get our room keys. A crowd had gathered around Ara and the hotel manager. Bailey, being one of our top players, had his picture in the paper the day before, and some of the hotel residents told the manager they didn't want him on the same floor with them. We had other blacks on the team, but the hotel guests only knew about Bailey from his publicity. Ara was incensed. "If we can't stay together as a team," he shouted, "then none of us will stay here!" The manager finally gave in.

Boxcar weighed 212 pounds and ran the 100-yard dash in :09.6 in a day when that was unheard of. He was becoming a legend. But sometimes he didn't use his head. The day of the game with Wichita was a good example. As we were warming up, some of the fans started to jeer at Bailey. He was still upset about the incident in the hotel the night before, and he wasn't going to take any more. So he looked up into the stands and flashed them the finger. In those days that wasn't good public relations in a place like Kansas, and the crowd booed him the rest of the day. Ara moved him to defensive end when we got back. He could contain Bailey's temperament more easily on defense.

We finished the season 7-3 and got a bowl invitation which the team voted down. Ara had his problems his first season, but he never lost his sense of humor.

We had a shot putter on our track team named Tom Jones. He could put the shot around 56 feet, and in 1952 the world record was only 60. During our spring practice sessions Ara wanted to have some fun with him. So he had Paul Shoults, his defensive backfield coach at Miami, Northwestern and Notre Dame, make a wooden ball the size of a shot and paint it black.

On the way to practice Ara and Shoults, who had the counterfeit ball concealed, approached Jones, hard at work on his specialty. "Gosh that looks easy," Ara began. "I bet any guy with some muscle and half a brain could throw that farther than you." Naturally that boiled Jones' competitive blood, and he challenged Ara to a match.

Jones went first and heaved a throw well over 50 feet. Shoults ran out to measure it and in the process switched shots. He brought the wooden one back to Ara. "I've never tried this before so the least you can do is give me a couple of warmup throws," said Ara.

Jones agreed, and Ara began fumbling with the shot, shifting it around several different ways in his hands. "Is this the right way to hold it?" he asked slyly. His bait was dropped, and he figured it was time for a toss.

The first one was totally effortless and went about 45 feet. Jones was amazed but not yet worried. Shoults came back, and Ara's next throw was nearly 55 feet. Jones was completely silent. "I think I've got it," Ara added. "This one will count." By now a crowd had gathered, and with absolutely no form at all Ara lunged forward and threw it well over 65 feet. Jones finally caught on to the hoax and broke up with the rest of us.

With one year's experience to his credit, Ara had the confidence to try some innovations his second season at Miami. Ara had a great background to draw from. He had played under Sid Gillman, the master strategist, at Miami. Gillman was one of the first coaches to put planning on a clock basis. He used to measure such things as the time it took the left halfback to get around the right end. From that he would devise strategy. Ara learned the importance of accuracy from Gillman.

Ara had watched one of the best organizers of all time in Paul Brown when he was with the Cleveland Browns. Through him Ara had seen the necessity of fitting the individual parts of a football team into a working whole.

From Woody Hayes Ara had seen the value of hard work and the significance of painstaking repetition. Ara took what he had learned from three of the game's greats and tested it.

By his second varsity year Ara had devised a system of audibilizing at Miami. Nearly every team has this capability today, but in the early 1950s wholesale audibilizing was unheard of for a college squad. The quarterback gave a single number and a double at the line of scrimmage. Sometimes the first one was the key, sometimes the second, and both represented a play. That was all built into the system. Technically we never had to huddle.

A lot of our players moaned when Ara presented it to us, thinking it was too complicated. It was risky. Certainly it is easier to give the players a signal that will hold up from the huddle. Changing the call in a split second at the line of scrimmage does require concentration. But after we got used to it, it was easy.

As formations changed with ends and flankers being split out and backs in motion, Ara had to revise our system. Crowd noise was a factor. Our split receiver might not be able to hear the signal, so instead of a verbal command Ara taught the quarterback to do it visually. Maybe he would scratch his nose or adjust his helmet as he looked over the defense. Later defenses began to conceal their formations, and the relative worth of making a change at the line of scrimmage did not out-weigh the risk. Once again Ara had to update the system.

In the early sixties Ara became conservative. Instead of creating a large repertoire of plays, Ara decided to concentrate on a few basic patterns and execute them to perfection. The opposition might have had an idea of what we would do, but if we did it well enough it would be up to them to try to stop us.

That theory is fine when you have the players to make it go. But in the seasons he didn't, Ara tried everything. Those years we would show hundreds of different formations. We would use quick huddles, slow cadences, draw plays, screens, reverses, double reverses. Ara knew he was playing with a little less strength than the opposition and that he would have to inspire the kids by playing more exciting football.

Ara's guiding principle was always, "Take the personnel, see what they can do best, and let them dictate strategy. Don't start with the strategy first." After a few years he had enough experience to come up with a style of play that suited any per-sonnel.

Ara never stereotyped himself as a coach. During spring ball we would try anything to see if it had worth. One particular play might not work, but it might trigger a related idea that wound up helping. Ara had the courage to experiment, the courage to try things in games and then the courage to admit he was wrong if they didn't work.

Eventually Ara developed a fantastic signalling system. His thinking was, instead of burdening the quarterback with field position, down, distance and wind condition, the coaches could more thoughtfully arrive at a call. This would allow us greater time to make a wiser decision and permit the quarterback to concentrate fully on performance.

The method had to be sophisticated enough so that the opponent could never pick it up. Some coaches thought they had ideas how to break our code, but they didn't. We changed the key from week to week and sometimes from half to half. Every year the system got more sophisticated, and we never wrote it down. We would commit it to memory and go over it with the quarterbacks during the week. We had over 200 plays, formations and assignments we could signal to them. Ara even had one signal that told the quarterback to look to me for the

36

Ara inspects his Miami varsity in action.

37

play, our ace in the hole if we thought our opponents were onto the code.

Ara and I used to laugh about some of the ways we considered signalling. There are only so many parts of the body you can use. Baseball coaches think they have it bad! One year the system was so unique it was merely a matter of where I stood in relation to Ara that tipped the quarterback. People who didn't know what was going on might have thought I was either a nervous wreck or angry with Ara.

Defensively Ara was just as innovative. He came to the conclusion that if offenses could change their strategy at the line of scrimmage after checking the defensive alignment, why not keep that alignment constant. Then within that formation, build in several variations.

Ara wasn't the originator of every play we used. But it's easy for assistant coaches to come up with theories. The head coach has to live or die with them. Ara always did one of three things with ideas. He either accepted them, which was rare; made them better, which was most common; or shot holes in them.

Ara's initial innovations brought him an 8-1 record at Miami in 1952, his second season of head coaching. With the great John Pont gone, Ara called on me to carry the ball much more that year, and I was able to gain over 1,000 yards. My teammates chose me captain for my senior year. That season was a difficult one for me. I was injured seriously in our final game against Cincinnati when I tore a muscle in my thigh.

The leg continued to bother me as I prepared for the most important event of my life. A few days after our last game I married my hometown sweetheart, Shirley Leib. We couldn't afford an exotic honeymoon, so Ara offered us his house in Oxford while he was away. That arrangement was fine until the day after our marriage. My leg began bleeding internally, and Shirley had to get me to the campus infirmary.

Several weeks later the leg was strong enough to walk on. Ara lent me his car to drive to a doctor in nearby Hamilton, Ohio. The doctor x-rayed my leg and discovered calcium deposits. "How do I get rid of them?" I asked him. I had just been drafted by the Cleveland Browns, and I was impatient to get back in shape. The doctor looked at me solemnly and told me never to play football again.

I don't know how I made it back to campus, but I headed straight for Ara's office when I did. I broke down as soon as I started telling him about it. He knew what this kind of news felt like and tried to console me. He told me about an outstanding orthopedic specialist in Cleveland.

Ara arranged an appointment, and the diagnosis wasn't all bad. The doctor told me not to run, jog or do anything faster than walk for six months. At that time he would reexamine my leg.

That spring I graduated and was drafted by the Cleveland Browns. Ara and I stayed in touch after that. I wrote him often and told him about any football prospects I saw or heard about. We also visited occasionally during holidays in Akron. Broken ribs ended my football career, and I was then commissioned in the Air Force for the next three years.

Ara coached at Miami two more seasons and had records of 8-1 and 9-0. Stu Holcomb, the new Northwestern athletic director, was looking for a head coach, and noting Ara's impressive won-lost mark, and the fact that he had recently beaten Indiana while Holcomb was Purdue's head coach, he offered Ara the job.

In 1958 I got out of the service and applied for the head football job at Akron North High School. Through the recommendation of Ara I got the job other guys were standing in line for. But after two seasons there I was ready for a change.

I had made up my mind to quit coaching, go back to work for Goodyear Tire and attend law school at night when I read that the freshman job at Northwestern was open. I thought Ara would call and offer me the position. When he did not I called him. He was distant with me but told me to fly in for an interview.

In the five years since Miami, Ara had changed noticeably. He was not the same radiant figure. He seemed subdued.

When I got to his office he came to the door and greeted me, but it wasn't the warm reception I had been expecting. We shook hands briefly, and Ara took a seat behind the desk. We were strangers. Without any personal dialogue he started asking me a list of formal questions. Then he moved to more specific inquiries. It finally struck me that our relationship was not like it used to be at Miami or when we got together during holidays at home. He was now my prospective employer, and he acted it. He quizzed me further and finally leveled with me.

"Look, Tom. I'd love to be able to hire you. But frankly, my position here is shaky. I only have one more year left on my contract, and our record hasn't been that good. I'd hate to have you move your family all the way out here and have you wind up without a job in a year. And besides that, I couldn't pay you much. Football coaching is an unstable business. But if the job means that much to you, it's yours."

I was elated not only to have the job but to find out why Ara had been so cool toward me and why he hadn't contacted me about the job. I didn't care what his situation was or what the job paid, I wanted it.

So I became the freshman coach, and Ara soon saw I was as much a competitor as a coach as I had been as a player. On Monday nights the varsity reserves scrimmaged my freshmen, always with the same result—a convincing victory for them. After one game I got so upset I said to Ara, "You get your jollies out of kickin' the crap out of me on Mondays, don't you?" I was shouting at him about an inch from his face. He stared at me blankly for a while and then started smiling. He probably thought back to the days he had said similar things to Woody Hayes. Finally he just laughed and replied, "What are you getting so hot about?"

In 1962 I moved up to offensive backfield coach. We played well that season considering the competition. In three successive weeks we had to meet Minnesota, Ohio State and Indiana in a year when they all had great teams. Minnesota had Carl Eller, Milt Sundae and Sandy Stephenson. We beat them in the final moments. I felt that Ara outcoached them because there was no way we should have stayed with them physically.

The next week we went to Ohio State and beat them late in the game, too, after trailing 14-0 in the first quarter. But we pulled it out, and Ara was in ecstasy. Naturally, he loved to beat Woody Hayes, the Ohio State coach he had formerly served under. Even the normal competitor would have felt that way, and Ara was far more than a normal competitor.

At halftime I spotted Woody charging over to the referee to file a complaint. "Mr. Official, Mr. Official," he hollered as I followed close behind to hear what he had to say. "That young man over there is signalling to his quarterback, and that's against the rules." It was, but everyone did it to some degree. Ara was amused when I told him what I had heard.

Matt Snell was a great defensive end for the Buckeyes that year. Ara devised an audible that completely stymied Snell and Woody. When Snell came in tight, our quarterback Tommy Myers was instructed to fake a run and then pass into Snell's vacated flat. The Buckeyes didn't know how to handle it.

After that we came back home and edged Indiana on the last play of the game. We threw a bomb that went for a touchdown.

We were in a great position to challenge for the league title and a Rose Bowl appearance. All we had to do was win one of our last two games. But we lost them both and were criticized. It seemed at Northwestern we always ran out of gas in front of the finish line.

Actually it was simply that injuries caught up with us late in the year. We had some good players but not a lot of them. We had no depth. If anyone got injured our strength was greatly diminished. People didn't realize what a great job Ara did at Northwestern. There were great wins every year but one, and Ara had title contenders. Northwestern fans were not accustomed to that.

I discovered that Ara was just as considerate to me as my boss as he had been when I played for him. Shirley and I lived farther out from campus than Ara. We had one car and two kids, so he insisted I take his car and leave mine home for Shirley. I could swing by on my way in and pick him up. That seemed fantastic, but there, was a hitch. I would have to wake up before dawn to get Ara. His routine included rising at 4:45 a.m. so he could stop at his favorite restaurant, read all the Chicago papers and still get to work by 7:00 a.m. I would slip off in some distant booth and sleep until he came over and tapped me.

I couldn't get to his house early enough. One morning I overslept. A storm that night had knocked out the electricity for several minutes—just enough to delay my alarm. It was still raining the next morning, and I drove like a madman to meet Ara. He was not at his house when I arrived. He had started walking, and I found him three blocks away—soaking wet.

In 1963 Stu Holcomb and Ara began to have differences about a number of issues. The most crucial factor was Holcomb's viewpoint toward coaching. Most athletic directors who have been head coaches like to remember how they did things and think those same techniques will work in any situation. In reality, no one but the current coaches are totally aware of the intrinsic problems of a team. Little comments from Holcomb disturbed Ara. It encouraged him to look around for job openings.

Ara knew that the Notre Dame job was open. We had beaten them four straight years, and Ara decided to contact Father Edmund P. Joyce, Executive Vice President and Chairman of the Faculty Board in Control of Athletics. Ara politely asked to be considered. Father Joyce was always one to keep his eyes open for prospective coaches, and he had followed Ara's progress for several years. He and University President Rev. Theodore M. Hesburgh met secretly with Ara at a south side Chicago motel. The men spoke for hours, and Fr. Hesburgh in particular came away tremendously impressed with Ara.

Coincidentally, letters and phone calls had been coming to Holcomb from the Northwestern alumni praising Ara. The alumni, the fans, the press all loved him. Holcomb got the message and offered him a new five-year contract. Ara left it unsigned on his desk and instead accepted an offer from Notre Dame. Immediately Holcomb named Alex Agase, one of Ara's assistants and best friends, the new Northwestern head coach.

That Sunday, Ara was supposed to be at Notre Dame to meet the press. The *South Bend Tribune* had carried a story the day before stating that Ara would be named Notre Dame's 22nd head coach. But Sunday, instead of posing for pictures in his new role, he read a brief statement to the media, telling them that the announcement of his acceptance had been premature and that he had not yet made a decision.

When I heard that on the radio I was shocked. Ara had agreed that he could bring three assistants with him to Notre Dame, and I was to have been one of them. Later that night he called and asked me to drive over to his house for an explanation. He did not have to explain anything to me, but I was anxious to see him.

At Northwestern.

There were many theories about why Ara changed his mind. The most popular belief was that his being a non-Catholic would cause problems. Ara tried to live the best life he could by a Christian code. He held so many things sacred and treated people with such respect he had to be religious...he just wasn't Catholic.

But when he came to the campus after accepting the head job, as he was heading down Notre Dame Avenue toward the Golden Dome, I suppose a feeling controlled him. "Do I have the right?" he might have wondered. There was a sacred atmosphere about Notre Dame, and Ara probably questioned his right to enter this shrine of Catholicism. A less humble man would not have given this a second thought. Notre Dame is the greatest college football job in the nation, and nearly anyone else would have grabbed at it.

But Ara met with Father Joyce and explained why he could not accept the position. Ara and Father Joyce stayed in close contact the next three days, and Ara eventually changed his mind. In the meantime speculation continued over what had happened. Had Notre Dame and Ara disagreed on the number of assistants he could bring? Had Notre Dame reneged on some promise? Did Notre Dame have second thoughts because Ara wasn't Catholic?

By the time his "era" ended Ara would stand side-by-side with Knute Rockne as Notre Dame's winningest coaches.

And so Ara finally took his place at the top of the college football world—at Notre Dame. Ara didn't show great elation about the decision. He remained concerned about it for several weeks. It wasn't until we were on campus solidly that he got caught up with the place. One night in January we were having staff meetings quite late, trying to familiarize ourselves with the players and the University. We heard a commotion outside our office, and I got up to look. I couldn't believe what I saw. I called to the rest of the group.

There in front of the Rockne Memorial Building were hundreds of students carrying torches. They were singing the famous Notre Dame "Victory March" and chanting, "Ara! Ara! Ara!" Ara turned to us with that faraway look. Maybe he recalled the inscription in his high school yearbook where a close friend predicted, "Some day, you'll be the head coach at Notre Dame!" He turned back to the scene for another moment and then smiled. We knew that he was ready.

1964 -
Cinderella Minus One

As the days went on, Ara's enthusiasm for his new position became even more apparent. But his excitement didn't approach that of the students. Notre Dame was electric from the moment we arrived in January. Athletics was the lifeblood of the all-male student body, and they looked to Ara for a transfusion.

Ara got books on Notre Dame and asked the staff to read them. His assistants were Paul Shoults (defensive backs), Doc Urich (offensive line) and me (offensive backfield) from Northwestern; lone holdover from Hugh Devore's staff, John Murphy (prep team); and Notre Dame alumni John Ray (linebackers), Joe Yonto (defensive line), Dave Hurd (offensive line) and George Sefcik (freshmen). We all familiarized ourselves with the legends—Knute Rockne, George Gipp, the Four Horsemen, Frank Leahy—and were getting caught up in it.

Life was fun for us. We'd get a special thrill just from walking around campus. At Northwestern we were tucked away behind the scenes, but here it seemed as if everyone who saw us knew who we were. Ara was not exactly a national figure at this time, but he had received quite a bit of publicity from Chicago's major papers while at Northwestern. More importantly to the Notre Dame students and players, Ara's teams had beaten the Irish four years in a row. That was all the endorsement he needed.

The torch rallies continued for weeks. The students implored Ara nightly to come out of the Rockne Building and

46

Three Notre Dame legends—Frank Leahy, Moose Krause and Ara Parseghian.

address them. Finally he did, and that is all it took to win them forever. The students listened and loved him. If he talks to you, you're his.

The players found that out the first time he met with them as a group. He never touched any gathering so deeply as he did that day. First he introduced the staff and then had each player get up and give his name, position and hometown. Then Ara took over for the next hour. He had a general idea of what he was going to say, but it wasn't a prepared speech. He captured the totality of what they felt, aspired to and dreamed of. He hit the nerves of every guy in that room. As soon as he began, they sensed that this was the start of something big, and they didn't want to fall behind.

"I've been around football nearly all my life and I think I

know what it takes to win," he opened. "You know what it takes? Let me show you. It's like my fist. When I make a fist it's strong and you can't tear it apart. As long as there's unity, there's strength. We must become so close with the bonds of loyalty and sacrifice, so deep with the conviction of sole purpose, that no one, no group, no thing, can ever tear us apart. If your loyalty begins to fade it becomes a little easier to go out and have a beer, to slack off a little in practice, to listen to those who tell you you should be playing ahead of someone else. If that happens, this fist becomes a limp hand.

"How do we accomplish success? You've got to make a believer out of me that you want to be football players! And I've got to make you believe I am the best capable leader for you! What will I promise you? I'll promise that you'll be the best conditioned football team Notre Dame has ever had. You will have absolutely the best strategy in football. I will constantly study and update our techniques. I will work as hard as I can. I will never criticize any of you in public but I expect the same in return. I will be fair with all of you as will each member of my staff. But I insist you respect us. I don't want you to put any of us on a pedestal. Call us by our first names.

"Notre Dame has a great football tradition. That's probably a big reason you decided to come here. This team had a fire that blazed to the sky in the past. Perhaps the flame has burned low of late, but it is not out. You guys could possibly be the first Notre Dame class ever to graduate without having a winning year. You don't want that and neither do I. Within this room we have the makings of a great football team. We'll have to work. It's not going to be easy. But if you want it badly enough we can do it."

I watched the faces of the players as he spoke, and every eye was riveted on Ara. No one moved after he finished, not that they needed to hear more, but rather that his message had them hypnotized. I listened to their comments when they did leave. This was such an important meeting. It would have a bearing on everything we did in the future, and I was relieved to find out that Ara affected them the same way he had me years ago. "Boy, if we had only had him earlier...." "That guy could get you to knock down a wall...." "I can't wait to get the pads on...."

48

Prep team coach John Murphy, with fullback Joe Kantor, was a valuable holdover from Hugh Devore's staff.

Somehow the thirst that lies dormant in all competitors rose first in the seniors. Guys that were apathetic in former years got the team together shortly after Ara's talk and decided to organize conditioning programs on their own. They broke the squad down by position and started to play basketball, lift weights and run the stadium steps. If someone didn't cooperate, the seniors put him in line. When they reported for spring practice they were in great shape.

By then most of the players had stopped in our offices, and we got to know them as individuals. We learned jokes about them, and from having watched our bloody staff basketball games in the Rockne they knew we were competitors. Ara was pleased with the progress. He admitted that all the contagious enthusiasm made this the most magical time of his life.

But he had not yet seen the full extent of that enthusiasm. At Northwestern we would be surprised to have four or five people show up at practice. Our first day out that spring there must have been four or five thousand fans clogging the field. Ara could not believe it. But it further inspired the players.

Ara wasn't a contact-oriented coach, though he understood the need for it occasionally. We had to find out that spring who our hitters were, so we used some special drills. At the start of practice Ara told the team that no one owned a position. That's all they needed to hear. They went after each other with a ferocity I had never before witnessed, but there were very few injuries. Ara gave the players a chance to work at the positions they wanted, but, as he warned them, if he felt that they were better-suited for another spot he moved them.

Ara was constantly alert for what he called the "skill players." He told us in our staff meetings that we would throw all types of offenses and defenses at them in the spring. He wanted to overwhelm them, expose them, try them and refit them until their abilities would dictate what style of play we were meant for.

One of Ara's first acts was to split up the old "Elephant Backfield." The previous season Notre Dame's running backs consisted of halfbacks Paul Costa, 240 pounds; Jim Snowden, 250 pounds; and fullback Pete Duranko, 235 pounds. Ara moved Duranko to defensive tackle and Snowden to offensive tackle. Both went on to play pro ball thanks to the change.

Costa became a defensive end. Ara made similar alterations at other positions. The players were appointed, moved, lowered, raised, praised and, most of all, taxed.

Through Ara's talks and his obvious organization, pride was developing during our workouts. It was a never-ceasing, growing and living thing. The players seemed to walk a little taller, speak more softly, and to fret over who might be tried at their positions. Ara remarked about the "hunger" he saw on their faces, the overwhelming desire to be a part of a Notre Dame team that would be remembered.

Ara sensed it was important to get their reaction to their new positions. He used to kid Pete Duranko. "Hey, Duranko, how do you like defense?" he would holler.

"I like it, I like it!" Duranko would shout back.

Jack Snow asked to play split end instead of halfback. Ara moved him there, and Snow was in seventh heaven. He was to become one of Notre Dame's greatest receivers. Ken Maglicic, who was always second-best his two previous years, could now see the light of day and drove himself at practice. We employed four separate teams that spring to give everyone an equal chance. That was meaningful to these players. They could see that Ara meant what he had said.

Our most critical search was for a quarterback. We had essentially two choices: Sandy Bonvechio, a 5-10, 185-pound senior; and John Huarte, 6-0, 180, also a senior. Bonvechio had backed up the graduated Frank Budka the year before with Huarte as the third-stringer. But Ara detected promise in Huarte. He saw his quick release and footwork and his ability to be on target. Ara cautioned me in all I undertook with John to make him confident. That was all John really lacked aside from actual game pressure.

Huarte's metamorphosis from a shy individual into an eventual Heisman Trophy winner was a privilege to watch. Ara referred to him as a Basque. Basques are shepherds, and that was a perfect comparison. Like a shepherd, John was quiet, introspective, lonely and reserved. When he first came out in the spring he didn't have enough dominance in his voice to call the signals in the huddle. But each day of performance gave him more confidence. His personality reflected it. He began to play more resolutely and talk with authority. His emergence was a

Ara saw promise in quarterback John Huarte.

lesson in psychology. Ara chuckled when he'd watch John make a great play. "We're going to surprise someone with him," he gloated.

The offensive backfield as it developed was a throwback to the glorious past. Joe Farrell, Bill Wolski and Nick Eddy were all runners, receivers and blockers with the pride of Notre Dame. They were under the direction of an unheralded, constantly improving quarterback. John Huarte, with greater days in front of him, was soon dubbed "Stevie Wonder" by his teammates because he never ceased to amaze them.

We began to realize we didn't have much depth, but we were emerging into a devastating defensive team. The threat from Huarte's arm allowed us the possibility of scoring from anywhere on the field. Scrimmages told us we could move against ourselves. They also told us we could stop ourselves. But with just intrasquad activity we couldn't be certain how good we really were.

Since 1964 was the first season of two-platoon football a healthy rivalry came to life between the offensive and defensive players. In practices we would never let the first offense go against the first defense. Simple logic suggests that to do otherwise is foolish—an injury on either side costs you a starter. But this isolation enabled both units to make mighty claims. "We'd run all over you guys if they'd let us," the offensive players would taunt. "You jerks wouldn't get past the line of scrimmage," was the reply of the defense. When we least expected it, one of the players might come out of the huddle and make up a cheer. Cornerback Nick Rassas was a defensive favorite. "Rassas, Rassas, knock 'em on their asses!" they'd exhort. Then someone on the offense would fire one right back.

Ara gathered the squad together once or twice a week after practice to talk to them. The subject would vary. Academics was a favorite. "You guys can't play a day for Notre Dame, not one play if you're not eligible," he warned. "This is springtime and I want you to get on it. If you're having trouble let me know and we'll get you a tutor. But by God I won't go to bat for you if you're not in class."

One of the few discouraging events of that spring took place the week before the annual Old Timers' Game. Huarte, the new ignition key of our offensive machine, separated the shoulder of his passing arm during our final scrimmage. The prognosis was for surgery. Through his own experience Ara realized that athletic injuries are unique, and he felt that more than local opinion should be sought. He did some research and came up with the names of three orthopedic specialists in Chicago. Huarte was in a South Bend hospital being readied for an operation when Ara called and got him out.

I knew he must have been gravely concerned about Huarte because he gave me a day off practice to drive John to see the doctors. Eventually I figured out why. Ara understood the need for us to build relationships with our players. I was John's coach and I, too, had known the disillusionment of injury. I could empathize with him, and during the course of the ride to and from Chicago John might need some consoling.

After meeting with the first two doctors, John needed all the consolation I could muster. They both told him surgery was a must. He was noticeably depressed. It would almost definitely rule him out for fall football. But he wasn't through yet, and hoped against hope that the third specialist's diagnosis would be different. Unlike any of the doctors who had examined John so far, this third specialist was a former football player. "This looks about like the injury I had when I was playing, John. There's no question in my mind," he said, as we both awaited confirmation of the other diagnoses. "I wouldn't let anyone touch this shoulder. Time is a great healer."

John turned pale and started wheezing like he was going to faint. He reached for a table, and I hurried over to support him. He couldn't believe what he had heard. The verdict stood at three to one, but at least he had hope. I looked him in the eye and grinned. "Come on, baby," I said. "I'm going to buy you the biggest steak in this town."

Our "Basque" really opened up on the ride home. We talked about his decision to come to Notre Dame and what we both had found here, his disappointments of the previous year and all the implications of his shoulder problems.

He had great admiration for Ara. He knew what a deep and sensitive man he was. John felt he owed him a lot. Up till now no one had ever paid much attention to him, but Ara had called him into his office and promised him a fair chance at the quarterback job. That gave him a new outlook—then came the injury. Ara met with John as soon as we returned. He laid it all out for him. "You're an adult and you have heard your alternatives," Ara explained. "Go home with your parents, discuss it and make your decision. We will live with whatever you decide."

Huarte picked the longshot and was advised to avoid all activity for six weeks. After that he started throwing the ball short distances. Receiver Jack Snow lived nearby in California, and they got together daily to work out. Gradually John increased his range, and by the time he came back for fall practice it was as though he had never been hurt. Thanks to Ara's foresight he salvaged a dream for an individual and our whole team.

Though we wouldn't be sure of Huarte's availability for several months, at least now there was a chance. The Old Timers' Game gave us one last opportunity that spring to examine our talent under pressure. This tradition at Notre

Dame brought back some of the illustrious performers of the past, a bit out of shape perhaps, but spirited nonetheless. Our varsity managed to beat them by the slim margin of one touchdown but without our spark plug.

Now that the spring session was over, Ara was able to thoughtfully evaluate his decision to accept the Notre Dame job. He liked the idea of this new challenge, of starting fresh. He had a stature here that was missing at Northwestern and people were cooperative because of it. He was pleased that he ultimately reported to Father Joyce and Moose Krause and not a whole athletic board. He was surprised at the low enrollment at Notre Dame thinking it was a huge school. But he enjoyed the small community atmosphere that gave it a feeling of warmth. The Catholicism issue never came up except in staff meetings when Ara asked John Murphy about past pregame format, which had been to attend mass before the team meal. Ara insisted on retaining that tradition and he, too, went to the masses. He continued to do so until the late sixties, then missed two weeks in a row. When he found out 20 or 30 of the players also stayed away, he got angry. After analyzing it he realized it wasn't right to insist that they go if he was absent. He never missed thereafter.

That summer Ara decided on several changes. He wanted to create a new image for our players. Green was the color of the jerseys worn by some predecessors, but Ara chose to return to Notre Dame's original colors—gold and blue. He did away with all ornamentation on the uniforms. They were lightweight, durable, protective and plain. "Plain is what we want to be," he said. "Our trademark won't be emblems or designs, it will be our great intensity.

"We need a motto," he continued. "Something that ignites great thought. You know, simple and direct, yet powerful." Joe Yonto came up with a paraphrase of the "Victory March."

What Tho The Odds
Be Great or Small
Notre Dame Men
Will Win Over All!

Ara liked it. We had a sign hung at the exit of our locker room.

Those were the last written words our players saw before they took the field.

Ara also planned to give his assistants more responsibility on the practice field that year. With the advent of the two-platoon system he felt a need to get a broader vantage point than he could from field level. So he had a tower built and conducted most practices from above. He'd spot a mistake and yell down to the player or coach about it. Even though it was effective, I know he didn't enjoy it as much as field coaching. I can still picture him up there on a typically windy day doing jumping jacks to keep warm.

It was strictly a functional decision, though many of the players started kidding about "God." He didn't realize it and certainly didn't intend it, but the players were gradually constructing the "pedestal" he spoke against in his opening speech to them. None of them took him up on the offer to call him by his first name. They were forming such deep admiration for him that he could not be just "Ara." It was always "coach" or "sir." That was only natural. Ara radiates an air of greatness! You can't be in his presence more than a few minutes without sensing that. And, ironically, that tower served as a symbol for all of this magnitude.

The players must have spent the summer soul-searching

The players came back in the fall ready to conquer.

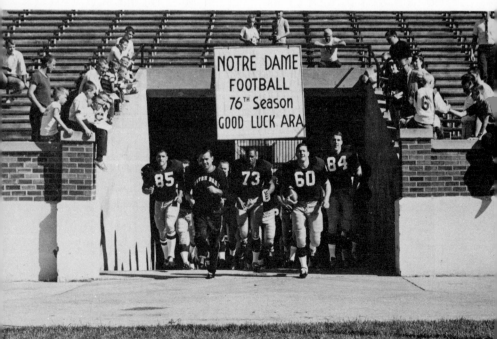

because when they came back in the fall there was only one thing they cared about—getting ready to win. They were all lean and bronzed and anxious to conquer. Ara presented the challenge. "To be great, to achieve, you must pay the price," he explained. "You must earn the right. This is true of everything in life. Everything worthwhile must be bought with sacrifice."

The message was well received. We couldn't ask too much of them. Two-a-day sessions in the fall are as demanding as any physical activity conceivable. The high temperatures and humidity of the midwest in August and early September encourage most people to stay in air-conditioned comfort. But in the heat of the day we drilled the players, in full football equipment, let them shower, eat and cool down for a few hours and then brought them back out for more of the same. After the first few days many of them found it hard to sleep they were so sore. But 8:00 a.m. rolled around quickly, and it was time for another session. Despite their discomfort they responded to Ara's constructive criticism with an humble, "Yes sir, I'll do better next time." And frequently Ara had to call in players who had remained on the field long after practice had ended.

Beyond being a taskmaster and psychologist, Ara befriended the players. He allowed them to laugh when the laugh was there. He clowned, and they clowned when the moment was right.

And the greatest example of that was "Rookie Night." After the completion of two-a-days, as a celebration of that fact, Ara kept the team together following our evening meal. The upperclassmen began yelling for the sophomores, the newcomers to the varsity. Evidently these rookies understood the tradition because they came prepared with skits. Most of them did impersonations of Ara. They'd walk like him, whistle like him, spit like him, yell like him, maybe even swear like him. The assistant coaches and trainers were other targets, but Ara was the favorite. Feeling safety in numbers, most of them got together to do their acts. It was amusing to see these big hulks like Alan Page, Jim Lynch, Don Gmitter and Tom Regner do their routines. They chose to picture Ara around the breakfast table at home with his family. "Okay!" they had him saying. "You'll have 10 seconds for the orange juice. Ready...Drink!

Let's show some enthusiasm over there, Mike. All right, stop! Don't try to sneak an extra sip, Kris!" By now the place was rocking. What a binding moment!

Ara had the sense to capitalize on this at the end of the evening. He pretended to be outraged by all the "insults," but the players knew he was kidding. He told them they had come a long way through spring and fall practice, but there was much work ahead. He asked them to remember pleasureable moments such as this. These, he said, would get them over all the rough spots they might encounter.

Ara knew how to plant the right seeds for pride to grow. In all practice sessions we made a premeditated attempt to boost each player's pride. Ara insisted on it; he knew we couldn't treat all the players alike. Not everyone responds to the same type of coaching. Some we prodded, others we patted on the back.

Every team forms a certain "personality." It grows in direct proportion to pride. Our players that year reflected the same actions and emotions, almost the same attitudes as Ara. Winning attitudes, work attitudes, enthusiasm and perfectionism were all generated by Ara's personality.

The 1964 team learned there was strength in this pride. It was the very thing that would give them an edge and exactly what had been missing before Ara arrived. It was not so much the blocking and tackling he taught them, but rather the inner strength that would catapult mediocrity into greatness. He constantly made them aware of what had to be done, and all of a sudden they became a prideful group of men ready to demolish. That day came on September 26, 1964. It was the day we played at Wisconsin to open the season.

Ara was understandably nervous about this trip. As his first with the Fighting Irish he had no routine to draw from, and he was concerned that everything would go right, including the outcome of the game. Arriving in Madison, we ate a private meal, boarded our buses and headed for a movie as a team. When we returned a throng of well-wishers had jammed our hotel lobby and were crowding into the elevators. They knew the players and coaches by name even though we had yet to play a game. Ara was disturbed by all this, but he would soon see that these Notre Dame fanatics would not be an annoyance

Ara was nervous about the Wisconsin opener.

to the team but an inspiration.

The next morning all of us went to mass. I sat near Dick Arrington, a non-Catholic, who told me he never missed these services. He claimed it gave him great satisfaction. A priest from campus always accompanied the team on the road, and after mass he gave a short talk dedicating the game. Then Jim Carroll performed the legacy of Notre Dame captains. He led us in a litany of prayer to Mary the mother of God. He prayed that we would play our best and spare Wisconsin and ourselves injury. We ate and shortly after left for the stadium.

The locker room scene before the game was as it would always be. The players were nervous and commensurately quiet. They made sure that each part of their equipment, each piece of tape felt comfortable. Many of them were chewing gum a hundred miles an hour and looking up through the barred windows at the arriving crowd. Number 7, John Huarte, was sprawled on the floor close to Number 85, Jack Snow. Their white jerseys with blue numerals sparkled and contrasted against the metallic gold pants. They looked neat, trim and well-conditioned. Meanwhile, Ara was pacing, pulling on his sleeves, patting the players on the tail and giving them a silent gaze that said he needed them and hoped they'd do their best. In the distance we heard their band playing "On Wisconsin." Moments later our band played the "Victory March," and it was reassuring to have them there. You can't be human and not get stirred by that sort of emotion.

When the time was right, Ara got the team together and reminded them of our objectives. This was not really meant to be a pep talk, though his voice rose from excitement. He merely intended to review key thoughts in power-packed phrases. He was like a cheerleader, a father, a priest, a general, a coach—all in one. He told them with clenched fists swinging how fierce he wanted them to be. "Games are not won in the first minute," he began. "They are 60 minutes long and that's what I'm asking you for. Are you going to give me 60 minutes? No matter what happens today there is no adversity we cannot overcome. Keep thinking that. The guy who gets knocked down and lets the opponent run 80 yards but who gets up right away and pursues him may make the tackle that saves the game. You be that guy. Don't wait for someone else to do it. Let's not have a breaking point. The great teams because of pride, coaching and loyalty are never broken, even in losing efforts. With them there is never one specific point in the game where the tide swings to the other team. Let's be like that. We are a good football team. I know it, you know it, now let's let everyone know it! Win, lose or draw, I'll be behind you guys all the way. Now let's hustle out there!''

A capacity crowd greeted us with a mixed reaction as we ran onto the field. We opened the scoring with six seconds remaining in the first quarter. Ken Ivan kicked a 31-yard field goal into the wind. That's the way it stood until late in the second period. Using the same play that had missed by inches earlier in the game, Ara directed Huarte to fake a run and then look for Snow. Snow raced behind the secondary at the Wisconsin 30 and cradled Huarte's perfectly thrown pass. He went

The Old Fieldhouse rocked when the band entered playing the "Victory March."

the rest of the way unobstructed for a 61-yard touchdown play. Wisconsin was the team being fooled by Huarte as Ara had predicted in the spring. Huarte and Snow connected on a few more patterns to put us in position for another Ivan field goal.

We went to the locker room with a 13-0 halftime lead. The defense was playing spectacularly, but a light rain was hampering the offense somewhat. Ara didn't say much, just a few important reminders. "Thirty minutes is not a football game," he said. "We have to go out there and make the Badgers reach their breaking point. Give me 60 minutes."

At the start of the third quarter Ara had reason to think that the team was asleep when he spoke at the half. Wisconsin took the opening kickoff and scored six plays later, highlighted by Hal Brandt's 45-yard pass to Jimmy Jones after our defense nearly dropped him for his third loss in a row. Instead of approaching their own "breaking point" this group of Fighting Irish heeded Ara's words and pushed the Badgers to theirs.

Capitalizing on a bad Wisconsin punt, Huarte hit tight end Phil Sheridan on a 23-yard pass, and reserve fullback Joe Kantor took it in three plays later. We came right back on our next possession and scored on a 50-yard drive. Huarte still had one left for Snow, and with three minutes to play the twosome combined for a 42-yard touchdown pass. The game ended that way, 31-7.

From the appearance of our locker room, you might have thought we had just won the National Championship. But the players' excitement was natural. They had known too well the frustration of defeat, and this new experience was something they wanted to savor. Spring and fall practice left them uncertain of their ability. This game proved it. Ara said things I had heard before as one of his players, but each time he used them he did so with sincerity.

"I've never been more proud of a group of guys in all my life. I want to thank all of you. That's the first time Notre Dame has beaten Wisconsin in the last three tries. One game doesn't make a season but we're on our way. Next week we play Purdue. Are we going to beat them?" The players' response left no doubt.

The reporters came in, and they all wanted to talk to Huarte and Snow. A year ago Huarte wouldn't have been able to handle such attention, but he was developing in more ways than one. I overheard all the players talking to the press. Huarte gave credit to the linemen who in turn praised the backs. The defense pointed to the offense. Everyone complimented some-one else, but no one tried to steal the limelight.

The next day the coaching staff got to the office about 1:00 p.m. to review films of the game and go over the Purdue scouting report John Murphy had drawn up. The players were to jog a mile and meet us for the evening meal. After showing them the film we came back to our offices for more discussions until 10:00 p.m.

The week wouldn't get any easier. Ara wanted us in at 7:00 each morning for our staff meetings. We would work until noon then break for lunch. At 1:00 p.m. we were back together and stayed that way until practice at 3:00 p.m. After the work-outs we always ate with the team, then met with them by positions, but we weren't through yet. It was back to Ara's office until 10:00 p.m. when we could finally go home and remind our families who we were and catch a *few* hours sleep. Such was the dedication Ara required, but none of us objected. In reality we all looked forward to going to work every morning because we enjoyed what we were doing.

Our staff meetings were held in Ara's office in the Rockne Memorial. "The Rock" is an archaic structure built to serve, not impress. However, the memorabilia, highlighted by a life-size bust of Knute Rockne, is eye-catching. Ara had a corner office with a view of the North Quadrangle from one window and St. Mary's Lake from the other. It was spacious though not plush. A long table shot out from the middle of his desk, and that's where we had our discussions.

Monday practice was brief for those who had played Satur-day. Ara pitted those who had not in a scrimmage against the freshmen. But prior to any of this he assembled the team for a ceremony that would become traditional. He congratulated them soundly for their impressive showing and warned them to continue their dedication at practices. He then presented the Wisconsin game ball to Jack Snow. It was his custom to bestow this award on a senior, not necessarily for his performance in that particular game, but for his career contributions. Ara had done this at Miami and Northwestern.

But he added a new twist at Notre Dame. He honored the best performance by a defensive back, linebacker, and lineman, and offensive back and lineman after each game. And as a form of "battle ribbon" he decided to recognize great plays, fumbles and interceptions with blue stars painted on the gold helmets. Beyond incentive this was a mark of accomplishment for men who had known only losing seasons before.

The Purdue game would be our first at Notre Dame, and it was certainly one that none of us would forget. Only after that weekend did we fully understand the essence of Notre Dame.

In our lifetimes none of us had ever witnessed anything like a Notre Dame pep rally in the Old Fieldhouse. We had been told about them, but none of us could imagine what we were to see. The far end of that facility was built for 2,000 spectators back in 1898, but during a rally five to six thousand crazed supporters would cover every inch of the dirt surface. We could have flipped a dime from the balcony where the players sat, and it never would have reached the ground; the people were packed that tightly. The students who wanted a better view climbed up to the building's rafters while others formed pyramids. Atop these shakily-built mountains of flesh climbed the more acrobatic students. When they balanced themselves they would tear away their shirts disclosing the word "IRISH" painted in green on their chests. I got dizzy watching the students shot into the air with blankets slingshot fashion by their accomplices. At the top of their ascent they would scream, "Go Irish!" I had to wonder what would happen if a sudden outbreak of food poisoning ever developed. All the toilet paper on campus was scattered across the Fieldhouse after these rallies. The unsophistication, the absolute abandon, the spontaniety of these people were incredible.

The throng was composed of South Bend residents, weekend visitors, faculty and students. Attendance was mandatory for the students. Anyone staying away was dumped into the lake afterwards by other members of his dormitory. There were not many who needed such a deterrent since nearly every student had at least one friend on the team. There are no fraternities or athletic dorms at Notre Dame, and as a result the players are truly regular members of the student body. They are not a bunch of "big apes" who stand out.

64

The players and coaches were already in their seats when the band entered. It had made a tour of the campus playing all the school songs and rounding up even more followers. When it marched through the side entrance playing the "Victory March" the place nearly exploded. When that had ended, almost as though they had been cued by some mythical director, the crowd clamored in unison, "We want Ara. We want Ara...." Ara took the hint, and when he got to the microphone the noise was beyond belief. They screeched and whistled with such volume and for so long that I was certain they must have done it in regimented shifts. Finally they allowed him some silence, but the most he could get out was a short phrase. "We wanted to bring you a winner," he shouted. Before he could complete his statement they chanted, "You did, you did!" Ara turned to us and laughed. He was astonished that a congregation that large could respond that quickly and forcefully in unison. He fired them up with similar dialogue then called on some of the players. After countless choruses of the "Victory March" the spectacle ended with the Alma Mater.

Ara was astonished that a group that large could respond so quickly in unison.

With every cell of our batteries recharged we headed for our night's lodging—Moreau Seminary on the opposite side of the lake. Ara figured that the crowd coming in for a weekend of merriment would not be conducive to the relaxation the players needed, either in the dorms or in local motels. Ara wanted a place where we could watch a movie, get a good, quiet sleep and have mass the next morning. He did some scouting and came up with Moreau. It was built for 400 seminarians, but attendance then was just 75. There we had our own separate floor, and each player and coach had his own room.

The seminarians loved the idea. We invited them to sit in on the movies, which were usually shoot-'em-up type shows. They were perfect hosts. When we arrived before the Purdue game they wanted to remind us of our objective. They had labeled everything in sight with "Beat Purdue" signs, including the toilet paper in our bathrooms. We had success over the years with this arrangement. Otherwise, chances are Ara would have had us camping around the lake. He would never admit to being superstitious, but he rarely repeated anything involved in a losing effort. He was touched by the scene when he awoke at dawn that next morning. His room faced the campus, and when he looked out the sun was just coming up, reflecting the enlarged splendor of the famed Golden Dome across St. Joseph's Lake. Ara went downstairs and strolled around the shore to collect his thoughts in the peace of the moment.

Taking the field for the first time in Notre Dame Stadium was another experience. When we walked down the steps of the locker room and started the climb up the tunnel to the field the band was still playing the "Star Spangled Banner." That minute of waiting sent all the normal thoughts running through our players' minds. "Will we be good enough? Will I play well? I wonder if my parents are out there? Look how big the guys on the other team are? I hope they didn't notice me looking at them. I wouldn't want them to think I'm scared." Then the signal came for us to go, and the noise was incredible. I found it hard to imagine, but it was even louder than the night before at the pep rally. Now I understood why playing at Notre Dame was so difficult. The players headed for the sideline and tried to contain the emotion that had been building. Ara got us in a circle and shouted some last-minute words of encouragement.

Ara wanted badly to win his Notre Dame home opener against Purdue.

He led us in prayer, and we were ready.

Ara often said that the mark of a great team is its ability to come from behind. With Bob Griese guiding Purdue to a quick 7-0 lead we had a chance to test that tenet. But with Huarte, Snow and Wolski shining on offense and Alan Page, Tom Longo and Kevin Hardy pressuring on defense, we got right back in the game.

The last score in our 34-15 win was Huarte's three-yard pass to defensive back Nick Rassas. It was his first Notre Dame touchdown, and the elated Rassas literally cartwheeled his way to the sideline, tears flowing unashamedly down his boyish face. "Oh God, how I've dreamed of that!" he conceded. Ara had not planned to use Nick on offense, but it was a gesture to reward this young man's spirit. Ara realized that Nick could have been a great running back, but he asked him to sacrifice his personal glory to fulfill a team need on defense.

The Air Force game gave us another chance to come from behind. It was here that Nick Eddy's sophomore immaturity ended. Ara knew of Nick's great potential as a breakaway threat, but there is no breakaway so difficult as the first. Nick found off-tackle daylight to his left, knifed through, and broke to the sideline out-racing all the cadets to give us the lead for the first time. It was the start of a great career, and it ignited us to a 34-7 win.

We returned home immediately but after landing heard some disturbing news. One of the planes carrying student supporters from the Air Force game had been circling the South Bend airport for 45 minutes, trying to get the landing gear down. By the time I got to my house I heard a bulletin reporting that the plane had landed, and that the passengers had exited vibrantly and confidently roaring, "We're number 1! We're number 1!"

Two California teams came to South Bend next, each with an explosive offense threat. UCLA had quarterback Larry Zeno, and Stanford featured nation-leading rusher Ray Handley. The two victories gained us national publicity. *Life* magazine wrote an article on "Huarte-to-Snow," *Sports Illustrated* gave us play and *Time* magazine called us the "team to watch."

The next week in practice we needed a special effort from a little publicized group of players—the preparation team. Ara always went out of his way to encourage these men. They rarely suited up for a game and almost never appeared in one. But they showed up every day at practice like the varsity players and went through the same conditioning with few of the rewards. Ara did his best to repay them when he could, dressing as many as possible and taking some on the road when there were openings. Their importance was never more obvious than the week before the Navy game. Through Ara's instruction they dressed in the same numbers and performed in the style of all our opponents to familiarize the varsity with its competition. Roger Staubach was Navy's Heisman Trophy candidate at quarterback and could scramble, run and pass better than anyone we would face. But thanks largely to the "preps" impersonation of him, our defense shut out Navy while our offense racked up 40 points, highlighted by Eddy's 74-yard touchdown pass from Huarte.

Our defense clung to a 17-14 win the next week over Pittsburgh. It gave us a healthy scare. That set up the match between the second of Notre Dame's three biggest rivals, Michigan State (Purdue and Southern Cal are the others). The University President, Father Theodore Hesburgh, as popular with the students as Ara, made a rare but welcomed appearance at the pep rally.

Father Hesburgh had recently made an announcement that Notre Dame would not alter its policy regarding postseason games. Since it would lengthen the season by six weeks and therefore interfere with the players' academic endeavors, Notre Dame would continue to abstain. But as Father Hesburgh approached the microphone that night, the students hollered, "Go to a bowl. Go to a bowl." He smiled and awaited their quiet. He then began a fantastically conceived tale about a dream he had on the war between the Athenians and the Spartans.

Ara was from Armenian heritage, and that sounds like Athenian. There was no mistaking the Spartans, and the crowd was quick to catch on to his analogy. He told how the smaller and quicker Athenians through the leadership of their great general had outwitted the bulky Spartans. The Athenian dedication, tenacity and spirit overcame all Spartan obstacles. The crowd cheered. Father Hesburgh then paused and asked, "Do you know what this great Athenian general told his loyal troops

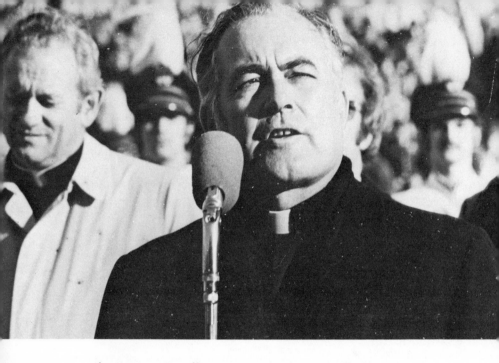

An internationally renowned educator, Father Theodore Hesburgh was nonetheless interested in the football program.

after this great victory?" Once again he paused, and before he could continue a voice from out of the silence shouted, "Yeah, go to a bowl!" The other fans then took up the chant. Father Hesburgh seemed stunned at first, but bowing to the humor of the remark said only, "Touche!" To this day no one knows what the Athenian general said. But Father Hesburgh's dream came true as we beat the Spartans, 34-7.

We whipped Iowa in 10 degree temperatures to close out our home season. The game cost us a valuable performer, though, in fullback Joe Farrell. His loss was a sad one. Joe had been operated on often during his career, and knee surgery was necessary again. He had been the embodiment of team spirit. His quiet, willing attitude was a great steadying force. We'd miss his contributions, but that was a secondary thought. After the game Farrell lay on the training table and cried. His lifelong ambition was to come to Notre Dame and play on a winner. We had tried to recruit him while at Northwestern, but he told us if Notre Dame wanted him that is where he would go. His tears were not from physical anguish but from a shattered dream, a dream he had clung to for a long time. "I'm not in pain," he stuttered. "I just hate to miss the end of this thing."

Ara saw Farrell's agony, and he hoped that wouldn't be widespread just one week later. None of us had any notion at the start of the season that we could challenge for the National Championship. We wouldn't let ourselves even think that way. Ara never went into a game he didn't believe he could win, but he constantly preached, "There's no game more important than the one you're playing today. What's the good of thinking about next week's game if we lose today?" And with that philosophy we never looked ahead. But now we could see where we were, and that was in the enviable position of being one win away from a national title. We had to beat Southern Cal.

The weather continued to be bitterly cold in South Bend. Ara knew we would play in a drastically different environment so he took us to hot and humid Phoenix, Arizona, a day early for acclimation.

The pregame emotion really was not any different for this game. We had played nine times by now, and we knew what we had to do. It was ironic, but I vividly remember glancing at the blackboard just before I went out on the field. Someone had written "60 Minutes" in big letters. That's what Ara had always asked them for. It would be such a critical factor in this game.

We got a break early in the first quarter. Don Gmitter recovered a fumble at the USC 46. Huarte hit Sheridan and Eddy on two long passes and moved us to the eight. The Trojans held us, and Ara called on Ken Ivan to kick a field goal.

We came right back on our next possession for a 51-yard scoring drive in 12 plays. Huarte spotted Snow open in the end zone and lofted the ball to him for the score.

Our amazing offense continued to click and put us up 17-0 at halftime. Huarte drove us 72 yards in 11 plays with Bill Wolski carrying it over from the five.

The first half had been pretty much ours as the defense, although not completely stopping USC's sensational halfback Mike Garrett, had at least prevented him and his friends from scoring. Ara pleaded with the team not to let up. "60 Minutes," he harped. "That's what a game is!"

We found out quickly that the Trojans were a long way from their breaking point. They started the second half by driving 68 yards in nine plays. Garrett accounted for 36 yards and carried over from the one for the score.

We had two excellent scoring threats but couldn't make them count. After moving from our own 19 to the USC 9, Huarte and Wolski got crossed on a pitchout attempt and Southern Cal recovered. But later and more significantly, with the ball on USC's six-inch line, second and goal, Joe Kantor plunged over left guard for an apparent score. The six points were denied us as we were called for holding. That moved the ball to the 16-yard line and in three attempts we couldn't push it across. That, quite possibly, could have been the breaking point of the 1964 season.

The Trojans, now fortified, took to the air and connected with regularity. With 5:09 to play in the fourth quarter, quarterback Craig Fertig threw complete to Fred Hill in the end zone for a 23-yard score.

Leading just 17-13 our offense tried to mount a drive. When we failed, Jack Snow punted to Garrett at the USC 23 with no return. However, we were again called for holding, and this time Snow could only get it to the USC 46 and Garrett ran it back to our 40. The penalty actually cost us 37 yards.

Fertig quickly hit Hill on a 23-yard pass, moving the

Nick Eddy couldn't evade the Trojans in the second half.

Trojans to our 17. We held them to two yards in t eir next three attempts. On third down Alan Page broke through to deck Fertig, jarring the ball loose for an apparent fumble. The officials ruled it an *incomplete* pass. With fourth and eight from the 15, Fertig dropped back to pass, and linebacker Ken Maglicic came within inches of tackling him. But Fertig released the ball toward flanker Rod Sherman. Defensive back Tony Carey was there, but in the scramble he fell, Sherman snagged the pass and streaked into the end zone. With just 1:33 to play, Southern Cal went ahead, 20-17. We tried desperation passes at the end, but it was no use.

One minute and 33 seconds! That's how close Ara had come from taking a 2-7 team to 10-0 and the National Championship. Privately we considered ourselves the National Champions anyway, but that was little consolation. We questioned three key penalties when they were called, and after studying the film we were certain they hadn't occurred. The most crucial one was the holding call against Bob Meeker on Kantor's touchdown run. Oddly, USC had a linebacker, not a lineman across from him on that play. Seconds before Meeker made any contact, and it wasn't holding, Kantor had crossed the goal line. Any infraction called after-the-fact has to be marked off on the next play. Ara never vocalized it, but he felt it was a terrible call.

The walk from that field to our locker room seemed endless. It was a blurry tunnel we walked through in the Memorial Coliseum, one full of tears. Quietly the players suffered the torture of total despair. The death of someone dear is the only comparable feeling.

And our locker room was the funeral parlor in that analogy. Joe Kantor, who had scored what would have been the winning touchdown, sat dazed and misty eyed. John Huarte and Bill Wolski, who failed to connect on a pitchout, both shouldered the responsibility for the loss. Bob Meeker was inconsolable. I didn't think he'd ever stop crying. He reasoned that his penalty cost us the game. I worried that Tony Carey might have a nervous breakdown. He felt he should have batted Fertig's pass down and prevented the final score. He was hysterical with grief. It went on and on, and each player who had participated blamed himself. It was the most humble moment we would ever know.

We had come so close, fought so hard, died so violently!
(Photo by Bill Ray, *Life* magazine)

As Fertig was completing his pass to Sherman I noticed a photographer angling onto the field close to Ara. It's strange what you think about at a time like that, but I tried to get in his line to shield Ara. I didn't want the naked image of a crumbled man exposed in an unfair moment. I failed in my attempt, and the picture appeared in *Life* magazine. It captured the heartbreak in his distorted mouth lines, his wrinkled brow and distraught arms grasping his head. His anguished body twisted, trying futilely to encourage an interception. The picture said it all. Why had we come so close, fought so hard, died so violently?

But Ara, in his perpetual driving fashion, composed himself rapidly. He entered our locker room and asked everyone to kneel. "Dear God," he said softly, "give us the strength in our moment of despair to understand and accept that which we have undergone." He stopped for a few seconds and then began again.

"I want all of you to realize one thing. What we do here and now will follow us for many years. There are thousands of things we could say. There are the officials and the calls we could blame. But when we won this year, we won as Notre Dame men—fair, hard and with humility. To be less than that at this moment, to cry foul, to alibi, would undo much that this season has done. For the next 10 minutes no one will be allowed in here. If you've got to scream, if you want to cry, swear or punch a locker, do it now. I can understand all those sentiments. But after we open the doors I want all of you to hold your tongues, to lift your heads high and in the face of defeat be Notre Dame men. I've never been associated with a greater bunch than you guys. No one will ever forget the achievements you made this year."

All this took a helluva presence of mind. With all his success Ara had never come anywhere close to a national collegiate championship. All this was new for him, too. But he fought through his dejection and thought of the proper thing to do in that situation, namely accept defeat graciously.

The writers came in and asked him all the painful questions. He answered them shortly but politely and gave praise to the Trojans. "USC was the best team we played this year," he told them. "I'm not just saying that because they beat us. They moved the ball well on us, both on the ground and in the air. Fertig hit key passes with defenders right on the receivers' backs. There were the normal number of penalties, but the play was apparently rough and I would not care to comment on that until I have a chance to see the game films. The worst penalty a team can suffer is a 15-yarder from the one-foot line that costs you a touchdown."

After they had gone, Ara seated himself on the corner of a travel trunk and stared out randomly for minutes. Perhaps his eyes did not see the gnarled balls of muddy tape, or the orange peel remains from our halftime energizer. Maybe he counted the sweaty towels strewn throughout the room. I doubt he noticed any of it. He was lost in disconsolate thought that only he could know or had a right to know.

We were scheduled to be in California an extra two days as a season-ending reward to the players. None of us considered it a bonus. Ara stayed in his room the entire time, emerging only to buy the papers and grab some coffee. He just didn't have the energy or desire to do anything.

The team had been invited to Disneyland, and the magic of Walt Disney's fertile imagination at least helped our young men thaw. The following day we toured Universal Studio and watched Gregory Peck film a scene. Afterwards he came over and seemed as excited to meet us as we were to see him.

Still, all any of us really wanted to do was get home. On the plane Ara was able to talk about the season. He had to admit it was a successful year despite the unpleasant ending. During the flight some of the seniors came to him and thanked him for the year. They had heard the same "We're going to win" phrases from other coaches in the past. But the difference was that Ara made them see *how* they could win because of all the elements that went into it—organization, strategy, conditioning and, mostly, morale. He had brought them farther than any of them imagined possible, from 2-7 to third in the nation in just one year. Their thanks gratified Ara.

When we landed that night we were asked to remain on the plane for a few minutes. We had no way of knowing what was planned, but the short delay made final arrangements possible. The route of the buses that would take us to campus had been publicized, and all along the way people had their porch lights on and were standing out applauding us in nine-degree temperatures. We expected to go to the main entrance of the campus as usual, but instead the buses headed straight for the Old Fieldhouse.

Assembled there was a larger crowd than for any rally. The overflow was forced to stand outside in the snow. As soon as the fans spotted us they erupted. We were escorted to our normal place in the balcony with the cheers still building. This lasted for at least 20 minutes. There were no speeches planned, but Ara made an attempt at one. He fought to get the words out as he considered the tribute these people were paying us. "We wanted to bring you back the National Championship...," he stammered. "You did, you did, you did...," they roared. He couldn't continue.

That had to be the most stirring event any of us ever lived through. I looked around at the team and the other coaches. None of us, including Ara, could hold back the tears. We were all that touched and hurt that we couldn't have pulled it off. The band played the "Victory March" and the Alma Mater, and the gathering broke up.

The next week we received word that John Huarte had won the Heisman Trophy. Huarte was ecstatic. We had watched him grow into that honor. He was a young, humble athlete, unassuming-looking with his slight frame. Everyone came to admire him because the rapid transition in his life hadn't changed him. All he needed was someone like Ara to show confidence in him, and he was set. He had fought his way up all along, and he now knew how to live with success. So off he went to New York to accept the award as the top collegiate player of the year—two weeks before he was to receive his first Notre Dame monogram.

Gradually the sting of Southern Cal wore off. We went out recruiting and resumed our staff meetings to discuss future strategy. Just because the season was over didn't mean we could relax. Ara had come close to the top, and a competitor such as he would never settle for close. That could only mean we would all work even harder from now on.

1965-
Thou Shalt Not Pass

Only now that I can look back 12 years removed from its occurrence do I really appreciate the accomplishment of that 1964 team. I suppose it could have happened at another school, a place where football tradition had once been grand and glorious and then diminished for one reason or another. But certainly regeneration of those programs wouldn't command as much national attention as it did at Notre Dame. And I doubt it would have as much impact if it were to happen today at Notre Dame. People have been exposed to too many Cinderella stories, too many last-second wins to be intrigued by them any more. No, the success of the 1964 team was perfectly designed.

However, in curing the ills of the Notre Dame football program and being named co-coach of the year, Ara did create a monster. The millions of Fighting Irish fans around the nation now expected miracles every year. After all, Ara took a 2-7 team to 9-1, so it should be a snap to go from 9-1 to 10-0. Unfortunately, it was not that easy.

One of the most common misconceptions about Notre Dame football is that recruiting is a matter of sitting back and waiting for all the "blue chip" prospects in the nation to knock on the door. Ara had a similar notion when he came here. We all assumed it would be our easiest chore, but that was far from true.

First, Notre Dame did not and will never get all or even most of the athletes it sets out after. The common thought is that all the Catholic priests and nuns in the country send their best players to Notre Dame, and if one quarterback gets hurt the coach just opens another "can of quarterbacks." But a recruit's academic ability instead of religious preference is the real clue to the school's program. At this leading academic institution many of the outstanding players can't meet admission requirements. As a school with integrity, players will never be induced to attend with anything more than a four-year scholarship. And with no dominant state loyalty to call on like most of the other traditional college powers—Oklahoma, Alabama, Michigan, Ohio State, Nebraska, Texas, Louisiana State, Tennessee—Notre Dame is forced to recruit nationwide.

That was one of our biggest problems. While other coaches had the luxury of being able to spend hours in certain schools, the best we could do was drop by for an occasional visit or more often just make a phone call. If you can visit six schools in a day, you can call at least 20. But since we were not always around trading football strategy with the high school coaches or taking them to lunch, we were often labeled "snobs."

The national scope of our recruiting was even more of a burden for Ara. While he visited recruits as the coach at Miami and Northwestern, he never once did it after we came to Notre Dame, and with good reason. "If I go see your top recruits in Pennsylvania, and yours in California and yours in Texas, I'm going to be involved in nearly 100 recruiting trips every year," he explained to us. "Other staffs can centralize their efforts, but we can't. If I go to one of our recruits, in all fairness I have to go to them all. I will never have any family life that way.

"Besides, I'm not convinced there is a need to make personal appearances to all the players. Maybe it will turn some against us. If they're playing games to see how many head coaches they can get into their living rooms, I'm not sure we want those players anyway. The right kind of young men will find their way here and not by us doing anything special. Some we will have to sell on Notre Dame, but we won't buy them. You bring me all the players you're interested in and I'll talk to them. If it will help, I'll call them and their parents."

When the young men visited, we didn't act unnaturally; we didn't get Miss Universe to greet them at the airport; they did not stay in the plushest hotel in town or eat gourmet cooking. Those who might have been waiting for the "Godfather" to shower them with gifts were disappointed when no one "made them an offer they couldn't refuse." Ara insisted that we let them make their decision based on true expectations. They saw the rooms, ate the food, met the people and felt the atmosphere that is Notre Dame. No facades.

Ara placed great emphasis on a personal interview with each recruit. If the player was lively and dynamic, wasn't in awe but had a certain humility, had the necessary physical station and a respect for family—these things impressed him. Those who came in brazenly, bragging about how many schools were after them and doing everything short of putting their feet on his desk, had no chance with Ara.

Before each interview we met briefly with Ara to discuss the player and go over his statistics and other pertinent details. Stats didn't mean much to Ara. He had to be impressed with him as a person. Many is the time a player would tell us something with authority only to melt in Ara's presence. "How fast do you run?" I once asked a recruit. "I ran a 9.8 100 in a track meet," he answered. Ara put the same question to him with the following response: "Well, I think I can run the 100 somewhere over 10 seconds but I've really never been timed exactly." That's why all the assistants sweated until hearing the outcome of the interviews.

Ara has a great sense for talent, and there are many factors to consider. A player may have been outstanding in high school, but perhaps getting a free ride to college was his goal and with that met maybe his desire is gone. Through Ara's detailed interviewing session, he subtly asked all the right questions. When it was over, he had a good feel for the total person. He took that into consideration with the recommendation of the high school coach, the player's grades and what kind of a league he played in. He alone made the final decision, but if the assistants differed and fought like hell for a kid, Ara usually agreed.

Before making contact with recruits Ara plotted personnel needs. While he tried to fill weak spots, he told us never to overlook a good athlete because we had depth at his position. Skilled athletes are adaptable. All Monday and Friday mornings during the recruiting period were set aside for meetings on that subject. We gave Ara a report on whom we had coming in the next weekend, whom we had seen the past week, and what

Ara paid close attention to the well-being of his players (shown with Tom Talaga).

phone contact had been made with other hopefuls.

Ara's underlying doctrine in all our recruiting activities was that no violation is necessary and nothing can be gained from one. Ara didn't want the kind of kid who had to be bought, though we played against some. He felt there were enough who would come because they believed in Notre Dame and the academic value of the institution. Not only that, but he had a deep feeling about doing anything that might shame the University.

Such was our recruiting dilemma. The 33 players we ended up with weren't always the best in the country, they may have had their faults, but generally they were respectful young men with a sense of direction. And they were always selected scrupulously. This, however, sometimes left our cupboard bare, and in 1965 we didn't have that "can of quarterbacks" to open.

The one-year pass-catch routine of John Huarte to Jack

Snow had ended through graduation, and we could not replace their skills at those positions. We did have a good running and blocking group, and we were solid defensively. The *thirst* of the year before was not lacking, and the leadership of captain Phil Sheridan was excellent. It could have been another championship contender, but we just couldn't pass well enough.

Ara's initial choice was among three sophomores—Tom Schoen, John Pergine and Dan Koenings. Schoen was the quickest, but his passing was erratic. Pergine was the largest, but though he had a strong arm he was inaccurate. Koenings was the best passer but didn't have the agility of the other two. We waited for one to take control, and it didn't happen. So Ara called on Bill Zloch, a senior who had been listed at quarterback when we came here.

Bill was a high school quarterback and really hadn't played there in college. He was hurt as a freshman and was well down the list his sophomore year. Ara had moved him behind Jack Snow at split end in 1964, so Bill was certainly rusty at his new position.

By his own admission Bill was not a good passer. He was a heady player who understood our offensive concepts. He could direct the team, take the snap from center, fake and run well. "Gator," as his teammates referred to the Ft. Lauderdale native, was a tremendous leader. The team knew this and responded positively. He turned out to be the best guy for the job.

As is always the case when a decision isn't clear-cut, we had our share of suggestions from the regular visitors to practice. Often the "volunteer coaches" were Holy Cross priests. They'd stop Ara on the way to the locker room with some kindly remark. "Things are really shaping up out there, Coach, but don't you think Tommy Schoen is starting to look better?" they might say. Even though Ara and the other coaches probably added some *new* words to their vocabulary during practice, the clergy continued to be our most loyal supporters over the years.

The priests not only followed our games and practices but were also frequent visitors to our offices. Doc Urich, Paul Shoults and I were having a discussion one afternoon when in popped a fast-talking clergyman who had surely lived through decades of Notre Dame football. "Oh, my boys, here you are

82

hard at work," he interrupted. "We're so happy to have you here doing your best for Our Lady. Kneel down now and I'll give you my blessing." As the only Catholic in the group I knelt right away while Doc and Paul, puzzled by all this, followed my lead. "And may the grace of God be with you, in the name of the Father, the Son and the Holy Ghost." The priest mumbled some other words of encouragement and departed. As he did, Doc grabbed me by the shoulders and with a terrible look of distress implored, "Tom, what the hell did he do? Did he baptize us? I don't want to turn Catholic!"

We would need all the prayers the clergy had time for. Ara pointed out our strengths to the squad when they returned that fall. He glossed over the weaknesses. "We'll be a different styled team than last year," he explained. "We'll play possession and position, relying on our kicking, defense and ground attack. We're Notre Dame. We can't win on past performances. We're coming along but we've got a long way to go. I see some things that please me but we've got to eliminate mistakes and penalties."

Ara warned us to be on the lookout for the players' tendency to foul. When we played Notre Dame while at Northwestern, the Irish were a rowdy bunch. They averaged close to 150 yards a game in penalties. That's 15 first downs. Yardage is too valuable to throw away like that. So Ara coached against it every way he knew how. He made our offensive cadence so simple that if we jumped, a defensive player must have drawn us. Clipping was probably our most frequent offense, but Ara cut the penalty average to about 35-40 yards a game. He detested penalties, and he screamed at those who committed them, "You're not worth 15 yards to this football team!"

Mindful of our deficiencies we flew to the University of California at Berkeley for our opening game. Zloch made us wonder what we had been worried about as he launched a 24-yard touchdown pass to Nick Eddy. But Ara realized that all our opponents wouldn't be fooled as easily. In reality we beat California 48-6 with those elements Ara had forecast to the team—defense and ball control. Nick Rassas intercepted two passes and returned a punt 65 yards for a touchdown. The backfield of Larry Conjar, Eddy and Bill Wolski ground out 381 rushing yards.

This was a talented rushing unit formed of diverse personalities. Larry Conjar took over at fullback for the graduated Joe Farrell and Joe Kantor. He had the build of a Greek god, 10.2 speed and a quick start. Before 1965 he was missing only one thing—desire. Football just had not been that important to him his first two years. It could have been a combination of factors. Maybe he hadn't made the transition to college ball, maybe the role of playing behind Farrell and Kantor stripped him of incentive. Whatever the reason, we put him with the prep team as a sophomore, and it was there, under coach John Murphy, that he became a football player. John made men out of a lot of kids during his time. And when he spotted a guy who was a player, he brought it to Ara's attention. Such was the case with

The 1965 backfield of Bill Zloch QB, Bill Wolski HB, Larry Conjar FB, and Nick Eddy HB.

Larry.

Ara advised me to watch Larry closely. It didn't take long that year to notice the change in him. He didn't have great lateral mobility and he wasn't much of a receiver, but his thrust made him a tremendous straight-ahead runner and he became our best blocking back. We tried to dump him short passes because once he had the ball in the open he was tough to bring down. In grading the films Larry played near-perfect games every time out. Ara respected him for his development.

After watching Nick Eddy work out shortly after we came to Notre Dame, I told Ara we had a running back like we had never known before. I had seen Nick catch the ball, then jiggle, hop, skip, pivot and side-step the way Gale Sayers did in his prime. Eddy had all the elements—great hands, speed, movement and the quickness of a cat. But Ara wanted to pin me down. "Are you willing to make a black box statement that he'll be a superstar?" he asked me. A black box statement was written and circled on the blackboard in our meeting room. No one ever erased it, and if it didn't materialize Ara would razz you in staff meetings. I agreed to make that one about Eddy.

And I was right as early as his sophomore season. Nick played an important role in our success that year, but he was never as effective thereafter for several reasons. His early accomplishments built expectations so high he could never live up to them. They also alerted opposing defenses to key on him. Beyond that were personal factors. Nick fell in love, got married and had a child after his sophomore year. There was another addition to the family his senior year, and his attention was naturally divided. His life was further complicated by the AFL-NFL bidding war. He was one player both leagues were after, and his worth ranged upward to $500,000. He tried to push that to the back of his mind his senior year, but he realized that one little injury could cost him, his wife, and his kids a comfortable future.

Never having experienced wealth, Nick dreamed of being a good provider for his family. His parents had troubles when he was growing up, and he came to Notre Dame with few possessions. During his freshman year he took part in a dormitory prank. He was an honest kid, and when asked about his involvement he confessed and was suspended for a year.

Nick Eddy—expectations were too high for him to meet.

Ara understood the pressures attacking Nick. He could see conflicts in his life, and he watched him do his best to handle them and contribute to our team. Nick scored points for us throughout his career that we wouldn't have produced without him. Even if he hadn't, Ara knew he had done enough for us in 1964 to pay his dues at Notre Dame.

While Eddy was a ballet dancer on the field, our other half-back, Bill Wolski, was a longshoreman. The team called him "Muscle Face" because of his strength. He had the kind of attitude that would have made him perfect to star with John Wayne in a war movie. Anything we ever asked him was carried out without a gripe. Bill was in no way a fancy runner. He would power his way along, dragging defenders with him. With Conjar he gave us a great blocking combination.

But it was not our offense that concerned Ara the week before the Purdue game; it was Purdue's great passer, Bob Griese. The current-day pro star had impressed Ara in our victory the year before, and we just didn't have anyone on our prep team who could prepare our defense for his threats.

Griese played better against us than we ever dreamed possible. His afternoon's work included completing 19 of 22 pass attempts for 283 yards, three touchdown passes, 39 rushing yards and one point after. Down 21-18 with less than six minutes to play, Griese took the Boilermakers 67 yards in four snaps. He connected on passes of 34, 13 and 19 yards before turning the ball over to his fullback.

"I didn't have to see this stat sheet to know what happened today," Ara told the writers. "Bob Griese had a sensational game. He hit 19 of 22? That's hard to do in practice, much less in a game. Passing is a percentage thing, like shooting baskets. One day you hit a lot, the next not as much. But what Griese did was unbelievable."

What Griese had done after only the second game was destroy our season's goal of going undefeated. That's the trouble with being an independent without hope of a post-season game. When visions of a National Championship have faded, the only incentive left is pride.

That Sunday in our meeting Ara advised us of our new task. "Losing is the most difficult thing a team must take in stride. It's easy to lose and easy to expect to lose. Coming back

Nick Rassas turned many a game around with his returns.

is our big job. You can ruin a squad very easily at a time like this. Harp, blame them, destroy their confidence, that's not our way. We'll start at the beginning, the fundamental things you win and lose with. We missed tackles, we blocked poorly, our pursuit was lacking and we violated our contain principle—bend but don't break. We'll start all over again tomorrow and do and redo those things that are football's bread and butter."

The next day at practice he expressed similar philosophy in a different manner to the squad. "When we lose, we all lose. There is not one of us who can feel good about the game. It's history and fretting over it cannot help us. We'll use the Purdue game to learn from our mistakes, but from here on we think in

terms of our next opponent—Northwestern."

This was just one more example of how Ara had the ability to sense a danger he had never before experienced. In the span of one day he considered it and devised a plan to overcome it. Because of his message to the staff and later to the team, none of us lost enthusiasm for the season. We settled for that last remaining incentive—pride.

Our next game would be a tough one to bounce back on. It would be Ara's first meeting with Northwestern and his former assistant Alex Agase. We had recruited most of the players we'd be facing. But by game time all that sentiment was lost. Zloch threw an early interception that Northwestern carried all the way in. Things weren't going well for us until late in the third quarter when Nick Rassas returned an interception 92 yards for a touchdown and scored minutes later on an 85-yard punt return. The game turned into a rout, 38-7.

Zloch suffered from tendonitis the next week so we prepared Tom Schoen to replace him. Schoen was performing well enough against Army in New York's Shea Stadium, leading us to a 7-0 halftime edge, until bruising his ribs. Zloch was forced into action, and we finished 17-0 winners.

That led us to the game all of us had been waiting for—Southern Cal. We had a week off after Army so for 12 days the campus vibrated with revenge from the miracle the Trojans had destroyed the year before. You couldn't walk anywhere on campus without hearing someone say or seeing written the word "Remember." I still don't know how it was done, but one of the students had climbed to the top of the Administration Building and hung a "Remember" sign from the Golden Dome. It was a term that pervaded our team and indeed the whole coaching staff. That past winter Ara lived with the USC game film, viewing it time and time again. It was a soul-search for him, and he dwelled on it. How could anyone forget it?

Whenever we recalled 1964, how the students and other fans greeted us in the Fieldhouse after the loss to USC, the same old lump came to our throats. The squad had asked Ara for special meetings. Phil Sheridan took the offense, and Jim Lynch and Nick Rassas the defense. We didn't really know what was going on in those conferences, but we could see incredible concentration and intensity on the practice field.

On the day of the game in a quiet moment before the officials called for Captain Sheridan for the coin toss and before Ara grouped the players for a last word, Tony Carey walked to the center of the locker room. Carey carried the heartbreak of falling on the Trojans' winning touchdown pass in 1964, and there was only one way to rid himself of that grief. "Look guys," he stammered, almost in a stage whisper, "I've been living with this thing for one whole year. No one's ever blamed me, but I've lived just to pay these guys back." He didn't have to say more. His supporters came to his rescue. "We'll get 'em, Tony!" "Make 'em pay for '64!" "Let's do it with class, though," Jim Lynch reminded, "clean, hard and fair."

Even though they had not come as far as we had last year,

this was our chance to ruin USC's undefeated season. And from the opening play we were prepared to do so. We kicked to Mike Garrett two yards deep in the end zone. After fielding the ball he took a couple of steps, lost his footing and fell violently, untouched by anyone. My wife later told me after that play someone near her remarked, "My God, I knew they wanted to win, but I didn't think they'd shoot him!"

The defense held the Heisman Trophy-winning Garrett to 43 yards rushing that day, his career low. They pursued, swarmed, gang-tackled and thoroughly disjointed the Trojan offense. The result was a 28-7 victory.

The offense, eager to regain its lost form, played near-flawless football. Larry Conjar was a classic battering ram, gaining 116 yards and scoring four touchdowns, all on the ground. Conjar outgained the entire Southern Cal offense by 42 yards. Eddy had 65 yards rushing, Wolski 64 and Zloch 50, giving every Notre Dame back more yardage than the highest USC rusher.

"Spirit plays an important part in any football game and today we were really up," Ara said in his press conference.

It took more than one USC defender to stop Bill Wolski and other Irish backs in 1965.

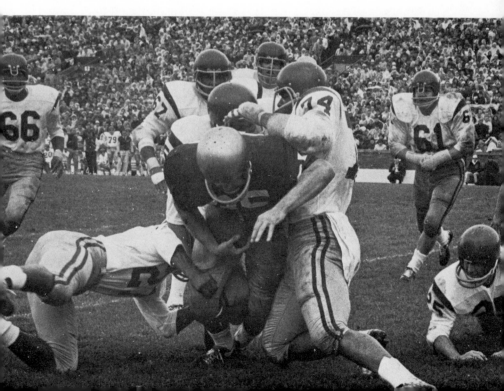

"At the outset of the game, we were happy USC elected to receive. If we had won the toss, we would have defended the North goal, giving them the first crack on offense. I think when a team is as emotionally high as we were it is better to begin the game on defense. If an error occurs due to over-anxiousness, your chances of being hurt seriously aren't as great. Garrett's stumble in the end zone spurred us even further."

An emotional letdown is common after a game like this, and Ara admonished the team Monday. "You just once get flat, you just once relax and someone will fatten up their reputation at your expense," he chided. "Now I'm proud of you. That game was a great win and you played the way you had to. But NO GAME, NO GAME is as important as the one you are going to play. Who do we play?"

"Navy!" the squad retorted.

"Who?"

"Navy!"

"Will the Southern Cal game help the score against Navy?"

"No!"

"Is there any game more important than Navy?"

"No!"

We soon realized there was no game more important than Notre Dame for Navy, either. Leading just 6-3 before the half, Ara's coaching genius led us to Navy's breaking point. Ara had taught the team the importance of utilizing time outs. Navy tried to run the clock out on its last possession, but we were able to stop it with the time outs and take over on our 45 with 13 seconds. Ara had time for one call, and it was a great one. Realizing that Navy expected us to throw long, Ara signalled for a flare pass.

Zloch dropped back, stuck the ball in Conjar's gut and pulled it out deftly while Conjar faked into the line screaming, "Draw." Nick Eddy moved unnoticed to his right, and Zloch lofted him the ball. Eddy started up field, breaking through an opening and squirming free from one defender. At the Navy 40 he reversed his direction, and Bill Wolski cleared out the lone remaining deterrent. Eddy had traveled 55 yards by covering nearly 100. The final score was 29-3.

Ara told the staff he was extraordinarily worried about the upcoming Pittsburgh game. The squad had looked loggy all

In the open field one man rarely stopped Nick Eddy.

week in practice, and he knew that the Panthers would be "up."
He needn't have been so concerned. We scored two plays into
the game, and with Bill Wolski racking up five touchdowns we
finished 69-13 winners. Ara's fears actually came one week
early as North Carolina threw a real scare into us. The Tar Heels
held us to a 3-0 halftime lead. We moved better in the second
half and won, 17-0.

At 7-1 we were in position for another great record. But
two of our toughest games lay ahead. Michigan State came to
our stadium undefeated and slated for the Rose Bowl. We
weren't moving the ball well, but neither were the Spartans. For
over a half it looked as if Ken Ivan's 32-yard field goal might
win it for us, but Michigan State had too many skills, too much
size and speed. They put a drive together midway through the

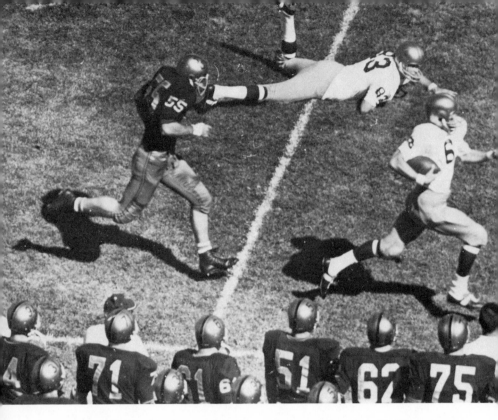

Bill Zloch—a poised field general and constant rushing threat.

third quarter and went up 6-3. With 10 minutes to play Zloch threw an interception, and MSU took over on our 19. Their quarterback, Steve Juday, immediately completed a touchdown pass and put us behind, 12-3.

This made their defensive team higher than ever. Individually they were screaming taunts at our players and flowing in force to every play. Some even yelled vulgarly at our bench and baited us to put the ball in the air. They had 11 men within three feet of the line of scrimmage on nearly every play. If Zloch tried to pass, they swarmed him for a loss. And he had already been intercepted three times. MSU had been containing our rushing game all afternoon. On the day we had a negative rushing yardage of 12 yards and gained only 24 yards passing. We had never felt our offensive impotency any more than in that game.

Bill Zloch shouldered all the responsibility. He felt he had failed everything that was Notre Dame. His body was a mass of bruises, but that didn't concern him. He was the last to leave

94

the locker room, and Ara went over to him. "Aw, Coach," he sobbed, "I let the guys down. I let all you guys down."

Ara had been Bill's greatest defender all season. He accepted the fact that Bill wasn't a great passer. Bill didn't claim to be, but he was the best we had, and he helped us out of a jam when we needed him.

"You didn't let us down, Bill," Ara consoled. "Ordinary players would have cracked out there today under all that pressure and physical abuse. But you didn't give up. I'm proud of you. We wouldn't have seven wins right now without you. Don't forget that."

Playing in the heat of Miami, Florida, our last game didn't help our offense. The best scoring shots for both teams were field goal attempts. Miami nearly scored on one of 52 yards, but it hit the crossbar and bounced back. Ken Ivan missed on three occasions, and the game ended without a score, the only time in 11 years at Notre Dame we didn't put points on the board. It was a frustrating finish to a spirited but agonizing season. We could not have asked for greater effort all season long from any of these young men. Ara praised them after the game.

"I'm proud of you guys, just so damn proud of the way you hung in there tonight and all year. Don't any of you hang your heads. Don't any of you alibi. There's no need to. You're Notre Dame men. You gave your best and you must concede something to worthy opponents. They played their best against us, too."

Two weeks later we honored the team at the banquet and said farewell to several seniors. Included was Nick Rassas. "I recently have been privileged to be elected an All-American," he told the audience. "I also have signed a pro contract for more money than I ever thought possible. But let me say here and now, I'd give it all up right this minute to play one more year for Notre Dame. My dreams all came true and I'm saddened that they are over."

Though we had no way of knowing it, our dream was just one year away!

1966 -
We Did It With Class

Coaches are probably the biggest pessimists around. I don't think any of us ever recognize the potential of our teams. There's always the fear that even though we might have players who can do the job, someone on our schedule will have even more.

Further, there's no such thing as a starting point for building a winner. The long-lived Notre Dame tradition triggers a great effort for the pursuit of excellence every year. It has become a self-evident dream, a pervading one, rekindled annually. The parade of players passes, the greats and nongreats, the graduating seniors and those ready to replace them. New leaders emerge, growing in their visions and aspirations, now more mature in their seniority than in former years. It is a continuous cycle which periodically produces a champion.

In retrospect I can see that the blend was perfect in 1966 for a championship caliber team. Ara knew that the only thing that kept us from having a superb squad in 1965 was a passing combination. We would have one of Notre Dame's greatest in 1966 plus the best of the previous year's team. Ten All-Americans would be named from this squad. The mixture of seniors and underclassmen would create the proper fervency, and the leadership would never be better.

Though Ara wouldn't allow himself to fantasize, our strengths were obvious. And so he encouraged the staff to push even harder. "Success won't happen by sitting here," he preached. "We've got to keep on striving. We've got to recruit,

There were seven pairs of shoes to fill on offense in 1966, but Tom Regner (76), Larry Conjar (32), George Goeddeke (54) and Nick Eddy (47) did return.

explore new ideas, improve old techniques and know, really know our players. We're not going to spoon feed them. Winning has to be as important to them as it is to us. It should be! It will be, or what we're doing will be wasted on them."

We would sense at the opening of spring practice that not only was winning as important to them now as it had been our first two years, but they had the added element of confidence. The winning tradition of Notre Dame had been restored after two consecutive prosperous seasons, and these players were sure they were going to be especially good.

After our year-long passing drought Ara's first concern that spring was our quarterback. Throughout 1965 he had his eyes on two outstanding prospects on our freshman team— Coley O'Brien and Terry Hanratty. Even at that early stage of development they could have given the varsity a lift.

Holdover Tom Schoen was pitted against O'Brien and Hanratty in the quarterback battle. But early in the spring Ara

asked Tom to make a change. His speed, good hands and knowledge of pass defenses made him a natural to become a defensive
safety. Tom had a desire to play, and where was insignificant. It
didn't take him long to fit in at the new position. Ironically, he
stymied O'Brien and Hanratty time and time again with interceptions on great second efforts. Paul Shoults worked with him
on punt returns, and his judgment whether to fair catch or
gamble on a run became masterful.

O'Brien and Hanratty were demonstrating a throwing
weapon far beyond the average sophomore level. Added to their
skills as passers were the counterpart skills of their receivers.
Sophomore Jim Seymour was showing the ability to find open
seams and catch the ball.

Tom Schoen—where he played was insignificant.

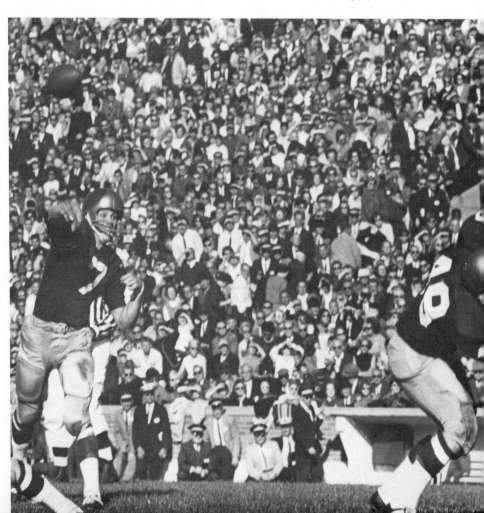

As freshmen, O'Brien had held a slight edge over Hanratty in performance. But that became less observable that spring. In terms of speed they were equal. Hanratty was the taller of the two at 6-1 while O'Brien tipped his toes to reach 5-11. Hanratty threw a tight spiral with a low trajectory and had a whiplike release. O'Brien relied more on an arched trajectory and did not have Hanratty's strength. We alternated both of them with the first team, but the slight edge of consistency was given to Hanratty. His speed away from the center, his rapid-fire release and ability to throw on the move improved with each practice. Having two such talented passers was a luxury we had never known.

After watching our young quarterbacks in action, Ara began to glow in our staff meetings. "Hanratty impresses me more than any passer I've ever seen at a similar stage," he beamed. "And O'Brien is as good or better than most quarterbacks at the same stage. I know we're going to have a good running game. If we can throw against our opponents, too, we're going to give them all a lot of problems."

At the close of spring ball, as had been Ara's custom in years past, the assistant coaches called in all the players for individual conferences. In these sessions we pointed out the players' strengths and weaknesses and told them what they must do to remain on or advance to the first team. We also mapped out a summer conditioning program. Then we gave them a chance to tell us about any personal problems or gripes they might have had. In this process we were able to establish a rapport with those we worked most closely with. We took notes during our interviews, and in the summer Ara reviewed them, considering the players' suggestions and often implementing them.

A major topic in these discussions was academics. Ara always took deep interest in the educational progress of his players. He knew as well as anyone that football is a temporary activity, whether a guy made it to the pros, which is the case with only a small percentage of players, or went directly into the business world. A degree is invaluable either way. Ara's involvement wasn't just peripheral. He worked closely with the academic counselors to see to it that his players were getting to class and making the required effort. And his concern paid off. Ninety-nine percent of all his players graduated. St. Petersburg sportswriter Hubert Mizell took a survey of all National Football League players in 1976 to see how many had actually graduated. Notre Dame had 24 participants (most of whom played for Ara), and all 24 had received diplomas. No other school came close to that mark. Of Notre Dame's frequent opponents, Southern Cal had 18 of 41 for a .439 percantage, Purdue 13 of 21 for .619 and Michigan State 7 of 17 for .412. This was one of our proudest accomplishments.

Anticipation of the upcoming season made the summer pass quickly. Before we knew it our 7:00 a.m. to 10:00 p.m. regimentation was upon us. This time when we met there were some new faces. Doc Urich had been hired by the University of Buffalo as head coach, and Dave Hurd left coaching to enter private business. Ara elevated George Sefcik from freshman coach to receiver coach and hired a man who had just led South Bend St. Joseph High School to a state championship—Wally Moore. Jerry Wampfler, a teammate of mine who had played on Ara's first freshman team at Miami, replaced Doc on the offensive line. Both men fit in perfectly.

Ara felt unusual confidence in the team after the way it had performed during fall practices. But it was time to make sure it was emotionally ready, too. Part of that responsibility fell to me. I had proposed that an anonymous letter be placed in all the lockers to stimulate our players to think about the game. I wanted to magnify Ara's and the staff's thoughts about the game in the form of a written pep talk. I signed it "The Phantom" so that I could say anything, even take potshots occasionally.

I got the notion for the name from a crude dormitory prank at Miami. We had some jerk who would sneak into our restroom, do his business in the middle of the floor and insert a coathanger with a notebook paper sign saying "The Phantom strikes again." We stayed up nights trying to catch the guy and racked our brains figuring who he might be. That was my intention here. I wanted to spur or applaud the players, but mostly just give them something to consider.

My toughest efforts were season openers and after losses. Ara constantly reminded us that after a loss you cannot punish your players. Then more than ever they need to know you're

100

John Pergine (50), Jim Lynch (61), Mike McGill (60) and Kevin Hardy (74) do their best to keep Bob Griese handcuffed.

with them. My writing always reflected his philosophy. Before Purdue I wrote, "Notre Dame, our training thus far has pushed several thoughts, but they are only of value when applied. Purdue will tax us. They have pride, and because of that we cannot play flat. We can never let up in any way. The will to win is in all people. Those with the most will always wind up winning. This will be on national television, the opener. We owe Purdue something for last year. But to ourselves and the nation that follows us, we owe much more. I have no doubt we will play poised—emotional with fierce pride and love for contact. If we do these things, we can start the long climb to greatness. Good luck!"

An outgrowth of "The Phantom" was the Clobber Board. I posted pictures of the opposing team on a locker room bulletin board in the formations they would line up in. Each player could then see whom he would be going up against. On the picture I wrote little items about each of their players. For instance, for Bob Griese I put "Best quarterback in the Big Ten.

Recently stated that Notre Dame couldn't stop me if I were handcuffed." I'm sure Griese didn't say that, but it was the type thing that incited our defense.

One other motivational technique had its origins in 1964 in the form of taunting between the offense and defense. Ara regarded their spontaneous chants as something to be preserved and eventually reserved a spot at the end of the practice day to capitalize on this.

"Now you defensive men hustled today and we got in some good work, but you offensive fellows are playing like the little sisters of the poor. All right, offense, let's have a cheer for the defense and their fine work."

One of them went like this.

> Roses are red.
> Violets are blue
> Ara thinks you're great.
> But that ain't true!

Ara then gave the defense a chance for retort.

> Mother, mother, does your son
> play football?
> No, No—He's on offense
> And they do nothing at all!

As time went on the natural flair of these young men took over. Then came bigger and better productions with choreography, music and lyrics. Ara assumed the role of "Ted Mack," judging the tunes or poems and selecting a winner. Eventually the cheers turned into attacks on the upcoming opponent. Drawing from current or traditional songs the players adapted their own words, like the one before the Purdue game.

> His name is Griese,
> He leads the Boilers,
> He throws the football,
> All over the field.
> We're gonna stomp him,
> We're gonna drop him,
> And we're never gonna yield!

Ara contended that all other things being equal, the winning edge goes to the team emotionally ready. He knew that all our opponents were motivated to play Notre Dame. So he wanted to build something to offset that—unity. All these activities may have seemed corny, but they did unite us.

Ara further united us with his pregame talk the morning of our game. With the exception of his opening address to the team in 1964, Ara never reached anyone any better than he did time after time in these lectures.

It had been his habit for years to print his thoughts on an index card in his lefthanded style. These notes were a compilation of the entire week, a list made when the concepts struck him.

Without fail his pregame meal would be finished long before anyone else. A pacer by nature, he then circled the dining hall, unaware of the hushed voices, the clanging silverware and clinking glasses. As though by a prearranged signal, he sensed the completion of the meal and took his position at one end of the room. "Let me have your attention, men," he said, and from that point on he had it.

His talk would highlight the offensive and defensive musts. He generalized what to look for against the opponent and what he thought the pulse of the contest would be. This was a concise, candid presentation, devoid of redundancy, laying our hopes on the line, squarely, openly and finally! He would wind up the 20-30 minute discussion by telling us why this game was so important. Under the heading "What we must do to win" his brilliant analogies and heart-felt sincerity held us spellbound. We had heard all this during the week, but his manner of summation always left a fresh taste, a hunger.

Ara then broke down the team by position, giving the assistant coaches one last opportunity for review. He always met with the quarterbacks, outlining their duties. Terry Hanratty and Coley O'Brien coordinated for one another; that is, the one not in the game would study the opponent's defense. The third quarterback, Bob Belden, had a sharp comprehension of football and helped with sideline organization, manning the phone to our spotters in the press box.

With our many young players at key positions Ara was naturally concerned about their opening-game jitters. National

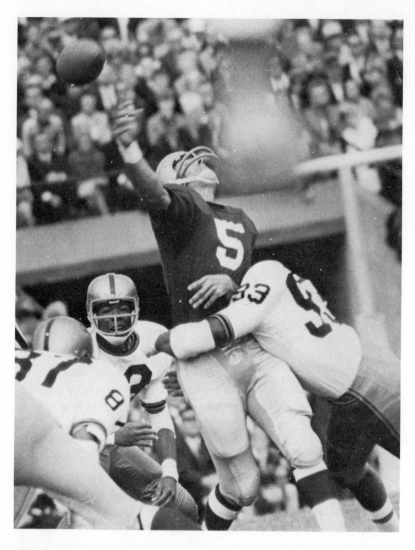

Terry Hanratty manages to get his pass away for a 42-yard gain to split end Jim Seymour.

TV did not help matters. The formalized introduction of players delayed us nearly five minutes, and to someone ready for action that is a short eternity. Ara tried to alleviate the problem somewhat by kicking to Purdue and giving our more veteran defensive group the first crack. When we took over Ara chose to ease in Hanratty and the other sophomores by calling for three straight rushes, allowing them to get a feel and maybe even take a few pops that would introduce them to college football.

On our next possession Ara opened up the offense. As Hanratty rolled right to pass, the Purdue cornerback blitzed from his blind side. Terry sensed the pressure and at the last instant dodged forward to avoid the tackle. He quickly regained his balance and threw to Jim Seymour for a 42-yard gain.

Later in that drive Hanratty tried to pitch to halfback Rocky Bleier but put the ball slightly behind him. Bleier did his best to get a handle but was hit in the process, jarring the ball loose. Purdue's Leroy Keyes snatched it inches above the ground and sped 95 yards for a score.

We needed to regain momentum, and Ara called for our special kickoff play. A five-man wedge of Bob Gladieux, Don Gmitter, Larry Conjar, Seymour and Bleier pierced the first wave of defenders just long enough to escort Nick Eddy through the opening. From there Eddy turned on his speed and headed for a 97-yard touchdown. Ara ran over to Eddy and grabbed him gratefully. "Thank you, Nickie," he beamed, "we had to have that." One exciting play such as that can spark a team. That's exactly what it did. Our sideline was 30 yards of elation.

Then it was time for our "Baby Bombers" to go into action. On the next series Hanratty was faced with a third and 14 situation on our 16-yard line. Seymour ran a deep pattern and broke free at the Purdue 30. Without breaking stride he gathered in Terry's pass and had no problems reaching the end zone for an 84-yard touchdown. The twosome connected again for a 39-yard score to start the fourth quarter. After Purdue had battled back within six Hanratty went to Seymour once more on a seven-yard touchdown pass. That gave us a 26-14 victory. Hanratty had completed 16 of 24 passes for 304 yards, and Seymour caught 13 of them for 276 yards.

Ara displayed his pleasure to the press. "I feel wonderful because we beat a fine team today—a dangerous football team. With Griese we knew they were explosive after last year's game.

"I was very proud of our team. In particular I was thrilled

105

to see the way they came back from that bad break in the first quarter when Keyes took our fumble in the air for a score. The way we blocked for Nick Eddy on the kickoff was really something.

"Both Terry Hanratty and Jim Seymour produced for us beyond my fondest hopes. Hanratty followed our game plan very well. I have been so high on those fellas that I feared I might be a bit over-confident, afraid I might be overrating them. But they showed everyone today just how good they are."

The next week against Northwestern Eddy got us off to an early lead with a 56-yard touchdown run. Somehow nothing seemed to click from then until the fourth quarter. We left 35-7 winners in Ara's first return to Evanston since coming to Notre Dame.

Injuries were beginning to deplete our ranks, but though the replacements were obviously not as capable as our regulars they were getting the job done. Coley O'Brien, however, began to concern us. Coley's speed seemed to have lessened. His footwork and running smoothness lacked the nimbleness that had earlier been his strength.

We scored early and often against Army, entering the locker room at halftime with a 35-0 lead. Ara used the reserves the entire second half but was disappointed with their ineffectiveness. The defense, led especially by Alan Page and Jim Lynch, played superbly as we held on to that 35-0 score.

As everyone knows from his fame with the Minnesota Vikings, Alan Page is a great football player. With us he was amazingly quick though not as strong as our opponents built him up to be. He intimidated offensive linemen because of the stories that had been spread about his size. In reality he was only 6-5, 238. He didn't become a devastating hitter until his last season, after Joe Yonto and John Ray worked with him on it. He was always cooperative and a true team player. Though quiet he was extremely articulate. He was one of the very few blacks at Canton (Ohio) Central Catholic High School so he was used to the small black population he found then at Notre Dame. On a team, more so than any other organization, race and religion have absolutely no bearing on acceptance. Performance is the only thing that marks a man.

Jim Lynch was Notre Dame's version of Jack Armstrong.

Alan Page receives last-minute instructions from Coach John Ray.

I'm sure he eats Wheaties, drinks milk, obeys his mother and father, loves God, country and Notre Dame. While that may sound a little far-fetched it's because you just don't find many like him. He was never on a soap box, but after listening to him for a few minutes you knew he was a leader. He wasn't gifted with an overabundance of talent, but as a wholesome, quick-thinking, hard-working individual he achieved far beyond our expectations. Jim came from a small town. His father had been ill for years, and both parents dreamed that he and his brother would make it to college. After his brother won a scholarship to Navy Jim began to work even harder to please his parents.

He never tried to dominate anyone, but as the captain he had the ability to keep the team in line. If he saw any of them out drinking he politely asked them to get back to their rooms, and because of the respect he commanded they did so willingly. We pleaded for him on offense because he would have made a great tight end. But he was needed on defense and went on to become a star linebacker with the Kansas City Chiefs.

The entire defense continued to play remarkably. We held North Carolina scoreless in our next game, 32-0. Hanratty had pulled a muscle in his throwing arm the day before the game with the Tar Heels, and we doubted his availability. Ironically, Hanratty awoke the next day ready for duty, but in short order North Carolina lost *its* top two quarterbacks to injury.

Our upcoming challenge figured to be the most difficult to date. Oklahoma was 5-0 and ranked ninth in the nation. The

Jim Lynch—Notre Dame's version of Jack Armstrong.

Sooner defense was anchored by middle guard Granville Liggins, referred to by the press as "Chocolate Cheetah." Liggins would play over center George Goeddeke, and line coach Jerry Wampfler wanted the prep team to work George as hard as possible all week. Jerry drafted two preppers to play the part of "Cheetah," and he made their instructions clear. "There are two of you," he said, "so that means you can spell each other. The guy who's in there has got to press Goeddeke. Rush him, side-step him, leapfrog him, call him names, taunt him, but work him. This will be the key to our offensive success."

They did their job well. "Ol' Granny's going to suck you up in exhaust fumes," one jibed as he knocked Goeddeke over. "You better look quick, Georgie Porgie." Goeddeke's hazing began Sunday night after North Carolina. One of the student managers had pasted a picture of Liggins' head to the body taken from a Mr. Universe magazine. Goeddeke's eyes swelled when he first saw it but soon discovered the fabrication. "I thought he rippled and bulged too much for a 205 pounder," he said, smiling to Wampfler.

Goeddeke was having a hit and miss time with Liggins come game day. Their sellout crowd of over 60,000 sensed an upset, and we did not score in the first quarter. With Eddy and Hanratty scoring on rushes and Joe Azzaro connecting on a 32-yard field goal, we managed to go up 17-0 in the first half.

But the scores were costly. Linebacker Mike McGill, not wanting us to use a time out, hobbled the entire width of the field in pain. The doctor immediately reported he had torn knee ligaments. Later Jim Seymour was tackled by a Sooner defender after a pass had sailed over his head. Seymour landed with all his weight on a twisted ankle, and the medical staff rushed him to the training room.

As our players filed into the locker room at halftime they could see our two injured stars being tended to on the examination tables. "They've hurt us," someone yelled, "those guys have hurt us. Let's go out and get even!"

Ara heard the remark and understood the intention. "Hold it, gang," he shouted. "No one hates seeing a player hurt more than I. It is the stinking part of the game no one can control. But whatever you feel, play clean. The worst thing you can do to any team is beat them. Let's do it hard and clean with class.

109

*Coley O'Brien—the kind of young man older women wanted to
mother and every girl fell in love with.*

Everyone will understand this—even McGill and Seymour!"

The team obeyed Ara and quickly scored two more touchdowns in the third quarter. This brought on our second team,
and it ground out one more score. Our 38-0 win over this excellent Oklahoma squad shot us into first place in the ratings the
next week.

But the next week also brought some bad news. On Tuesday morning Dave Haley and Frank Criniti, Coley O'Brien's
roommates, came to my office. They were concerned about
Coley's health. It seemed he had an unquenchable thirst and
couldn't sleep at night because of his constant urge to urinate. I
explained the situation to Ara, and he agreed that Coley should
be checked. We sent him to the infirmary for tests, and the
doctors informed us Coley showed signs of diabetes. Ara called

him in and broke the news.

Coley didn't flinch. He was aware of diabetes strains throughout his family, and he accepted it as a fact of life. Coley's father was a commander in the Navy, and Coley was mature beyond his age because of his worldwide travels.

Coley reminded me of Dobi Gillis. He had an angelic face with a peaches and cream complexion. He was the kind of young man older women wanted to mother and every girl fell in love with. He was well built though short for a football player. Still he was a good athlete. Scholastically Coley was a wiz, but he didn't grasp football concepts as quickly as Terry Hanratty. Politicians and dignitaries didn't awe him because he had always been around them, but he was never cocky about his experiences.

Coley was an unselfish individual. As a freshman he was the heir apparent at quarterback. But he could see Hanratty improve over the course of the year and realized he had fallen a notch behind Terry. Coley then became Hanratty's cheerleader.

As might have been expected his teammates did everything they could to make life easier for the ailing Coley, but he had to do most of it himself. Dr. Howard Engel became his mother hen the next few weeks. He tested and balanced Coley's blood sugar level and showed him how to administer the necessary injections. He was amazed at how quickly Coley adapted to the situation. Engel warned us to take it easy on him at practices, pulling him to the sidelines periodically for juice or a candy bar. With those guidelines Coley was back in action in a week. Most players would have been through for the season.

Suddenly it dawned on us why Coley's performance had dropped off and his coordination had been encumbered. In a way it was reassuring to find an answer.

We added wins with relative ease the next three weeks. If it weren't for a blocked punt and a resulting touchdown yielded by the offensive team against Navy, we would have been able to run our shutout string to four. The important thing, however, was that we left Philadelphia with a 31-7 triumph over the Middies.

Ara sensed that the team might let up in preparation for the next two opponents, Pittsburgh and Duke. He hoped to combat any lackadaisical attitude. He started Monday to

111

explain the complete situation facing us. He knew that the players could appreciate all the facets of our position and weigh them well enough to judge the true predicament. With each day of preparation Ara spent a few moments reiterating our goals. It is a strange man, indeed, who hears over and over a logical concept and blanks his mind to it. He admitted that Pittsburgh and Duke were not having successful seasons, but he also warned that such knowledge lent itself to a relaxed state. Ara's faith in the team to uphold its desire to win was his plan for combatting any ripeness.

And it worked—but not without some additional encouragement from Ara along the way. Leading just 7-0 at halftime of the Pitt game Ara felt the need to "stimulate" the offense. "I didn't believe you would get flat. I thought you'd realize more was at stake. You're giving them courage. They're thinking if they can contain you for a half, then they can conceivably upset you! You won't make yourselves believe that, that's why defeat is possible. Let's wake up and fire up! We've come too far, worked too hard, to throw it all away." The final score showed the effects of Ara's admonition: Notre Dame 40, Pitt 0.

Ara needed only to watch the second play of the Duke game to see we weren't going to make the same mistake twice. Nick Eddy took Hanratty's handoff and rambled 77 yards for a score. Fifty-seven points later we closed the home portion of our 1966 schedule and readied ourselves for the GAME OF THE CENTURY—Notre Dame versus Michigan State.

It was finally here! All season long that's all everybody talked about, but we fought to surpress thoughts of it lest it interfere with more immediate objectives. Now such thoughts were legal and, even though it would be the most hectic week any of us would ever know, it was a relief to finally be here. The Spartans had not lost a regular season game in two years, and since they couldn't repeat a Rose Bowl appearance this was their chance for the National Championship. They were rated number two. We were challenging for the national title for the second time in three years. We were ranked number one.

The campus was absolutely chaotic the entire week. The students held dorm meetings and rallies every night. Even though it was a road game the campus was covered with spectators hoping to see something—anything that might take them behind the scenes of this game. The players and coaches were besieged with requests from reporters. We couldn't imagine that many papers, radio and TV stations existed. We tried to keep practices closed, but it seemed impossible. Everybody knew Rockne, Father Hesburgh or Ara personally, and the three combined couldn't have had that many acquaintances.

After 1965 Ara became guarded about our workouts. During that season he was sure one of our opponents had spied our practices from their quick reactions to our formations. Thereafter he was especially watchful before certain big games. And there was none bigger than Michigan State. We sent a manager to check for intruders on upper floors of the library—a perfect vantage point. Another manager was constantly on the lookout for trailers parked on the back roads behind our training area. By now our entire practice complex had been surrounded by a padded fence.

Ara realized that the team didn't need to be pepped up for this one. His brief comment to them at the beginning of the week seemed needless on the surface, but in reality it made them analyze their dedication. "Let's not be guilty of not wanting it badly enough!" The practices reflected a combination of a little fear, a lot of respect for the Spartans, tremendous tension and yet confidence that we were a better team than last year when MSU beat us. The world suddenly dwindled in size and became a plot of ground 100 yards long. Time spent on anything but game preparation felt wasted.

The students organized one last rally Thursday night, and they and the townspeople packed the train depot Friday morning before our departure. Our freshmen were accompanying us on this trip to play the MSU frosh. The fans sought to mingle with the players and coaches, posing for pictures with them and asking for autographs. The mayor of South Bend and virtually every service club in the area showed up.

On the way to East Lansing Nick Eddy came over to sit with me. He had been hurt in the North Carolina game and reinjured himself against Duke. By Thursday his shoulder had been slightly healed but was still tender. His arm felt numb and we worried about his ability to carry the ball. Psychologically it would be bad to start him and then have to pull him out. This could add fuel to Michigan State's fire.

The students held rallies every night.

"Coach," he said, "I want to play, but I've been concerned about just how much I can help or hurt if I'm not right. My shoulder has another whole day to rest and I'll go as long as I can."

"We want you in there, Nick, but only if you can play without jeopardizing yourself," I told him. "Just being on the field you have to be defensed. If it feels better and you can, that's fine."

The weather was cold and rainy when we arrived. Busses met us at the station to take us to the Jack Tar Hotel, and Ara and I were already seated when Rocky Bleier charged up to us disconsolately. He reported that Nick had slipped descending the wet steps of the train. As he braced his body for the fall he caught all his weight on his elbow. Ara and I searched for Nick and found him slumped in a seat on the other bus. As we approached him the pain he suffered manifested itself in his tears. The fall had ripped his shoulder upwards and destroyed any healing that might have taken place. "I'm sorry," he sobbed, realizing this ended any chance he had of playing tomorrow.

That night Ara gave the players the choice of watching the freshmen play, going to a movie or staying in the rooms. Most just wanted to relax. Both varsity coaching staffs assembled in the press box of Spartan Stadium to observe our rookie freshman coaches in action. This gave Ara and Spartan coach Duffy Daugherty a chance for some humorous interplay.

Leading 14-0, Ara felt enough confidence to get the ball rolling. "Wally Moore is a fine fellow," he told Duffy. "He has a keen football mind and he's doing a marvelous job. Yes, Wally's hiring was another great decision on my part!"

We had scored on a kickoff return, but the Spartans came right back with a long pass. "Nothing to worry about," Ara continued. "But I must speak to Wally about that pass defense." After Michigan State scored again Ara's concern grew. "Wally, baby, what are you doing!" he shouted. Duffy gave Ara some of his own medicine after MSU converted an onside-kick recovery into a touchdown. "Yep," Ara insisted, "like I've been saying, that Wally Moore has got to go."

With the score tied at 27 after both teams had missed point-after attempts, Notre Dame had the ball on the MSU 32 with 75 seconds left. Ara moaned as he saw one of our players heading to the field with a kicking tee in his hand. "How the hell do you expect him to kick a field goal from this length, Wally, when we can't even make the extra point?"

No sooner had Ara verbalized his thought than it was answered. Ed Ziegler, a powerful fullback who had dominated the game, brought his leg through the ball in a jerky motion. It had no trajectory, but it was straight and true and sailed well past the goal posts.

Back in Ara's room that night the conversation centered on the thrilling frosh game. Ara was now singing Wally's praises again. When Wally arrived Ara congratulated him saying, "I just want you to know I hired, fired and rehired you all in the span of two hours. I'll tell you what saved you, though. It was that cool, calm, collected way you bore the pressure of the moment, made a decision and selected Ziegler to try for that field goal. That showed me something!"

"Oh that was easy, Coach," Wally answered innocently. "I

just turned and screamed at the top of my lungs, 'Who can kick a field goal?' Ziegler said he could and I sent him in." The room fell apart with hysteria. "I hope we can be this loose tomorrow," Ara uttered, bidding us all good-night.

That was an impossible dream. At this point no amount of psychology could undo what the unfolding drama of the season had created. The players were tense and so were we. This game meant the difference between being "also rans" and "the best." Immense tackle Kevin Hardy sprawled his frame on a mat covering the floor in our locker room, gazing pointlessly at the ceiling. Pete Duranko sat close by, running his fingers through his dark, coarse Croation hair. Larry Conjar was fiddling with his chin strap, nervous, quiet, intense. Then the officials broke the silence by calling for Jim Lynch. "Okay, let's do it!" the players shouted. "We've got all the marbles on this one!" "This is the game we need!"

Ara's voice summoned the remaining players to attention. For 17 long seasons he had "knocked on the door." There were times at Miami when his teams were the best in the conference. There were seasons at Northwestern when his nerve carried as far as six or seven victories before injuries allowed the bottom to drop out. But right here, right now, he was knocking again. This team had character, it had skill and most of all, knowing full well that Ara Parseghian never faced anyone he didn't think he could lick, it had a chance to be the National Champion.

Nothing will ever compare to this game for intensity, hard-hitting aggressiveness and absolute excitement from one second to the next. The stadium was overloaded. People were seated in every aisle, and some even managed to filter down to the field. The police couldn't contain them. So many fans, photographers, and cameramen were spilling onto our sideline that we had to employ our freshmen to hold them back. The usual splendor of college football was missing from this game. No one cared about the bands or cheerleaders, just the grim, deathbattle emotion of the game.

Neither team could mount a drive in the first quarter. On our second offensive series Hanratty rolled out to pass, but a Spartan blitz flushed him out. When he tried to run, middle linebacker Charlie Thornhill got an arm on him, slowing him for the onslaught of Bubba Smith, State's heralded defensive end.

Ara gives each player his usual pregame "stare" while they prepare in their own fashions.

The great jolt of Smith's weight knifed Hanratty's shoulder to the ground.

I could see that Terry was hurt, but before I could fight my way to Ara through our players, the police and intruders on our sidelines, the next play was underway. In the meantime George Goeddeke had been blocked hard, and he limped off the field with a severely wrenched ankle. Hanratty would be finished for the season with a separated shoulder. While the defense was holding the Spartans, we were quickly trying to warm up Coley and get him to take snaps from Goeddeke's novice replacement at center, sophomore Tim Monty.

The Spartans put 10 points on the board in their first two possessions of the second period. But little Coley kept his composure. His linemen made sure he was protected— anyone letting a defender through was chastised by the other offensive players. Coley came through for them. On our next series in just four plays he took us 54 yards, all in the air, for a score. He completed passes of 11 and nine yards before spotting Bob Gladieux on the goal line for a 34-yard touchdown.

When Coley came to the sidelines, Terry ran to him and hugged him like a brother, sore shoulder and all. The two of them were all that young men could ever be to one another—friends, competitors and admirers. "You were great, baby, you were just great," Terry grinned. "They really pour in at you, though, don't they?"

"You know it," Coley concurred. "But the line has been amazing. And that Conjar, he's beautiful. He's my personal bodyguard!"

The locker room was alive with concentration at halftime. Our players, far removed from their pregame tenseness, were wrapped up in the heat of battle. Ara grouped the staff around a blackboard to discuss what he thought would "go" against them offensively, and "stop" them defensively.

Coley was drained from his lengthy activity in the first half. Dr. Engel was trying to balance his blood sugar in a far corner. Just before we took the field again Larry Conjar voiced his feelings. "We can beat these guys," he raved. "Let's get after them this half!"

"Did you hear that, defense?" Lynch added. "Let's show some pride out there. We've got to carry the fight to them!"

Ara then took over. "We're not out of this, men, not by one helluva long shot. We can't let up, though. We've got to pour it on. Sell out—play your hearts out for one more half!"

The defense was as tough as Lynch had asked. Offensively we were doing our best, too, but the Spartans were unyielding. Late in the third quarter Coley took us from our 20 to the Spartan 30 with three long passes. Coley then turned it over to his running backs, Bleier, Conjar and Dave Haley, a reserve who had played little until forced into service when Gladieux was added to our growing list of casualties. We moved it to the 10, and Joe Azzaro opened the fourth quarter with a game-tying field goal.

Midway through the final period Tom Schoen came up with his second interception of the day, giving us our last real scoring opportunity. Taking over at the MSU 18 we lost six yards on the next two plays. Coley had been shuffled on and off the field in a flurry the last few minutes, and this really taxed him. He was dragging by now but playing as courageously as any Notre Dame player ever. His pass attempt to Seymour was wobbly and well off the mark so Azzaro had the pressure on him again. He was faced with a 41-yard attempt into the wind.

"He can do it," Hanratty was screaming on the sideline. "He's done it hundreds of times in practice. C'mon Joe!"

Azzaro's kick had the power and height, but it slid by inches to the right.

Michigan State then elected to punt on a fourth and four situation, giving us the ball on our 30 with three minutes to play. Three rushes by O'Brien, Bleier and Conjar left us a yard short on fourth down. Accepting the serious consequences, Ara signalled O'Brien to go for it. Drawing on his last bit of strength Coley kept the ball himself and picked up two yards.

There was roughly enough time for two more plays. Ara called for a pass, but Bubba Smith broke through Tim Monty's block and sacked Coley for a seven-yard loss.

So there we were. One play left. Our second string quarter-back drained from the fatigue of his disease, taking a snap from an inexperienced center, playing without two of his best back-field receivers and looking into the wind at Michigan State's rugged prevent defense. Ara signalled for a quarterback sneak to end the game.

His decision was not between a win and a tie, but between a tie and a possible loss. Ara would not allow the gallant efforts of many substitute players to fade through misplaced emotional thinking. He had no second-thoughts about his play calling, and it never dawned on him that anyone would challenge it.

After the game some of the fans were booing. One of the Michigan State assistant coaches charged across the field toward our bench and started to jeer. "You guys played for a tie!" One of the world's largest "Irishmen" now down on the field heard the remark and told him to shut up. The loudmouth coach ran to his locker room, but just as he had spoken I noticed two Spartan players set to shake hands with our guys. When they heard the charge they pulled their hands away and took up the chant. "What kind of cowards are you that you play for a tie?" Our players said nothing.

A quiet, indefinable air of emptiness hung in our locker room. The players had done their best, and they were spent, hurt, angered. No one was undressing. They all waited at their stools, not really sure for what. Ara entered and he, too, needed

119

some time for composure.

"Men, I'm proud of you," he said softly. "Get one thing straight though. We did not lose. We were number one when we came here, we fell behind and had some tough things happen, but we overcame them. No one could have wanted to win this more than I. Some of the Michigan State people are hollering about the tie, trying to detract from our efforts. They're trying to make it come out a win for them. Well don't you believe it. Their season is over. They can't go anywhere. Time will prove everything that has happened here today. And you'll see that after the rabble rousers have had their say, cooler minds who understand the true odds will know that Notre Dame is a team of champions."

When the press came in, no one mentioned playing for a tie. They knew they had seen a great game, one that Notre Dame had fought valiantly to win. But in days to come, spurred by a story in a national magazine, the venom that only Notre

Coley O'Brien to Jim Seymour (85) connected frequently against the Trojans.

Dame evokes spilled into many newspapers and onto the airwaves. Detractors accused Ara of being "gutless." Even some longtime Notre Dame fans began to question Ara's tactics. The hypocrisy of people came to the surface, and letters contained remarks like "I told them they shouldn't have hired a non-Catholic." The fair weather friends overlooked the thousands of thrills, the miraculous turnaround that Ara and only Ara could have directed the last three years.

Ara answered the attacks by reviewing his thinking throughout that final series. But never once did he mention Coley O'Brien's physical status, and that was the most important factor in his decisions. Never once did he apologize for any call he made. It was heartbreaking for him to bear the brunt of something that wasn't justified, and it grieved him for years.

But Ara managed to push his feelings aside because he had one more important confrontation left. We entered the Southern Cal game ranked first in one poll and a close second in the other, and a win over the Rose Bowl-bound team would probably clinch the national title. Injuries from the State game would make that a real challenge. Hanratty, Goeddeke, Bleier and Gladieux were definitely out.

Some of the players had been with us on our last trip to Los Angeles to meet the Trojans. They remembered the hope we went with and the desolation of our return trip. "The Phantom" tried to describe the experience to the newcomers. "I remember the Irish squad walking the long empty walk from the field to the tunnel. I remember their full grown bodies, shaking with sobs of dejection. I recall the fantastic turn of events that robbed us of a National Championship. We are fighters, hurt though we may be. We are aware of the obstacles, all the memories."

Jim Lynch called a team meeting that week. He asked for total dedication from every player. He beseeched the offense to protect Coley and the defense to play its greatest game. He had been a regular on our 1964 team and knew that the trip to Disneyland and tour through Universal Studio were appealing–but only in victory.

The offense got off to a good start, driving 80 yards for a score in 18 plays. The defense had a hand in the scoring, too. Tom Schoen perfectly timed a pass from Trojan quarterback

Toby Page, caught it in full stride and flew toward the end zone. He was met solidly at the three by a USC defender but fought forward for the score. Joe Azzaro kicked a 38-yard field goal midway through the second quarter to put us up 17-0.

When the offense came to the field John Ray hollered, "My God, you guys, we just have to get another score before the half," recalling the 17-0 halftime score two years earlier. We not only got another touchdown before the half, but we added 27 more points after intermission while the defense gained its sixth shutout of the year.

Our celebration began on the field late in the fourth quarter when we knew USC couldn't make up 51 points. When we got into the locker room the players doused all the coaches with soft drinks and threw them into the showers. Paul Seiler shouted to Ara, sopping wet by now, "You didn't even resist, Coach!"

"I've waited for this shower long enough, Paul, and I'm not about to fight it off now!"

Our return flight stopped at Chicago's Midway Airport. While there we received the pleasant news that both Associated Press and United Press had voted us National Champions. The busses meeting us at the South Bend airport had been ordered to proceed to the Fieldhouse. A typical Notre Dame crowd was assembled there and went typically crazy when we arrived. Their chants of "Ara! Ara! Ara!" drew him to the microphone. He introduced the entire coaching staff and team and then started to speak to them.

"We wanted to bring Notre Dame a National Championship," he began.

"You did! You did! You did!" they cried.

Somehow I had the feeling we had been through all of this before.

But this time it was even better!

1967 -
Encore, Encore

There is a frustrating side to achievement. While all of us scratch and struggle to climb to the top, those of us who reach it never really have a chance to enjoy it. At the very instant we succeed, the fight for retention must begin. Ara Parseghian has had his rags to riches and riches to rags experiences. But none of them were as traumatic as in 1967 when he went from the peaks of being the coach of the National Championship football team to the valleys of telling his daughter she had multiple sclerosis.

None of us on the staff had the slightest notion anything was troubling Ara. He reserved any preoccupation or moodiness for himself. In the staff meetings and on the field he was the same old Ara. He was and always will be a taskmaster, and when he yelled you never knew how to take him—he could be dead serious or joking. Ara is not the most readable guy in the world! In this traumatic era we noted that he wasn't quite as accessible. We didn't have as much "selfish" time with him. His door was shut more often, and he seemed to be on the phone constantly. We reasoned that he had become a celebrity, not that he acted that way, and it was only natural he would have more obligations.

One day after practice while Ara and I were showering I asked about his daughter Karan's health because I had noticed she was having mobility problems. I sensed that it was MS, but there were two characteristics of the disease I wasn't aware of. First, I didn't realize that it is extremely difficult to detect and second that it is incurable. If I had I wouldn't have opened my mouth. But I can see now why I shocked Ara when I brought it up.

He must have dwelled on that all night as was his habit. There were so many occasions when the assistants battled Ara in meetings and thought sure we had lost by the way he turned us off. Then at night he would go home, replay the discussions and come in the next morning and say, "You know, you might have something there."

In this instance Ara brooded about how I learned something Karan didn't know and the doctors weren't even certain about. When I explained my deduction he accepted my concern and let his true feelings come out. Ara was devoted to his family. Karan was the first born, and though he didn't love her any more than Kris or Mike, he had a special feeling about her that every parent would understand.

Ara was coaching at Miami when Katie gave birth to Karan. Of course football coaches, the big, rugged he-men we're pictured to be, are expected to have male offspring as a sign of masculinity. Naturally Ara got ribbed about having a girl, but he was ecstatic. As soon as she was old enough to get around, he took her with him everywhere he could. I vividly recall Ara bringing her to a bonfire pep rally one night at Miami. She was still in diapers, but he carried her around on his shoulder, stopping to show her off to all his acquaintances. He asked me to hold her while he spoke to the crowd, but he released her with great reluctance.

Ever since I can remember, no matter what the time of day, Karan had a book in her hand. She has a keen mind and has never been a rambunctious kid. She seemed like a little adult—mature, passive and serene. As the years went on she grew into a stunning young lady. She has that raven black Parseghian hair, a soft complexion and penetrating eyes. She began her college education at Miami and finished up at Notre Dame where she later earned her master's degree in communications.

Kris was born two years later and was just the opposite of Karan. She was a live wire and had the facility to get into all kinds of youthful mischief. When she was little she lived on the telephone. It wasn't unlike her to call and order a pound of weiners or phone the local radio station to tell them what they

Ara, with Katie, Mike, Kris and Karan, has always been a devoted family man.

were doing wrong. She was much more outgoing than both Karan and Mike and not nearly as wrapped up in academics although she did well at Miami and St. Mary's. All her life she was everybody's buddy at school—both a clown and a friend.

When it came time for his daughters to date, Ara wasn't the "over-protective" father. He had faith that they were sensible enough to meet the right people, and he knew the day would come when they would get serious about a young man. But that was a choice he left to them.

Mike was the male version of Karan—studious, quiet, introspective, a bubbling inferno inside, perhaps, though he never showed it outwardly. Mike was named after Ara's dad, and it was no secret that Ara was delighted to have a son. Ara didn't force Mike into sports, but he became a well-rounded athlete.

125

Mike Parseghian could have been a starting halfback at many schools.

He took up football, basketball, and golf, and though Ara helped him with the basics he didn't go beyond that unless Mike asked for assistance. Whenever he could Ara arranged his schedule to be in the stands like all the other proud fathers, but he was atypical by refraining from making "suggestions" to Mike's coaches. He might needle them when he saw them. "Hey, how's my boy doing? He's got great blood in those veins—thoroughbred breeding, you know? If you need any tips just call me." Ara really did not have to do any politicing for

Mike. Mike made all-state in football and played on the state championship golf team strictly on his own merit.

Mike could have been a starting halfback at a lot of colleges even though at 5-7 he isn't big by football standards. But he didn't plan to make a career of the game. Medicine appealed to him, so he chose to stay close to his family and friends and get a good education at Notre Dame. He came out for the football team his sophomore year. When aligning personnel in staff meetings Ara always played him down, saying, "He's a good kid, but he's just too small to play football here." Mike had been working well with the prep team, and John Murphy told Ara that he was underrating his son. Still, Ara continued to do so. Mike had to earn everything and then get clearance from his dad. Ara went further than called for to avoid favoritism.

Mike got into some home games, deservedly so, and performed credibly. I know that pleased Ara, and it gave him an opportunity for levity at our weekly Quarterback Club luncheons. "I keep telling our backfield coach about this little Armenian kid, but he just won't listen to me."

Paradoxically, Ara was both stern and liberal as a father. When he said something to his children it had better be done. Yet he saw the need to give in occasionally, letting them go their own ways to experience life.

It would have been easy for them to be haughty. Ara worked his way up in life, earning frighteningly little at Miami and not much more at Northwestern. After a few successful years at Notre Dame the monetary rewards and the resulting station in life followed. His kids were seeing the biggest names in football and show business right in their own living room. They were traveling throughout the country and the world. None of this spoiled them, though, and that is attributable to the respect Ara had shown them. He believed that children are people and that they should be treated as vital members of the family. Though they are younger and not as wise and don't have the same responsibilities as the parents, nonetheless their opinions must be considered. Having been given such freedom, Ara's children realized they were fortunate to be in a family that had become successful, but that didn't make them better than anyone.

127

Katie was the perfect match for Ara.

It was important for Ara to spend time with his family. He planned getaways whenever he could, but his job kept him tied down more than he would like, and Katie assumed the major responsibility of raising the children. She accepted his position in life and never tried to steal the limelight—but she was always there when called on. They met while she was a sophomore at Miami after spending her freshman year at the all-girls Western College across the road.

Katie was the perfect match for Ara—petite, cute, but most of all, sharp-witted enough to stay one-up on him. There are only three people I know who can get ahead of Ara—his mother, his brother Jerry and Katie.

Not based on time at home, Ara was a good husband. He

loves to needle and play practical jokes, and Katie has the tranquility to understand his humorous side and absorb it.

While still at Northwestern Katie suggested to Ara that they have the coaching staff and their wives over for an Italian dinner. As a concerned hostess Katie asked Ara for frequent progress reports. "Did you invite everyone? Should I send invitations? Are they excited? Is everyone coming?"

After hearing this for a few days Ara plotted a way to cure her of her anxiety.

The day of the party, Ara laid out his plan in our staff meeting. "Katie has bugged me about this all week and here's what I want you guys to do," he smirked. He planned to tell Katie he had chewed all of us out that day and instructed us to call and cancel at an assigned time. One of us had illness in the family, another had a last-minute appointment, another couldn't get a babysitter.

Meanwhile Katie was at home busily preparing pounds of spaghetti, salad, garlic bread and meatballs. When our calls started to come in Ara made sure he couldn't get to the phone to take them. Katie answered, and she was understanding toward all of us. After the last coach had called, Katie began to cry. The prospect of a dismal party saddened her. The normal guy would have cracked up by now, but continuing the role Ara walked over and put his arms around her and said he was going to call us back and insist we show up. Even before he could, we started arriving and Katie turned to him, shook her head, and offered a Mona Lisa smile, all the while plotting revenge.

As the head coach's wife Katie felt it was her duty to be of assistance to the other coaches' families. Like her husband she was a great organizer. She hosted the wives at coffees frequently and sat around empathizing with the other women about the life of a coach's wife. Whenever a new coach joined the staff she helped him and his wife look for houses, shop for furniture or shoulder any other burdens they asked of her.

No one took more interest in Ara or his work than Katie, but after a few years at Notre Dame she stopped going to football games. With all her many duties as mother and hostess she found it less hectic to send everyone off to the games while she stayed home to organize her postgame party. Since all the games were televised, she enjoyed the freedom of being able to pace, scream, pray, or even turn the game off. If Ara had wanted her to be present in the stadium she would have, but Katie hated the restriction of a *seat*.

Despite an unlisted telephone number, the Parseghians received several crank calls over the years. Ara eventually pulled the phone jack most nights before going to bed, but Katie had to listen to a lot of abuse while Ara was at work. If a caller was courteous, gave a name, and had a legitimate gripe, Katie took time to talk. But she could be the master of the perfect squelch. One caller, upset because he had lost five dollars on a game, woke her up one evening demanding to speak to Ara. "Well, he's asleep now and I don't want to wake him," she said. "But he'll be up tomorrow at five if you'd like me to have him call you then!"

In the end I think Katie played a major role in Ara's resignation. Ara is not the kind of man to be dictated to by a wife, so Katie tried to point out what she saw and let it be his own decision. She is far too intelligent to do it any other way—if it hadn't been *his* choice he never would have been satisfied.

Later, the summer after Ara's resignation in 1975, the Notre Dame Alumni Council wanted to honor him and Katie at a dinner meeting. It was a small gathering with a relaxed atmosphere—no formal speeches. Ara addressed them briefly and then I, in my role then as director of the alumni association, introduced Katie. The council members gave her a standing ovation and Ara, realizing Katie's reserved nature, antagonized her by screeching, "Speech! Speech!" Well, it was Katie who had the last laugh, because when I leaned over to ask if she wanted to say a few words, she said, "I think I'll do just that." Ara's jaw dropped about two feet.

"Everybody is mystified why Ara got out of coaching," she began. "A lot of you think it was the pressure or that he's ready to move on to the pros, but neither of those are true. Ara and I just returned from the West coast after making a commercial for the Ford Pinto. When he discovered my potential for stardom, he thought he'd give up his own career and let me become the breadwinner." Ara, caught completely off guard, laughed admiringly at his wife.

Katie and Ara stayed close to Karan's health matters, and only after the doctors were positive about her diagnosis did Ara inform the coaching staff. It didn't come as a formal announcement or in a way that was meant to evoke sympathy. He was straight and to the point as always in our meetings. "I think you guys have a right to know this," he said. "I've been spending a lot of time these last few months doing work for the Multiple Sclerosis Foundation. Katie and I have just found out that Karan has developed the disease." That was that, and none of us ever brought it up again.

Such was the burden he had to bear in 1967 and thereafter, one that only a few people knew about. Combined with our early performance on the field, Ara had more pressure on him than ever. Our fans were more expectant after the number one finish of 1966. Unfortunately, our players didn't have the enthusiasm to match. There were many returnees on the 1967 squad, and another National Championship just wasn't the dream it had been in 1966.

The season began impressively enough. California came into Notre Dame Stadium for the opener and left with a 41-8 loss. Odd as it may seem, offensively we weren't sharp. Hanratty wasn't nearly as stunning as in his debut one year earlier against Purdue, but he did complete 15 of 30 passes for 205 yards. Every team is pleased to get by the first game with a win, no matter what the showing.

Purdue had some good news and some bad news for us. The good news was that Bob Griese had finally graduated and moved on to the Miami Dolphins. The bad news was that sophomore Mike Phipps replaced him. Phipps threw 14 completions for 238 yards and two touchdowns. Hanratty connected 29 times out of an amazing 63 attempts, accounting for 366 yards and one touchdown. We hadn't planned to put the ball up that often, but we were playing catch-up all day. And it resulted in four interceptions. The last one sealed our fate. Trailing 28-21 with 1:29 to play at our own 38, Hanratty looked for Seymour once too often, and Purdue had the play figured all the way. We had *outgained* the Boilermakers 485 to 349, but we also *outmistaked* them, too, 4-0. This was a good example of a trend Ara frequently mentioned to the team. The team with better statistics wins only 50 percent of the time, while the team with fewer turnovers wins 90 percent.

We snapped back from the loss right away. Both the

offense and defense played with precision against Iowa, resulting in a 56-6 win. With halfbacks Rocky Bleier and Dan Harshman and fullback Ron Dushney combining for most of our 242 rushing yards and Hanratty chipping in for another 200 in the air, we looked like we could lick the world.

But we found out the next week we could not even handle a team at the far end of our continent. Despite the Trojans' number-one billing, we were 12-point favorites. The oddsmakers must not have taken Orenthal J. Simpson into consideration. Somehow USC coach John McKay managed to find another running back better than his Heisman Trophy-winning Mike

Ara never lost the urge to stay active in the game he loved.

Garrett. That shouldn't be surprising, though, because a quick look at any NFL roster will prove that talent was never lacking at Southern Cal. We had a 7-0 halftime lead thanks mainly to USC's ineffective passing, but McKay chose to stay on the ground in the second half, usually with O. J. carrying. That strategy gained them a 24-7 victory. On our side of the ledger Hanratty had thrown four more interceptions, and these turnovers were costly. So here we were, the defending National Champions, at .500 after only four games.

It was time for some soul searching, and this was one occasion when Ara was very familiar with the situation. He had seen a "get-rich-quick attitude" on a few Miami and Northwestern teams. The danger of having a strong-armed quarterback and elusive receiver who have had success is that both your offense and defense tend to relax. Both units think that even if the other team goes ahead, the passing combination will be able to come to the rescue.

Additionally, a quarterback who gets used to throwing to a certain receiver often overlooks more open candidates in the pass pattern. When opponents sense this, frequent interceptions result.

Ara felt we were guilty of both sins and took corrective action. First he decided to utilize our running game more. Second he called Terry in for a conference. "Coach, I've been lying awake nights thinking about all this," Terry admitted. "What am I doing now that I didn't do last year?" Ara explained his theory and told Terry if he would only follow our instructions his confidence would return.

The logic was good, but unfortunately things didn't go as planned. We beat Illinois the next week, 47-7, and Terry did as directed. He did have one pass picked off early in the game but only because of a great play by an Illinois defender who carried it in for a touchdown. Ara didn't want Terry to get down on himself, so on the very next play he called for a short, simple pass pattern. Damned if it wasn't intercepted again. He had two more that game but then didn't throw another one the rest of the season.

Rocky Bleier was our captain that year and being a natural born worrier our 2-2 record before the Illinois game had him distraught. He had been a vital member of our 1965 and '66

133

O. J. Simpson—the best in Southern Cal's distinguished line of running backs.

teams, and he could see that some spark was missing from last year's team. He faulted himself for that. Not being a fire-'em-up type guy, he had decided to lead by example. Now he thought that strategy was harming the team.

Ara once heard a saying that was perfectly applied to Rocky. It went, "Never worry about a worrier." Rocky was another in what was becoming a long line of strong, moderately-fast, hard-blocking, good-receiving running backs under Ara at Notre Dame. Rocky joked that Ara searched for backs in his own mold—short and stocky.

Rocky was the first offensive back in six years to be elected captain. He was the only logical choice. He was a hard worker who filled in whenever needed. We didn't have anyone else to punt that year, so Rocky volunteered and did a respectable job. All the players had high regard for him because, though he was concerned about the team's development, he didn't try to get heavyhanded with anyone.

Rocky was good enough to be drafted by the Pittsburgh Steelers after our season. He played for them in 1968 and was then drafted again—this time into the service. Unlike other athletes of that day, Rocky didn't try to pull any strings to avoid military duty. He didn't profess to be a super patriot, but he did believe in obligation. That obligation meant going to Vietnam and carrying a grenade launcher. One day on patrol he was shot in the left leg but managed to crawl to cover. He hadn't averted danger, though, as an enemy grenade exploded nearby, shattering his other leg.

The army doctors did everything they could, but when he got his discharge he was rated 40 percent disabled and told he would always limp. The Bronze Star he was awarded wouldn't impress NFL defensive linemen.

But Rocky set up an intensive training program, with his

Terry Hanratty listened to our advice but still threw four interceptions against Illinois.

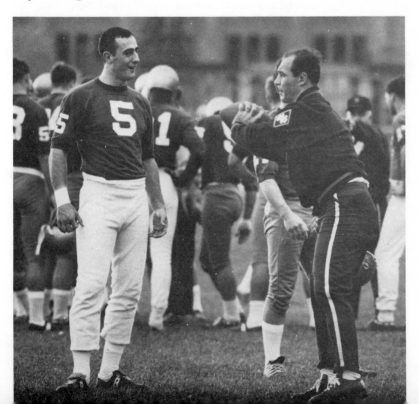

goal another shot with the Steelers. After his discharge he returned to Notre Dame for the 1969 Southern Cal game to be honored during halftime. He limped badly and needed a cane for support. Even though Fridays before home games are hectic, Ara found plenty of time for Rocky. He talked about his war experiences. "When I got shot I saw my blood spurting out in disbelief," he related. "I just couldn't believe it was happening to me. I remember scrambling to cover and trying mentally to make a pact with God. Desperate as I was, I didn't want to make a rash promise like becoming a priest or recluse of any kind. I just prayed and said if I got out of this and back home I'd live a life that tries to help people."

He kept that vow and today is dedicated to several causes benefitting children. He's always been able to charm them and never been too busy to give them attention. He also reached his goal. Against the advice of the coaching staff, Art Rooney, the lovable old owner of the Steelers, insisted that Rocky be added to the team in 1970. He may have been dead weight for a season or two, but after that his total determination made him a better player than he had ever been. He was a significant factor in the Steelers' two consecutive Super Bowl victories in 1975 and '76.

Rocky's influence went a long way toward bolstering his teammates, and we won our last six games. Michigan State followed Illinois on our schedule, but the interest wasn't remotely what it had been the year before. The Spartans had three losses. Still, it was an important game for both sides because of the 1966 outcome. We jumped ahead 17-0, but MSU worked its way back with 12 points. One more Notre Dame touchdown put the game out of reach, and with fullback Jeff Zimmerman gaining 135 yards rushing and Hanratty completing eight of 15 passes we won, 24-12.

After beating Navy 43-14 and Pittsburgh 38-0 our confidence was thoroughly renewed. That left us with our "Southern swing" to close the season. Playing Georgia Tech in Atlanta we wondered what had happened to "southern hospitality." As we were awaiting word to run onto the field, we heard one fan shriek, "Kill those Catholic bastards!" Several others spat on players. During the game someone threw a dead fish onto the field, and all night long our bench was pelted with filled beer

Against Georgia Tech Rocky Bleier scored two touchdowns with torn knee ligaments.

and pop cans. One hit Ara on the shoulder. I suppose this was a reenactment of the Civil War for them, and though it really hadn't been for us before the game, their actions unified us more so than any other game in 1967. We gained Notre Dame's 500th victory by a score of 36-3.

The win hadn't come without consequence, however. Sometime during the first half, Bleier seriously injured his knee. He didn't mention it to anyone, so we didn't realize he was hurt. He scored two touchdowns for us with torn ligaments. Only after we had the game securely tucked away did he come to me and ask if I could get someone to handle the punting for him because he was hurting a little.

Rocky was operated on the following Wednesday and traveled to Florida with us two days later for our finale with Miami. The Hurricanes had a six-game win string going and were plenty mad that the local Orange Bowl had snubbed them. Their coach, Charlie Tate, had publicly stated that "Notre Dame is our bowl game." His team had allowed only 14 points in its last four games and, with several of our top players either out or nursing injuries and playing in temperatures we weren't used to, we had to wonder how many points we could score.

Miami put us in the hole quickly, going ahead 13-3. We cut the margin to 16-10 at halftime and moved ahead 17-16 midway through the third quarter with Jeff Zimmerman carrying most of the way. After John Pergine got us the ball with an interception at Miami's 38, Bob Gladieux, contused leg and all, scored in two plays to give us a 24-16 lead. Miami scored with three minutes left and tried a two-point conversion. The play was well executed, but linebacker Bob Olson tipped the ball at the last instant and the game was ours. Our record was 8-2, good enough for a fourth-place ranking.

A defensive lineman from Miami paid us a great compliment after the game. "In the fourth quarter, I was really hanging and figured they're not as used to the heat as I am. But they'd break the huddle, sprint to the line and bust a gut coming after you. I knew then why they were Notre Dame."

We were all drained as we entered the locker room. Straggling behind, hobbled by his cast and crutches, Rocky Bleier was the last to arrive. As he did, his teammates cheered for him. "Rocky! Rocky! Rocky!" they chanted. Ara walked over to him and placed the game ball in his hands. Rocky stood motionless, pulling the ball tighter each second. As we went up to congratulate him, his tears were freely flowing.

The season was a success even after our startling start. But one personal development during the year would leave a mark on Ara, one that would eventually contribute to his resignation.

Rocky Bleier — 1967 Notre Dame football captain.

1968—
When You Have
Nothing Left But Pride

Knute Rockne had the "Four Horsemen" and the "Seven Mules" while he was at Notre Dame. One of Ara's most noteworthy Fighting Irish groups was the "Three Owls." They were named by trainer Gene Paszkiet, a parttime philosopher who warned the team, "You can't soar with Eagles if you fly with the Owls." Their real names were Ron Dushney, Bob Gladieux and Terry Hanratty.

The Owls had much in common with the students not active in varsity sports. Rumor held that they frequented the social spots and freely discussed anything from humor to world problems. When it became apparent that they were substituting such seminars for early morning classes, the conscientious nun teaching the players brought the problem to Ara.

So right before exam time Ara asked George Sefcik and me to keep tabs on them. Getting them up for breakfast and classes was a real trick. Alarm clocks didn't work. The Owls either shut them off or slept right through. George and I made it part of our daily routine to check in at Sorin Hall. Awakening them was easy—keeping them there was the difficulty. Maybe they weren't meant to function in daylight.

The Owls weren't troublesome. They didn't start fights and didn't get into any. They were super kids and great competitors, but in their case the "athlete" came before "student."

This is not to say they were not also students, because certainly they were dedicated to graduating with a degree, which they did. They just happened to enjoy one more than the other.

Dushney was always the clown, and our first impression of him was that he probably wouldn't play much. He was only 5-10, and that was pretty slight for a fullback. He was not as talented as some of our other backs and had to sweat for whatever he accomplished. He was pressed into duty in 1967 when starter Jeff Zimmerman's career was ended by injury. Ron worked so hard and played so well that he held off all other competitors.

He was a good natured kid but was prone to mistakes in practice. One day Ara watched him commit the same errors on successive goalline plays and hollered at him. "Dushney, you know what you need? You need a good swift kick...." I must admit I was worried about how Ron might take that, but he replied, "Coach, you're exactly right!" So Ara told him to bend over, and he gave him an innocent swat in the seat. Ara called the same play, and Dushney ran it in for a score. Ara, delighted now with the improvement, snickered, "See, Dush, all you needed was a little encouragement." Dushney smiled and continued in his carefree way.

Bob Gladieux was a stellar high school performer in several sports. He scored four or five touchdowns a game, setting career records in Ohio. At 170 pounds he was a fast runner by high school standards. I saw him star in the state all-star game and made the mistake of telling Ara what a great prospect we had coming in. It was a mistake for two reasons. At the end of the summer Bob caught mononucleosis and came to school weighing only 155. Ara kept asking me where I was hiding this "superstar," and I kept trying to get Bob to spend more time in the dining hall.

He beefed up by his sophomore year, and he attempted to make up for lost time quickly. We were playing him at right and left halfback, and he had to learn the assignments for both positions. Ara observed the offensive backfield at least part of every day, and without fail, whenever he came around, Gladieux would head to his alignment in a quandary and do something wrong. Eventually Ara exploded. "Damn it,

141

Bob Gladieux made one circus catch after the next.

Gladieux, don't you ever look at your play book?"

After practice I called him over. "Hey, Bob, I know you can play better than you've been showing," I said. "Just relax out there. You know what you're supposed to be doing, don't you?"

"Yeah, Coach, I do," he answered. "But every time that man gets near me I just freeze up." I had to laugh because I knew what he meant. It happened to a lot of us as players.

I mentioned it to Ara, and though he promised to talk to Gladieux he explained to me why he wouldn't alter his tactics. "If we make it really tough on them on the practice field, keeping them under constant pressure, they'll get used to it. If they can hold up and fight off petty peeves, they'll know how to handle any situation they face in a game."

142

Terry Hanratty's membership in the trio might have surprised most Notre Dame fans. His public image was one of dignity and grace beyond his years. Notre Dame traditionally protects and enhances the reputation of its quarterbacks. Terry was an abundantly talented athlete, but one who didn't take himself seriously. Terry's personal life was his own, but on the field he was all business and gained the respect of his teammates through his success.

Terry was as easy going as his accomplices. He took endless ribbing his sophomore year as a "green horn" leading a veteran team. His upperclass teammates dubbed him "The Rat" and played one pratical joke after the next on him. George Goeddeke was a frequent culprit, and Terry finally decided to even up the score. One night after the team meal, Terry ran over to Goeddeke's dorm, climbed into his room and hid in the closet. He expected him to arrive momentarily, but it was two hours later before Goeddeke entered with several other players for a bull session. Terry didn't get overanxious and instead waited for a more opportune time to play his hand. Minutes later Goeddeke walked over toward the closet, opened the door and Terry leaped out. Goeddeke and the others had a good long laugh, and Terry had the lifetime endorsement of his teammates after that.

All the Owls were clutch performers. Hanratty was a sharp quarterback who could dodge tackles, check his intended receiver and if covered shoot the ball to someone else. Gladieux made one circus catch after the next during his career, many of them in clutch situations. Even at 195 pounds Dushney was one of the best blocking backs we ever had, capable of knocking 225-pound linebackers on their tails. These men sparked our opening game win over Oklahoma in 1968. Terry was 18 of 27 for 202 yards and two touchdowns. Gladieux had 56 yards rushing and caught six passes for 45 yards. Dushney gained 55 rushing yards and returned two kickoffs for 34 yards. We rolled over the Sooners impressively, 45-21.

We must have impressed Oklahoma coach Chuck Fairbanks. "I have to take my hat off to Notre Dame," he told the writers. "They are a very good team. They are stronger offensively than when we played them in Norman in 1966. They have a lot of talent defensively and should improve there as the season progresses. I'm not sure they're better in that phase than in 1966. Possibly they have a better pass defense."

He couldn't have been more wrong about that as Purdue's Mike Phipps proved the next week. When Phipps had finished for the top-ranked Boilermakers, he had picked our defensive secondary apart 16 times in 24 tries for 144 yards and one touchdown. Multi-talented running back Leroy Keyes scored two touchdowns and threw for another on a halfback option play. Hanratty played well in a catch-up effort, connecting on 23 of 43 for 294 yards. We gained 454 yards offensively but couldn't seem to push it over once we got within the 20. The result was a 37-22 loss.

Our pass defense wasn't much better against Iowa, but our offense put 51 points on the board to the Hawkeyes 28. Consecutive wins over Northwestern, 27-7, and Illinois, 58-8, gave

Ara was at his best on the field with the players.

us new confidence in our defense. In the latter game Hanratty moved ahead of the immortal George Gipp as Notre Dame's all-time total offense leader.

That brought us to our annual clash with Michigan State. Never will a game in this series be more significant than in 1966, but both teams play with full emotion every year nonetheless. For this particular meeting with the Spartans, Duffy Daugherty leaked word to the press that he intended to start the game with an on-side kick if Notre Dame elected to receive. Ara questioned the credibility of that statement but warned the team to be alert just the same. We did win the coin flip, and Duffy was true to his word. Even though our players were on the lookout, they could not handle the on-side kick, and the Spartans recovered. Six plays and 42 yards later they had a touchdown. They had teased us and gotten away with it, and momentum was on their sideline.

Trailing 21-17 with less than two minutes to play and the ball on the MSU three, Ara signalled Hanratty to pass on third down. Two previous rushing plays had produced nothing against the inspired Spartans. Hanratty dropped back, spotted Jim Seymour with a slight edge on his defender and sent the ball his way. Before Seymour could catch it he was knocked to the ground. Everybody in the stadium could see it except the official responsible for the call, who had slipped and fallen. Ara argued, but it did no good. Hanratty tried carrying the ball on fourth down, but MSU's Al Brenner jarred it loose and State took over to run out the clock.

Ara's remarks to the press after the game were unusually critical. "I'm deeply concerned about the third down call they missed," Ara announced. "Jim Seymour was tackled in the end zone and nobody called it. Seymour beat his man to the outside. One official fell down on the play but there were four others to make the call. It disturbs me that they missed an out-and-out violation. It influenced the outcome of the game. We would have had the ball at the one-foot line with first down. I don't plan to lodge an official complaint because nothing can be done about it. They can't change the call or game.

"State's on-side kick didn't surprise us. We discussed it at pregame meetings, both at the hotel and in the locker room. We were yelling at our players about it before the kickoff. The ball

145

just bounced right for Michigan State."

This was a bitter loss for Ara. He was a hard loser by nature, and that might have been his biggest fault. Losing made him a tyrant around the office. He used to slam film cans, harp on poor officiating and snap at all of us in the staff meetings. He was impossible to live with. "What the hell are you teaching that kid?" he would bellow at the top of his lungs during film sessions when he spotted an error. It never got any better. He never lost any easier.

Sometimes his anger would carry into Wednesday or Thursday of the following week, a time when it was essential to be thinking strictly about the upcoming game. That Michigan State game was the best example. He looked at that game film over and over, rewinding it endlessly until I thought it would break. "You mean to tell me that isn't interference," he screamed. "You're damned right! I'm going to write the Big Ten office. Cut out that excerpt and splice me together a film. I'm going to take it to the Big Ten meetings. I'll show them how they cost us that game!" In a cooler moment he chose to drop the issue.

I think the intentions of his temperament were twofold. First, he wanted to vent some natural frustration. But second, he tried to spur us to correct mistakes and work harder to improve the team. Even if that hadn't been planned, it resulted. We treaded lightly and did everything carefully and were never late for meetings after a loss. Then hopefully we would win the next week and Ara's sting would be healed.

All the assistant coaches looked at Ara from a different vantage point. Paul Shoults, for example, had played in the same backfield with him at Miami and then worked under him for 24 years. I had played for him and later joined his staff. Others knew him only as a boss. All of us had great respect for him, and though some may have approached it, I do not believe any of us actually feared him. Those of us who had experienced his human side for years weren't in awe of him.

Ara was a motivational master with his staff. He had several approaches. One time he might holler, another time he might taunt, but his message always got through. He would explain what we absolutely had to accomplish and, for whatever our individual motives, we went out and did it. If it meant

146

putting in extra hours, it made no difference as long as we could show him what we could achieve.

He didn't pat us on the backs for this. That wasn't his style, and some of us felt insecure because of it. We would have given anything to hear him tell us we were doing a good job. In public Ara described all of us as the world's greatest assistants, but there were very few complimentary words behind closed doors. As a young coach, that troubled me until Ara and I talked about it one day. "If that's the way you look at it you're building this up as an employee-employer relationship," he said. "It isn't that at all. We're in this thing together. It just so happens fate says I call the shots. You're as much a part of this program as I and any success we have, we have together. Your perspective is all wrong if you're looking for compliments." When I thought about his words I appreciated what he was saying. Hundreds of coaches dreamt about being on the staff at Notre Dame. By hiring us he paid the highest compliment of all. It *implied* confidence in our ability.

Periodically, we all smarted from some criticism Ara made of us at practice. I brooded on those occasions and apologized to him afterward if I felt I had made a mistake. "What mistake? "What are you talking about? Oh, I had forgotten all about that," he would answer. I think we had the notion he kept a scorecard on assistant coaching errors when in reality we were the only ones who dwelled on them. Ara wanted us to be aware of error when it occurred, but then for him it was over.

Those on the administrative staff of the athletic department had their misconceptions about Ara, too. Many were either afraid or in awe of him. Ara didn't detect that, and he wouldn't have understood it if he had. Therefore, he didn't try to manipulate anyone. However, he felt that the football fortunes were his responsibility and that ultimately he had to call the shots. He listened to advice from the athletic staff and didn't try to make decisions in every phase of the operation, but if he was against anything that involved his team he wanted it stopped.

The world seemed right again after we won our next game over Navy, 45-14, but a real disaster was only days away. In his efforts to re-enforce the sharpness we demonstrated from the 20-yard line against Navy, Ara felt the need for some contact

Ara was a motivational master.

drills during our preparation for the Pittsburgh game. "We have to get mentally tough and practice scoring," he told us. "There's no other way than repeating it over and over again." So we ended practice with "live" goalline stands. Ara selected the sloppiest part of the field for this duty; it is rare for anyone to get hurt seriously in the mire.

Ara wouldn't call any quarterback option plays in these drills. He didn't want to expose Hanratty to injury by sending him into the line at that time of the day when the fatigue factor must be considered. Too many teams have lost great players that way.

Ara's first call was a quick fake to the fullback with a pitchout to the sweeping halfback. Hanratty took the ball from center, pivoted, slipped just a little and recovered too late to meet the faking fullback. Terry also realized that the halfback was too wide for the pitch. So he did what he should but exactly what we were trying to protect him against in practice. Terry took off, and as he splashed toward the end zone he was hit. He gave out with a war cry that numbed everyone in earshot.

We all knew what the scream might mean. We had to live with the risk of serious injury, but Terry was our All-American quarterback, our field leader, agonizing in the mud. The season had not been a distinguished one, but this would certainly ruin it.

Trainer Gene Paszkiet charged over and examined Terry. Undoubtedly he realized instantly that surgery was inevitable. A great college career had ended for Hanratty—all because of one freak play. Paszkiet drove him to the training room on a golf cart, and as he pulled away Ara shouted, "Theismann, get in there and run number one."

Ara couldn't end practice then even though he doubtlessly wanted to. He didn't want to send the squad to the showers with nothing more than the spectre of its offensive catalyst crippled in the muck. The guard had to be changed literally as well as figuratively. And it was quite a new guard at that.

The contrast between Hanratty and Joe Theismann was marked. Although Terry didn't fool around at practice, as a charter member of the "Owls" he could hardly be termed authoritarian. While Terry wanted to "soar" and "fly," Joe took no chances of being anything but an "eagle."

From what we had seen on his high school film, Joe was an outstanding runner but not much of a passer. When he reported to his first practice we discovered four other things not obvious in the screening room. Joe could throw much better than we thought; he was fast as well as quick; he had large hands for a small man; and he had extraordinary football sense.

Joe was small. He weighed no more than 160 pounds and was six feet tall. Pro teams seem to be convinced that body mold is everything, but to Ara it wasn't his prime concern. We didn't pass from the pocket, so Ara wanted an athlete, a quarterback who could roll out and pass on the run. Theismann showed himself to be a superb athlete his freshman year, even if he looked like a high school boy who had been given permission to fool around during freshman practice.

Seeing Joe for the first time some pro scouts would wonder, "That kid's a quarterback?" But after watching him awhile they said, "Yeah, that kid's a quarterback!" Up close Joe was sinewy. That kind of player is more durable than a guy built like a sculpture.

So seven games into the 1968 season another memorable chapter of Notre Dame history began. Theismann took over for Hanratty. Joe ran one play, and Ara screamed at him. He wasn't hollering because Theismann made a mistake, but in the distance the golf cart was slowly carrying away an Owl—one who had brought us through on so many occasions. Ara's shout was one of frustration.

Theismann looked at Ara and sensing the message in his voice said, "C'mon, Coach, it isn't that bad."

That was Joe. He knew that the season wouldn't be lost even though Hanratty was gone. Joe knew what he could do. The guy hasn't been born with more confidence in himself than Joe Theismann. He felt he could do anything he set his mind to. And the hell of it is he was almost right. Confident though he was, we were pleased that the youngster would have two games at home before Southern California at Los Angeles.

With only 30 minutes of varsity experience, Joe opened against Pittsburgh. Ara kept the offense on the ground until we had a 7-0 lead. He then gave Joe a chance to play his game. Rolling, ducking and darting, Theismann completed passes for

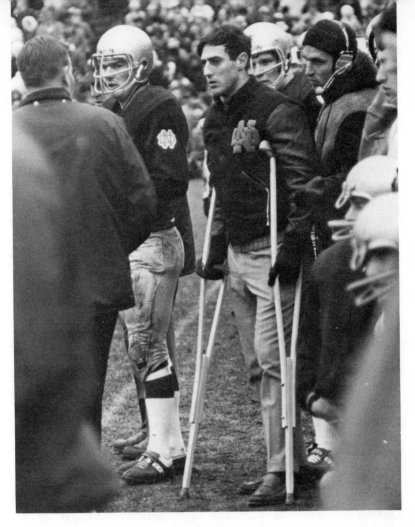

A crippled Owl, Terry Hanratty, shows concern.

20 and 29 yards on keeper plays and threw two touchdown passes to Coley O'Brien, playing halfback during the 1968 season. Only by having outstanding reserves like Theismann and Bob Belden behind Hanratty were we able to make that change. The final was 56-7, and Theismann's performance inspired old timers to reminisce about another late season when All-American quarterback Angelo Bertelli went off to war and was replaced by a sophomore named Johnny Lujack.

Comparisons with Lujack proliferated when Joe guided us to a 34-6 victory over Georgia Tech. With 10 days of Theismann behind us and two weeks to wait for Southern Cal, we had to face the fact we had a boy despot on our hands.

Given the reins, Joe grabbed them. Although older players hardly knew him, he didn't defer to their seniority. He wasn't awed by anybody, including Ara. He believed that the quarterback was in charge of the team on the field, and he was convinced he knew more about running the offense than a senior tackle or halfback possibly could.

Theismann did not suffer mistakes with Hanratty's equanimity. When a receiver made an error, Joe would say, "Damn it, you broke the pattern" or "What's wrong with you? Are you going to go your own way all day?" He was right, too. The other players knew it, and the coaches knew it. It wasn't a case of the kid trying to be a wise guy. He simply knew all the plays and all the patterns.

Ara saw the need for a buffer between this cocky quarterback and the older players who were sensitive to criticism from a sophomore. Since I was Joe's coach it was my duty to keep him in line. If he resented me for it he never showed it. After all, Hanratty had nothing but friends on the squad. So when Joe yelled at a receiver, blocker or running back, I would yell even louder, "Theismann, would you shut up! You run the team and let us coach it!" Every once in a while he did.

Joe had a firm belief that he would be a legend before he was 25. It wasn't idle talk to him—he meant it. If such a thing is possible, Joe wore his cockiness well as a college player. Ara had brought to coaching an intense appreciation for a quarterback's feel for the game. His appreciation increased during the time of Little Joe. "Don't ever overlook the magic of Joe Theismann," Ara often said. When things were dragging during practice or a game Ara would holler, "Do something exciting, Joe." And he rarely let us down.

Joe was anything but an all-talk, no-action kind of guy. In 1970 he was chosen for the Academic All-America team as well as the Associated Press on-the-field All-America squad. While critics predicted he couldn't play pro ball, Joe made a killing in the Canadian Football League and then returned to the NFL for an even larger contract.

But for all his efforts there was one goal that eluded Joe. Under the guidance of Sports Information Director Roger Valdiserri, Joe made a determined bid for the Heisman Trophy.

Joe Theismann—that kid's a quarterback.

153

As Joe began to shine his freshman year, Valdiserri pulled him aside and asked if he'd mind changing the pronunciation of his name. Joe's last name was pronounced "Theese-man" when he came to school, but Roger wanted to make it "Thighs-man." His idea was to market Joe in later years as "Theismann, as in Heisman." Naturally Joe didn't need much persuading. Unfortunately, Joe finished a close second to Stanford's quarterback Jim Plunkett. Joe's world didn't end when he got the news—it couldn't have because he felt somehow, someway he'd come out of anything on top.

He probably felt that way in his first game against Southern Cal in 1968. On our first offensive series in the Coliseum, Joe threw a pass intended for Jim Seymour at our 16-yard line. But Sandy Durko, a Trojan defensive back, cut in front of Seymour and had no problem scoring from there. After just two plays, 40 seconds into the game, we were behind 7-0. Staying on the ground on all but one of the 18 plays, Theismann brought us right back 86 yards for a touchdown. Bob Gladieux scored on a 57-yard, off-tackle play on our next possession.

A two-touchdown bulge was within reach when we came to second-and-goal at the USC seven as the first half was nearing an end. One play later it seemed unlikely after Theismann, rolling to pass, was tossed for a six-yard loss.

Southern Cal's players and coaches might have thought they had rattled the sophomore quarterback, but nothing rattled him. Ara sent in a play calling for Joe to hand off to Coley O'Brien. Coley ran a sweep to his right, pulled up, looked to his left and threw a spiral to Theismann, who had continued unnoticed into the end zone and who now caught the pass for a touchdown. It was a flawless play that put us in excellent position.

The defense was doing a great job of coping with O. J. Simpson, a running back destined to baffle all pro defenses. After watching the film of the 1967 USC game, Ara reasoned that it was a mistake to have the defense penetrate against Simpson because it created a bubble through which he could easily find his way. So Ara instructed the defense to float at the line of scrimmage. The Heisman Trophy winner did score USC's next touchdown in the second half, but we held him to 55 net yards in 21 carries, the worst production of his distinguished season. The Trojans scored again to tie the game, and when field goal attempts of 41 and 33 yards by our Scott Hempel were both wide, the game ended at 21-21.

That made us 7-2-1, fifth-ranked nationally. That was far from what we had hoped for at the beginning of the season. But as we would discover in the months ahead, we were now dealing with a new emotion on our team.

1969-
Someone Else's Gipper...
For A Change

Whenever I made a speaking appearance, many of which had been arranged by Ara, the audience always wanted to know about the guy I worked for. In later years I had a story I enjoyed telling. It went like this.

"I remember the adversity Notre Dame fans experienced before Ara came here in 1964. But after we won our first five or six games the students became drunk with their newfound power. One game late in the season it began to snow and the students started chanting, 'Ara stop the snow! Ara stop the snow!' Ara walked over to me with a puzzled expression and said, 'That's ridiculous.' He paused for a moment and gazed back quizzically, 'Do you think I *could*?'

"Just to show you how the years change a person, during one of our games last year it was snowing off and on and at one point the students renewed the cry of their predecessors, 'Ara stop the snow! Ara stop the snow!' This time there was no hesitancy in his voice as he asked me, 'Do you think I *should*?'"

Though the students did make such pleas over the years, Ara certainly wasn't vain enough to act as portrayed in that account. The anecdote does point out one thing, though—Ara's attitude did change.

In any business there are the idea men—the creative geniuses—and the doers—the organizationally-minded who know how to implement those ideas. It's rare to find both com-

156

modities in the same person, but thanks to the wealth of experience Ara gained at such an early age from some of the top minds in football, he is blessed with that combination.

Ara came from French-Armenian heritage that taught him to be respectful and gave him a feel for people. His father was an intelligent man, fluent in four different languages. He came to this country after the Turkish Communists overran Armenia. He was experienced in the banking and finance business and secured employment in the travel bureau division of a bank over here. Ara has the keen mind of his father, and through imitation he learned to be analytical in all that confronted him.

Ara has a hard, tough exterior. He often counselled me about my disposition, saying I had to be like a "duck." "Your problem is that you're like a sponge," he philosophized. "When water hits you, you absorb it, get heavy and eventually sink. When water hits a duck, it rolls right off his back and he stays buoyant."

Someone once told me he couldn't fault Ara's record as a coach, but in terms of building relationships with his players Ara was a failure. That couldn't be farther from the truth. Ara knew that every successful organization has a leader, one person

They believed that Ara could stop the snow.

who must dominate. He didn't try to make friends with his players at practice or during games. But one-on-one, if anyone ever came to him with a problem, complaint or request, Ara was ready to help. If he couldn't take care of the situation, he tracked down someone who could. Seniors who planned to continue in pro ball often called on Ara to help in contract negotiations—free of charge, of course. Others who sought jobs asked him to use his influence.

Ara is generous, almost to a fault. When we first came to Notre Dame I was badly in need of a car, and Ara tried to give me his 1956 Oldsmobile. I wouldn't take it for free so I gave him everything I had in my pocket at the time—a whopping $35. Every Christmas he hosted the staff at his house for a party. Sometime during the evening he presented all of us with a check—a considerable sum of money. He had earned it from his television and radio shows and then divided it equally among us. The shows cut into his time at the busiest point in the week, but he accepted the inconvenience to benefit us.

It wouldn't surprise me if the money he makes doing his Ford commercials is donated to the MS fund. A lot of people razzed him or made sarcastic remarks about his involvement in the campaign mostly out of jealousy. He refused to brag about his contributions to the MS cause or any other. That is the greatest act of love—to give anonymously. A local shopping center sponsored an MS drive at the start of our two-a-day practices one year. They asked Ara to speak. So he quickly cleaned up between sessions, dashed to the location for the talk and pulled out a $100 bill from his wallet to kick off the campaign.

Ara was considerate enough never to criticize a coach or player in public. In a staff meeting he might be wrathful with us over errors that cost us a game. That was justified, but as far as the world knew from what he would say to the media, all losses were his fault. He always shouldered blame and shared credit. Sometimes in a lighter moment during the school's weekly Quarterback Club meetings he would joke, "You saw our difficulties moving the ball in the first half. I guess I shouldn't have let my assistants run the team then but I took over at halftime and you could see the difference from then on." The crowd came to expect him to rib us that way.

These qualities of Ara Parseghian were tested and refined

in the late sixties. The face of all college campuses, or at least the personality of schools and students, was changing. The world and its values were being rearranged, and the college people were the ones most responsible for it. Campus unrest, demonstrations, draft evasion, peace, anti-establishment, pollution, women's liberation, gay liberation, race relations, marijuana, freedom, personal identity, relevance—these were the topics affecting their lives.

In all it was a very tumultuous time on college campuses. The seething unrest, the tide of change, the uncontrollable upheaval of values, the realigning of priorities, the constant pursuit of the young to live placidly, to remove barriers and *hang-ups* involved our players, too.

The beauty of Notre Dame as we remarked in 1964 was the total integration of players into the student body. We didn't have athletic dorms, and we didn't want them. Our players had been just like any other students. They were admired but not idolized. Now, however, student involvement was waning. Snake dances through the snow and spontaneous torch rallies were no longer fashionable. We strove to uphold all the values and, therefore, all the restrictions of past years. But while we only had the players for two hours a day, they were with their peers for the other 22. And our guidelines made them the "odd," "established," "Uncle Tom," "jocks." They were *out of it* by new student standards.

On the practice field in the spring of 1969 the impact of our young lions was being felt. Their manes flowed freely beyond their helmets. Maybe they were on time, and maybe they weren't. For the first time in our careers the players responded to our criticism with, "You screamed at me, Coach. I don't think that's right. I'm a person and I have feelings."

Our staff meetings were filled with more sociology than football strategy that year. We had three replacements joining us—George Kelly, a Notre Dame graduate who had been on the Nebraska staff for eight years; Mike Stock, one of Ara's players at Northwestern; and Denny Murphy, son of prep team coach John Murphy. All of our biases came to light during these sessions, and for most of us the generation gap was a reality. We had to decide how to cope with this new dilemma.

Ara is conservative by nature, and we fully expected him

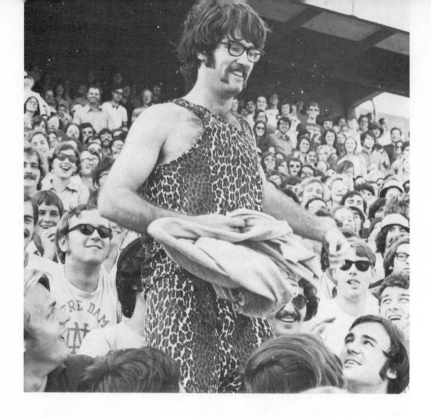

Some student traditions, like the "Stripper," never did change.

to take that type stance in this turmoil. In a sense he did. Ara resolved not to alter his coaching style. He felt that there was nothing he could change that wouldn't sacrifice a principle. He was going to yell at the players, laugh with them or hug them—whatever the situation called for. To do otherwise would have been contrary to his personality. He had seen the outcome of what he taught too many times; he had witnessed men molded by the discipline he imposed. Football is a challenge because every player must spend himself in order to achieve excellence. There are no shortcuts. So his word would be law at practice.

But simultaneously Ara forced himself to live with a difficult fact of life. With all the distractions and liberalism the late sixties dangled in front of our players, football wasn't as important for many of them any more. Their desire was fading, and it didn't stop with three or four of them. The secret of our success at Notre Dame was rarely that we had vastly superior talent, but rather that Ara understood the importance of and then developed morale. Up till 1969 that was the edge he had been able to generate.

Since we didn't have that same spirit then and the years that followed, Ara probably did his best job of coaching during this period. We went back to the basics in our meetings and made certain every small detail had been cared for. We were doing our best to build a "team" out of 100 or so "individuals."

Insofar as it didn't affect the team, Ara let the players be individuals off the field. A group of them approached him to get permission to march in a "Stop the War" demonstration. Most of the assistant coaches would have refused, but he told them, "If you feel in the depths of your heart it is meaningful for you to do that, I have no objection. Make sure it's a peaceful demonstration and don't allow yourself to be coerced into doing this."

If he got a report that a player was a nuisance, he called him in to check it out. None of them got away with lying to Ara. Not only did he have a way of seeing through it, but more than that he commanded such respect that no one risked lying. If he asked a direct question he expected an honest response. He admired the player who didn't try to alibi or skirt the issue and who was contrite in his admission.

161

Ara hadn't led a sheltered life when he was growing up, and he had a son and daughters the age of our players, so he could be tolerant of temptations. When we first came to Notre Dame we had a line in our rule book for the team that read, "No drinking, no smoking—that's a 24-hour proposition all year long." With the current "revolution" Ara felt that rule was no longer realistic. He wasn't naive enough to believe that our players over the years abstained entirely. He was just hoping they would be moderate in their drinking. But now there was such an outcry for "freedom" and "relevance" that he explained his stand.

"If you have to drink, you're in trouble," he told them. "If you're going to be moderate about it, do it privately and discretely so you don't cast a poor reflection. If you get into a drunken brawl at the bars, don't look for my sympathy. I expect you guys to be sensible about this because any of you could be the weakest link on the team."

We had our share of drinkers over the years, which is only natural for young men that age. Usually they were the reserves because making it to the first team demanded a certain dedication. However, this particular year Ara did get a call about one of our frontline players being drunk at a local night spot. He brought him into his office before practice the next day and tore into him. "Is it true what I heard about you last night?" Ara asked.

"Yeah, Coach," he replied timidly.

"You know what I've told you guys about this," Ara continued. "Why the hell didn't you use your head?"

"Well geez, Coach, I didn't have much choice," the player answered. "It's either drinking or drugs."

Ara's eyes dropped downward, and his head shook. His disappointment was apparent. "You know," he said with soft sincerity, pausing momentarily, "there is *one* other option...! How the hell can you call yourself a leader when you follow the crowd?"

Drugs were death in Ara's mind. There was absolutely no way he would tolerate their usage, and he made that clear to the team. We had a couple of kids who developed a need for drugs, and when Ara found out he saw to it that they got the proper medical assistance. Listening to coaches at other schools our

162

problems in that area were miniscule.

Ara didn't try to preach morality, because he knew that wasn't his right. The moral issues he did confront were only brought up because they affected the performance of the team. And when those rules were violated, he tried to be fair in dealing with the players. His guiding principle was, "Always a second chance, sometimes a third, but never more than that." He wasn't out to hang anybody, and discipline was never considered punishment. Ara made sure that the player understood his mistake and tried to handle it in a manner that would prevent recurrence.

He demanded that the player apologize to his teammates, a difficult requirement. Sentencing was then determined by the team—a vote of peers. The captains handled the proceedings, and most times Ara upheld the decision. If it was too stringent, however, he tempered it.

Fans are seldom aware of this human side of football. They just expect the coaches to teach the players to run, block, pass and tackle better than the opponents. And despite all the obstacles in 1969, we pretty well fulfilled their demands.

But the way we started in our opening game against Northwestern the team seemed to be lost in deep meditation. An early interception cost us a score, and the Wildcats jumped up 10-0 in the first quarter. Ara decided to grind it out as much as possible the rest of the game, and with a rushing corps of fullback Bill Barz and halfbacks Denny Allen and Ed Ziegler we went on to a 35-10 victory.

That was probably one of the slowest but "guttiest" backfields we ever had. None of them was exceptionally big, but they worked as hard as anyone. Speed was never anything we had in large doses. The fastest players we did get were tried first on defense. This was a situation attributable to our recruiting difficulties. The really fleet players usually weren't the quickest in the classroom, and so we lost out on many of those.

In this year of change one thing did remain the same—Mike Phipps' dominance over us in the Purdue series. His 12 completions were good for 213 yards, and even though Theismann countered with 14 completions for 153 yards we lost to Phipps and the Boilermakers for the third consecutive season, 28-14.

In 1964 John Huarte had Jack Snow to throw to, Terry

163

Hanratty had Jim Seymour, and now Theismann was working with another outstanding receiver, Tom Gatewood. Against Michigan State Theismann threw 10 times to Gatewood for 155 yards. Our game plan had been to go to the air from the outset because of the Spartans' great defense against the rush. Altogether Theismann threw three touchdown passes and accumulated 294 yards with 20 completions. We were back on the winning track with a 42-28 victory.

After beating Army 45-0, Southern Cal came to town with yet another great running back, Clarence Davis. Our defense, which usually played its best against the highly regarded runners, held the speedster to 75 yards in 30 attempts. Neither team scored in the first half. Bill Barz put us up 7-0 to open the third quarter, but the Trojans drove 75 yards in 10 plays to tie us. Quarterback Jimmy Jones completed his second touchdown pass of the day less than a minute into the fourth quarter, and we started our uphill climb.

Little Joe took us from our 22-yard line to USC's 3 before the alert Trojan defense dropped him for a 15-yard loss on fourth down. With the clock against us, our defense allowed USC one first down, but then forced a punt. Even before the ball was snapped we could sense what was to come. All-American defensive tackle Mike McCoy had his eyes peeled on punter John Young, and as though oblivious to the blockers between them he put his 6-5, 275-pound frame in motion and batted down the punt. We took over on the USC 7, and on fourth down Denny Allan scored the tying touchdown with 6:41 to play.

Our defense got the ball back again, and with Theismann directing us to the 31 Scott Hempel entered the game to attempt a field goal. It would be a 48-yard effort with the wind at his back. He seemed to catch it solidly, and there was no doubt it was on line. We heard the "oohs" and "aahs" of the crowd as the ball glanced the top of the crossbar, bounced up and then just short of success. For the second straight year we tied the Trojans, this time 14-14.

"Gentlemen, it was a helluva football game and no place for the timid," Ara announced to the press. "Both teams were very well prepared and they performed extremely well. It was a great college football game.

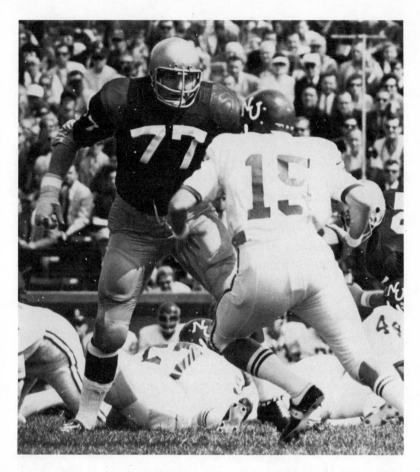

*All-American Mike McCoy—look out when he had his eyes
peeled.*

"I wasn't tempted to go for two points after our second
score. I noticed Big Ten statistics show 91 percent effectiveness
in kicking the extra point but just 18 percent in two-point
efforts."

We played our next four games with the confidence of a
great team. We beat Tulane 37-0; Navy 47-0 with a total offensive output of 720 yards; Pittsburgh 49-7; and Georgia Tech,
according us the same rude treatment as years previous, 38-20.

That left us with one game to play, but during preparation
for Air Force a significant announcement was made. The Uni-

versity had amended its policy toward bowl games and voted in favor of considering an invitation. The Cotton Bowl extended a bid, and all that was needed was one more win.

Ara had championed this cause since coming to Notre Dame. With no conference standing to compete for, the national title was our chief goal. But now, bowl consideration gave us something else to shoot for even in those years when we had one or two losses.

University officials always realized that bowl games gave the nation's top teams an opportunity to stake their claim to the National Championship. They were also aware of the hundreds of thousands of dollars bowl participation could generate, but their major objection was the academic detriment to the players under the calendar that had existed for years. In 1969 that academic calendar was changed, and the last stumbling block had been removed. It's ironic that a decision students had been supporting for 45 years would be made at a time when interest was waning.

The victory over Air Force came grudgingly, 13-6, and with an 8-1-1 record we prepared for the top-rated team in the country, the Texas Longhorns.

There were problems galore in planning for an excursion the school hadn't taken for so long. There were regulations governing the trip that none of us were familiar with. How many players could go? Which ones? Could they take their wives? How about the wives of the staff? Where do we stay and for how long? How do we arrange our practice schedule here in the face of our brutal winter weather? Do we let the players go home for Christmas? If so can we fly them to and from the bowl site from there? All these things plus a thousand others came up. So Ara, along with Business Manager Bob Cahill, did some fast research and quick planning and laid out our course. They came up with the most equitable arrangement for the players and staff under NCAA and financial guidelines.

Minor problems arose along the way, but all that aside our main concern was how to stop the vaunted Texas Wishbone Offense, subtitled the "Triple Option." They ran it to near perfection, and virtually no one had stopped them.

They ran fullback Steve Worster at you all day with their quick line thrust. When your defensive tackle closed to shut him

Joe Theismann dodged tackles all season long.

off, it allowed an alley for quarterback Jim Street to keep the ball. If your defensive end closed for Street, he pitched at the last instant to either Jim Bertlesen or Ted Koy, his halfbacks, who were by now well beyond the defensive end with blockers in front of them.

The execution and poise of this team made up a 14-point deficit to previously undefeated Arkansas in a nationally televised game that ended the season and clinched the Southwest Conference title. This prompted President Richard M. Nixon to walk into their locker room immediately after the game and pronounce them National Champions.

So here was our opponent, the proclaimed king of the mountain, undefeated, playing in its home state. Our players were anxious for the unveiling of this new experience. We practiced indoors six times before Christmas and then reassembled in Dallas on December 26. Even there conditions were cold and wet, but with all the parties, parades and other social events, the players and our families were enjoying the graciousness of the

Texas hospitality.

The media played up the Longhorns and their super back-field, but the player we feared most wouldn't even suit up. They had a defensive back by the name of Freddie Steinmark. He suffered a contusion of the leg in the Arkansas game, and close examination detected cancer. Surgery was performed immediately, and the leg had to be amputated. His presence on crutches the week of the game began to affect our players. We really admired his determination to be up and around so quickly, and he soon became a symbol of the Texas goal. We had our "Gipper," but our players were too "sophisticated" in this day and age to be moved by nostalgia. Steinmark was a here-and-now motivation for Texas.

There weren't many viewers, even our own fans, who gave us much of a chance to win, but seconds into the second

Bob Olson—the Cotton Bowl's top defensive player.

quarter those odds were entirely reversed. Scott Hempel put us up 3-0 six minutes into the game with a 26-yard field goal. With first and 10 on our 46-yard line, we tried a power fake to the split end side. Our line fired out, our backs faked beautifully and split end Tom Gatewood appeared to be a blocker on the play. He sucked the defensive backs in and in the meantime sped into the open where Theismann rifled him a pass. Gatewood went the distance, 54 yards and a touchdown.

Our defense had been disrupting the Texas offense for the first 15 minutes, but in the style of champions the Longhorns made adjustments. Mixing in some short passes with their other three options they put together a nine-play, 74-yard touchdown drive.

With 1:56 to play in the half and the ball on the Texas 12, our defense, led then and all day by co-captain Bob Olson, moved on the snap and cornered Jim Street. He bobbled the ball and we recovered, but the officials said that time out had been called by a 12th player coming off the bench. Over Ara's protestation, Texas got the ball and the down over with no penalty.

The sellout crowd of over 73,000 and the largest television audience that had ever watched a sporting event up till then were treated to a classic defensive struggle in the third quarter. Then Texas kept the ball for 18 plays and over eight minutes and drove for a go-ahead touchdown, 14-10 with 10:13 to play.

That enlivened our offense, especially Joe Theismann. Little Joe got us back on top three minutes later on an eight-play, 80-yard drive. Along the way he ran the ball twice for gains for 14 and 11 yards. On the caper Joe sprinted out to pass on third and four, looking primarily for Gatewood. Gatewood and secondary receiver Jim Yoder were both covered, and Joe was feeling the Texas pressure. He almost got caught but dodged out of it thanks to a timely block by reserve tight end Tom Lawson. Gatewood remained covered, but Yoder escaped in the end zone and Theismann sent him a 24-yard pass. With seven minutes to play we had a 17-14 lead.

Then the Texas Steers packaged one of the most thrilling drives in football history—76 yards in just over five minutes. There were squeakers every third down. There were measurements and decisions and penalties, but all falling the way of the

169

Longhorns. The game came down to a must-play with fourth and two at our 10. Street threw a quick pass to split end Cotton Speyrer. The throw was short and low, but Speyrer snagged it just before it hit the ground. They had a first down at our two, and three plays later they had a 21-17 lead.

With a minute to play and Texas expecting passes all the way, Theismann pinpointed the ball for a 16-yard completion to Denny Allan and 22 yards to tight end Dewey Poskon. That moved us to the Texas 39 with 38 seconds left, but then the percentages caught up with us, and defensive back Tom Campbell intercepted Theismann, aiming for Poskon, at the 14.

It couldn't have been a closer game in any regard. We had 410 yards of total offense in 70 plays while they accumulated 448 yards in 78 plays.

After the game former President Lyndon B. Johnson went into their locker room to congratulate the Longhorns. "It was a great privilege for me to watch these two great teams play today," he told them. "It was inspiring to see strong men fighting for every inch. I was proud of both teams, but I was especially proud of Darrell Royal and every man on his Texas team. Notre Dame fought to the last play and we just had some good luck. God bless you all."

President Nixon phoned to compliment Texas on its victory, one which he said he was pleased to see and which substantiated his belief of the team's supremacy.

"Well, Mr. President," Royal replied. "I'm glad we didn't embarrass your selection."

"You would not have embarrassed me even in defeat, for this was truly a great performance by both teams," Nixon said.

During the course of all this activity Freddie Steinmark, hampered by his crutches, inched his way through the crowd and into the Texas locker room. President Johnson walked over to him and invited him to his ranch. Halfback Ted Koy, observing the scene, told reporters, "We're not a real rah-rah team, but everyone is deeply concerned about Freddie and when he came into the dressing room before the game it picked us all up. He didn't have to say anything, just being here was communicating enough. Everybody shook hands with him and having him around was a big lift."

Steinmark lost his battle with cancer several months later.

Ara never did get a convincing explanation on the Cotton Bowl's "12th Man" controversy.

His death grieved us nearly as much as his Texas teammates.

Over in our locker room we weren't plagued by the depression so noticeable after key game losses in the past, and it wasn't just because of the "new" attitude of our players. We had been a decided underdog, we played our best and gave Texas the scare of its life. President Johnson eventually made his way over to our quarters and praised our efforts.

Overall the bowl experience had been a good one. The players, to a man, agreed it would be a fond memory. Our hotel rooms, the food, the social gatherings all contributed to making it an enjoyable paid vacation for our families. And of major importance, the University gained over $200,000 for its minority student scholarship fund. Except for the loss, everything about this venture had been positive. It was one rewarding *change* that took place in 1969, and we hoped it would be the start of a great tradition.

1970-
Many Stout Hearts
And A Road Runner

By now Ara's postseason responsibilities were beginning to involve him nearly as much as his on-the-field duties. He was in constant demand as a speaker, either for multiple sclerosis benefits or in general for professional seminars and banquets. He didn't have time to accept all the offers, and in keeping with everything else he attempted while at Notre Dame, that ruffled some feathers. People thought just because they called him under the guise of the MS charity, Ara couldn't refuse. But there were nights when he had to weigh a potential donation for maybe $300 against another for $3,000.

Ara improved tremendously as a speaker over the years. When he started out in his days at Miami he lacked only training. He didn't have any flaws, but his talks then weren't flashy. He was articulate, sincere and dynamic. People who hadn't heard him before had to be surprised when he spoke. He looked like such a bull of a man, and his high-pitched voice didn't fit the body. The more excited he got while speaking, the higher the voice rose.

As he became more experienced he developed a sense of timing and was able to feel the pulse of the audience. He saw the appeal of humor and learned that art by watching some of the top performers in Las Vegas and Hollywood.

His thoughts became more and more powerful as he emerged as a public figure. People were anxious to hear him

Ara improved tremendously as a speaker over the years.

comment on almost any issue because they realized he was a success in life. As Ara discovered this, his speeches reflected it. The best way to make any point is from a base of confidence.

Polished as he became at the rostrum, his public appearances were never as forceful as his talks to the team. It would be impossible for him to communicate as well to an audience seeing him for the first time or knowing him vaguely. The team had grown with him, it had gone through bitter and rewarding experiences with him, and Ara could draw on that background when addressing the players. Still, I don't know any organization disappointed by booking Ara.

Whenever he wasn't out of town during the winter Ara enjoyed attending some of the other sporting events at the school, especially basketball. There was a time when he nearly became a basketball coach before he took over the football team at Miami, so he had a fondness for the sport. In 1968 the Athletic and Convocation Center opened, and not only did we move our offices into the spaciousness of the new complex but the basketball team went from the 4,000-seat dust bin in the Old Fieldhouse to the 11,345-seat capacity of the ACC. Naturally with that many people Ara was besieged with autograph requests and handshaking. He was polite and took care of as many fans as possible.

That sort of attention tends to be an ego thing for many celebrities, but during Ara's entire career he never went anywhere just to be in the public eye. A lot of coaches seek publicity and actively court newspaper feature stories and television interviews. On more than one occasion I've seen Ara cut short members of the media, not that he wanted to be uncooperative but because at that time he felt that there were other "team" responsibilities more pressing.

It was funny to watch fans pay homage to Ara. Some of their techniques embarrassed him. I was in his office one summer day and happened to look out the window toward the parking lot. There, in front of Ara's car, was a young father carefully aligning his wife and two sons so as to capture in a photograph not only Ara's Thunderbird, but also the name "Parseghian" painted on the curb. Ara chuckled in disbelief when I called him over to witness the ceremony.

We used to razz him in recruiting meetings about running into his "roommates" while we were on the road. He must have had at least 100. The funniest part about it was that most of them couldn't even pronounce his name. "When you see *Aaron* tell him Bill said hello." "How is *Ira* these days?" Even more hilarious was how people butchered his last name. That ranged anywhere from "Parchesi" to "Parmesan."

Ara found it impossible to walk into an airport without being recognized—except on one occasion. He flew to New York for a speech during a cab strike. He was in a terrible hurry, and fortunately a friendly Fighting Irish fan noticed the ND insignia on his briefcase and somehow deduced that this was the head football coach. He led Ara outside and started hailing cars. After a few moments he got a driver to stop.

"I've got the head coach of Notre Dame over here and he's got to get downtown right away," he sputtered frantically.

The driver consented, so Ara, a little amazed by the fan's forwardness but thankful nonetheless, hopped in the back seat as his "angel of mercy" followed behind and sat up front. During the course of the ride the fan, proud of his accomplishment and regarding himself now as a lifelong friend of Ara's, leaned over to the driver and tapped him on the arm.

"See, buddy, aren't you glad you decided to stop?" he blurted. "Now tonight when you go home you can tell all your friends you drove Joe Kuharich around."

Ara kept himself from laughing and didn't burst the fan's bubble.

There were times when his fame got in his way. Fridays before home games were a big headache for him. The players' parents, graduated players and managers, alumni and hordes of others clustered between our dressing room entrance and the practice field hoping to get his permission to watch practice or have a picture taken with him. It was impossible for him to remember the names of some of those he had met only briefly or so long ago, and he didn't want to insult anyone. Normally he went out to practice early to jog, do calisthenics, pass with the quarterbacks and try field goals with the kickers. But on those Fridays he waited until just prior to the start of practice and asked us to move out with him en masse.

Ara was an excellent public relations man for the University, making a conscious effort to be pleasant whenever he was "on display." He always had time for kids. He'd pat them on the head or lift them onto his shoulders. Often he'd give them some article of his clothing as a souvenir. But like all celebrities there were times when he just wanted to fade into the crowd and be unnoticed in a restaurant or at a movie with Katie and his children.

Amazingly, none of this changed Ara's relationship toward people. He was a living example of something he told more than one of his players, "My life's experience has taught me one thing well. Never try to imitate or envy anyone. Always be yourself."

Trying to preach this or any other philosophy to our student-athletes during this time was a hit-and-miss procedure. But after undergoing one year of the *revolution* Ara decided to "get with it" and make ours a *free* society. "Football at Notre Dame is, was and shall be a voluntary sport," he announced at our first fall meeting. "You don't have to play. But if you want

Ara always had time for kids.

to there will be some team rules that will override personal ones. You make that choice, then let's begin."

Looking at our personnel we figured to have an outstanding team in 1970. Defensively we were as solid as ever, and except that we didn't have a breakaway threat among our running backs we would be explosive offensively. The team was much more responsive than one year previous, but as Ara pointed out in our meetings, "It's easy to be loyal when you're winning. The real test of attitude is when things turn sour." This was a likable group of kids. Still, their approach to the game was more businesslike, not nearly as spontaneous as it had been our first few years. Many of the traditions that had strengthened morale were now lost.

A 35-14 win over Northwestern got us off to a good start in 1970. Then a rarity occurred—we beat Purdue. Theismann threw three touchdown passes to split end Tom Gatewood. The defense held the Boilermakers to 144 yards and six first downs. After three years of frustration we exploded all at once. We scored 10 points in the first quarter, 14 in the second, 7 in the third and 17 in the fourth. All our reserves got to play in the 48-0 game.

The Theismann-to-Gatewood combination was becoming a superb weapon for us. Tom came to Notre Dame as a halfback and tight end. We tried him in the backfield, but he didn't distinguish himself there. Ara could see, however, that he had good hands so he gave him a look at split end, a position that needed filling. Tom didn't have great speed, but he was quick with his feet. Jack Snow had been a fluid genius of a split end. Jim Seymour was a long-distance gazelle who could out-rebound nearly anyone for the ball. Gatewood was a combination of the two—he was quick, shifty, caught the ball and knew where to go afterwards.

Tom was always friendly and respectful, but he was a loner off the field. As one of the few blacks in the community at that time it was a natural condition. His teammates admired him enough to vote him co-captain his senior year. In terms of records set he could have become Notre Dame's all-time leading receiver that year, but unfortunately some lunatic interfered with that. Tom never found out who it was, but someone was making threatening phone calls to him all year. That affected him psychologically and athletically. He missed a few practices because of it, and Ara asked for an explanation. Tom admitted he was troubled by the calls, but he felt it was a burden he would have to bear himself. Despite these difficulties he continued to be a reliable performer. Today he is the executive vice president of the Mutual Black Radio Network.

Winning the Purdue game was cause for celebration. And as usual after every home game Ara had an open house at his place for the football and administrative staff, special alumni, townspeople close to the program and his own personal friends. Many of those invited brought other guests, so his house was jammed with people. Katie served hors d'oeuvres and drinks and tried to greet everyone on hand.

When Ara finally got home he pitched right in and tended to his guests. Even after the most draining game he called on

Tom Gatewood—a combination of Jack Snow and Jim Seymour.

178

some unimaginable reserve energy to entertain his company. He mingled with all of them and talked mostly about the game. The first few years the parties literally lasted all night. Eventually he listed time limitations so he and Katie could unwind over dinner. But no matter how long he stayed up, he still arose at 5:00 the next morning.

Ara was a totally different personality on social occasions. He was whatever the moment called for without any unnaturalness. At the office he could chew you out and complain, and you expected that in his role as head coach. But at his home he greeted you with a handshake and smile saying, "I'll make the first drink and after that you help yourself." Nothing was too good for his guests, and they had the run of the house. Sometimes he might even break down and amuse the crowd with a piano recital. Liberace didn't have anything to fear, but Ara was good enough to enjoy himself behind the keyboard, and the visitors got a kick out of seeing him in this new light.

No matter what else Ara had on his mind he always found time for his friends. He made friends easily, and he was religious about staying in touch with them either through correspondence or over the phone. He is very close to his brother Gerard and sister Isabelle. Gerard is the big brother who offered a thoughtful and concerned point of view throughout Ara's life. He could tell Ara anything. Jerry is a success himself, having started his own company in Toledo, Ohio. However, he never let his business ventures get in the way of any of Ara's games.

Assistant coaches who moved on to other jobs—like John Ray, Bo Schembechler, John Pont; some of his former players; Paul Brown and Sid Gillman, his coaches; Tony Androwski, his college roommate; Eddie Niam, his boyhood buddy—these were people he talked about frequently and was delighted to hear from. If you were part of Ara, not just a passing acquaintance, you never dropped from his concern. Anytime you gave loyalty to him you could expect it in return. Wealth, political position and prestige had nothing to do with his determination of friendship. He had deep relationships with people at all ends of of the spectrum.

Socially and athletically Ara seemed on top after the Northwestern and Purdue games in the 1970 season. But the week before the Michigan State game we had a 21-year win

Katie and Ara—the perfect hosts.

drought staring us in the face. Not since 1949 had a Notre Dame team defeated the Spartans in East Lansing. However, in 1970 we did it in style, 29-0. The thrill of victory was tempered by the loss of our offensive captain, guard Larry DiNardo, who would require knee surgery and be lost for the season.

Larry had a rare blend of viewpoints working within him. He was raised in an old world tradition where the word of his parents was law—no questions asked. Yet he was intelligent enough to adopt some modern concepts that were more practical. He was marked for leadership, being opinionated and outspoken but knowledgeable of what he was talking about. Athletically, he started as a sophomore and improved each year. He wasn't exceptionally big or quick, but he developed his body and had great strength. When he became a captain his senior

180

year he was one of our best ever. His enthusiasm and competitiveness didn't change with the captaincy, and he really was a unifying force for the team.

After his junior season he went to Vietnam with several other scholar athletes as part of an NCAA good will tour to visit wounded service men. He left the states violently opposed to war, especially the current one, but returned with another outlook. The soldiers he spoke with over there convinced him the U.S. was serving a purpose in Vietnam, and Larry was open-minded enough to admit they had more right to make that judgment than he.

Larry was the guts of our interior offensive line, and our performance was never the same after his loss. We needed his field leadership and fiery play. The injury crushed Larry, but he remained our captain off the field. He was always at practice, helping the younger players, encouraging and joking.

After handling Army, 51-10, we traveled to Columbia, Missouri, to meet Dan Devine's Tigers. They shook us up early in the third quarter, pulling out in front, 7-3. But then Theismann threw touchdown passes to Gatewood and halfback Ed Gulyas, and Gulyas rushed for another in the fourth quarter to give us a 24-7 win.

Ed Gulyas was one of a handful of "walk-ons" who played key roles during Ara's years at Notre Dame. He wasn't a starter in high school, but it wasn't because he lacked ability. He was quicker than most Notre Dame players and made a skillful receiver. Ed's limitation in the game was that football was just that—a game—something to be done for enjoyment. As a result he didn't take it seriously. He came to Notre Dame without an athletic grant but decided to try out for the team anyway. With his speed we tried him first in the defensive backfield. That didn't work out because of his lackadaisical attitude. During punting drills in the spring one time he would break out for a 35-40 yard gain while the next punt might drop through his arms. He'd head for the sidelines unaffected and say, "Well, I guess I didn't do so well on that one." Paul Shoults, his secondary coach, is a perfectionist, and he couldn't find a spot for Gulyas.

So Ed came over to the offensive backfield and, when he reached the stage where he could see he had a chance to start,

Larry DiNardo—a rare blend of viewpoints.

his whole attitude changed. Once he tasted success he got caught up in it, and he battled to eliminate flaws in his performance. His happy-go-lucky personality never did change, though.

Ara defended walk-ons, many times over our objections. We used to gripe, "Hey, Ara, do we have to have this little 98-pounder out there? The guy doesn't even know how to put on his helmet. He's going to get hurt." Ara would smile and reply, "If he's not hurting anybody, just keep him out of the heavy drills. If the kid's got the heart to stay out there it may be the biggest thing in his life." Some who showed up had virtually no athletic ability. Ara talked to them and tried to channel them in another direction, possibly into the student managers' organization. He didn't want anyone to be injured.

Over the years Ara's perseverance paid off. Percentage-wise we didn't uncover many frontline performers, but we did develop valuable prep team players. These kids just wanted to be part of the team even though they wouldn't be rewarded by renown or financial aid.

Mike Oriard is probably the greatest tribute to the walk-ons. He came to us as a freshman at 6-1, 190. He ate wheat germ, lifted weights, practiced snapping year 'round and in 1969 became our starting center and offensive captain. He won a Rhodes Scholarship for his grade-point production and signed with the Kansas City Chiefs. During the off-season he earned his doctorate degree.

We beat Navy, 56-7, and Pittsburgh, 46-14, for our sixth and seventh wins of 1970. Theismann in the Pittsburgh game became Notre Dame's all-time total offense leader with a career production of 5,432 yards.

It was well he set the record then, because our offense didn't shatter any marks the next two games. Before our game with Georgia Tech both wire services picked us number one in

Joe Theismann (7) receives congratulations from Denny Allan (22), Ed Gulyas (12), Mike Creaney (91) and John Dampeer (67) after becoming Notre Dame's all-time total offense leader.

the nation. And the Yellow Jackets were convinced they could bump us from that spot. They felt that our running game was the secret to our success and decided to set their defense to shut that off. They played an eight-man front most of the way, confident that their secondary men could handle our passing threat. Their strategy was working as the 0-0 halftime score indicated.

But Ara pondered their methods in our locker room and devised a play to counter them. Trailing 7-3 with nine minutes left, Ara decided it was time to try his scheme. The idea was to send two backs and two ends out as receivers to flood their three-deep secondary. The play had been set up perfectly until an alert Tech linebacker knocked Gatewood down. Theismann was being rushed heavily, but he held out long enough to heave the ball in Gulyas' direction. The crafty little halfback broke his pattern to go after the ball. He was diving and sliding in one motion, but the ball thudded on his chest and he hung on—a 46-yard gainer, moving to their 34. Six plays later Denny Allan carried it over, and the game was ours, 10-7.

"To have a successful season a team must win the type of game we won today," Ara told the press. "I was particularly proud of our club the way they continued to come back. They drove 80 yards in the final quarter with the wind in their faces and that's the sign of a great team. This was the third time this year we've had to come from behind and we've done it each time.

"I am interested in the polls on November 28. It's nice to be number one as we were this week, but the only ranking I want is when we close our season."

Ara thought that the polls were good from an incentive standpoint. He made the players aware of our position in the polls as the season progressed, showing them how it was possible to advance by winning our games. Our goal was the National Championship which is determined by the polls, so Ara valued them as motivational tools. But he never tried to run up a score to "beat the spread," hoping that this would enhance our ranking. A one-point win would have satisfied him in every game.

We were fortunate to win by three points in our next game against Louisiana State, 3-0. We knew this would be an emotional game for them. The sports editor of the Baton Rouge newspaper had called Notre Dame "my most hated college team. If Notre Dame were playing Russia tomorrow, I'd be right out there waving the old hammer and sickle."

This was a game of thwarted drives, interceptions and superb defense by both teams. It took 57 minutes and six seconds to produce a score, that being a 24-yard field goal by Scott Hempel. The points were set up by an incredible punt by Jim Yoder. Yoder boomed one from the LSU 44 that bounced out of bounds on the LSU one. In three rushing attempts the Tigers moved it out to their seven but then punted to Clarence Ellis who returned it to the 36. Theismann got us to the seven, and Hempel handled it from there.

"This was just a tremendous defensive performance by two of the top college teams in the country," Ara said afterward. "I feel LSU is probably the finest and quickest defensive team we have faced here at Notre Dame since I've been here.

"Scott Hempel has been in a slump for a couple of weeks. He kicked more in practice this week than normal. I wasn't sure if I should use him or Scott Smith for the field goal attempt. However, I considered the contributions Hempel has made to our team over the last three years and the fact that this could be his last attempt in Notre Dame Stadium. I guess sentiment helped me make this decision to some extent—thank God!

"The squad will meet with the coaching staff sometime tomorrow to make a decision on a bowl game."

That decision was to accept a return trip to the Cotton Bowl to face a team nicknamed the "Longhorns." We had been anxious to get another crack at them, but there was a *little* matter of playing Southern Cal in Los Angeles before we could worry about that game. It seems we had been in a similar position once or twice before—headed for California undefeated with one regular season game to play. We had experienced both the "agony and the ecstasy" and this was one rubber match we had to have.

For some reason, it just wasn't meant to be. We outgained the Trojans by 200 yards, and Joe Theismann turned in the most amazing performance I've ever witnessed by a quarterback. Playing on a day when it rained four inches, we had to come from behind nearly the whole game. Under those conditions anything can happen, usually nothing good for the team that's trailing. We had eight turnovers, two of them enabling USC to drive only a total of 17 yards for scores.

We scored first, highlighted by a 25-yard touchdown run by Theismann. But the Trojans took it in the next three times they had the ball for a 21-7 first quarter lead. By now our game plan was useless, and Joe had to think pass on nearly every play. Midway through the second quarter he completed three in a row to pull us within seven. Even after USC added a field goal we felt we were in range at halftime.

Only three minutes into the second half the Trojans got the first of their big breaks. Darryll Dewan fumbled the slippery ball at the 17, and after four snaps we were down 31-14. Two plays later Joe dropped back into our end zone to pass, unaware that a USC defender had shot through our line without resistance. The Trojan lineman knocked the ball loose from Joe and recovered it for yet another score, 38-14.

With the rain pouring even harder, Theismann still hadn't conceded. Joe went to halfback Larry Parker the very next series and completed a 46-yard touchdown pass. We had nearly 14 minutes left when Joe ran in another touchdown, bringing us to 38-28. From that point on Joe attempted a pass on every play and completed 12 of 21. But we just couldn't score. For the day he completed 33 of 58 passes for 526 yards and two touchdowns. If the Heisman Trophy balloting had taken place after this performance I wonder if Joe would have still finished second to Jim Plunkett? If we hadn't given USC 14 cheap points perhaps the outcome of this game might have been different. If, if, if....

Speculation wouldn't help us. Our locker room was a mass of dejection but not like it had been in 1964 under similar circumstances. No loss would ever cause that much despondency. Ara praised the team for fighting all the way. He told them they had played well enough to win. No one could accuse us of giving up in this game.

Ara was heartbroken the next few days. As usual he didn't understand the defeat, but he didn't dwell on it. Ever since our narrow loss to Texas the year before, Ara had been analyzing the Wishbone Offense and toying with ways to harness it. He came up with a plan that was masterful, but risky. He called it

186

The lure of Notre Dame brought many celebrities.

the "Mirror Defense." The basic principle was to focus certain defensive backs on the Texas halfbacks and quarterbacks and certain linebackers on the fullback. These defensive people "mirrored" the running backs. This would be a defensive look the Longhorns hadn't seen before, and Ara figured that this unfamiliarity would ruffle them enough to stall their offense. But as a man-for-man defense, one mistake by any player could cost us. More than any other defense, this one demanded per-

Ara had the team well-prepared for our rematch with Texas.

fection.

Ara had his faith in that strategy tested on the Longhorns' initial offensive play. Their quarterback, Eddie Phillips, faked to fullback Steve Worster and then kept the ball himself. Mike Crotty was the safety man assigned to Phillips in the Mirror, and he committed himself too soon, allowing Phillips to cut back on him. Cornerback Ralph Stepaniak finally hauled him down after a 63-yard gain. Texas got a field goal out of the drive.

Ara refused to scrap the defense, however. He had spotted Crotty's error, and he gathered the defense around him to explain it. "We're okay, we're all right," he shouted. "We were in great position for that tackle, Crotty just overran it. It'll be all right, let's stick with it." That sales pitch helped, and the defense kept the Longhorns off-balance the rest of the day. They fumbled nine times, losing five, and soon abandoned their rush-oriented game for a passing attack. That's what Ara had been hoping to achieve. Texas was a great running team, but passing was something it didn't have much experience with. Not only that, but our offense was moving so well that Texas was thrust into a score-or-else situation, a problem for a Wishbone team.

Theismann threw a 26-yard touchdown pass to Gatewood right after the Texas field goal. In an effort to elude the Texas defender Gatewood pulled a hamstring muscle and was out for the remainder of the game. We recovered a Longhorn fumble on their 13 and turned that into a touchdown with Theismann carrying from the three. Joe scored again, this one on a 15-yard run, to open the second quarter.

After Texas mounted its last scoring drive of the afternoon, Ara called for the do-or-die play we had been working on all year. Using our strongest quarterback, Jim Bulger, and our fastest runner, Clarence Ellis, the concept was simple—Bulger would throw the ball as far as he could, Ellis would run as fast as he could, and hopefully the two elements would link. This time they did, and we picked up 37 yards, moving Scott Hempel into field goal range. His 36-yard kick wrapped up all the scoring, 24-11, with 24 seconds to play in the first half.

With Theismann nursing an injured finger on his throwing hand and Gatewood sidelined, our offense wasn't effective in the second half. But with the defense playing the mirror in the fashion its creator had envisioned, we had all the points we needed. This was probably as well as our team had ever been prepared for a game. Our strategy offensively and defensively was imaginative, and the players were totally receptive. Because of it Texas' 30-game winning streak, the longest in the nation, had been ended.

Nebraska looked like our main competition at that point for the National Championship. They were to play LSU in the Orange Bowl that night, and if the Tigers could only win, the national title would be ours. They gave it a great try, but Nebraska pulled it out. Most of us watched the game from our rooms and were disappointed to see Nebraska squeak by. Just to make sure the pollsters wouldn't regard our win over Texas too seriously, Nebraska coach Bob Devaney told the press, "Not even the Pope would vote Notre Dame number one."

Clarence Ellis was our fastest man.

The outcome of Cotton Bowl II was much more joyous.

He didn't, and we finished second. But the prospects for 1971 were encouraging, especially on defense. One severe graduation loss, however, would be Joe Theismann. Only in the months to come would we fully realize how valuable he had been.

1971 -
A Tiger At The Tail

Even though the worst problems lay ahead, I really believe the 1971 season was the most trying of Ara's 11 at Notre Dame. We had what should have been one of our best defenses, a good offensive line and an experienced corps of running backs. We lacked only two elements—an established quarterback and intensity.

We would be starting 14 seniors backed up by 10 more. Overriding the advantage of experience was the disadvantage of complacency. Most of these players had filled significant roles in our Cotton Bowl Championship the year before. They had been to a bowl, come within two fumbles of the National Championship, appeared frequently on national television and earned their monograms. Because they were playing for Notre Dame they had been asked to extend themselves game after game to rival the emotion of our opponents who could make their seasons by beating us. In short, the incentive just wasn't the same for them anymore.

Those are factors coaches can appreciate but fans find hard to understand. If there is a way to coach *desire* to a team that has known nothing but winning, the inventor ought to patent his solution.

We wrestled with the problem frequently in our staff meetings. Thank heaven for those sessions. They were the most meaningful moments of our lives. The content of the meetings

Ara coached the kickers...but sometimes even he needed a little extra push.

depended on the time of the year. During the spring they were especially enjoyable. We weren't quite as pushed then, and we were able to bring topics unrelated to football into our discussions.

Ara was a genius when it came to football, but his interest and knowledge went well beyond just that one subject. For instance during the year he probably flew an average of 75,000 miles, so he studied aircraft and could dissect every working part. He met politicians, lawyers, businessmen, doctors, athletes in other sports and people in many other professions. Therefore, he made it a point to stay abreast of developments in all these fields to be able to converse intelligently with these acquaintances. The average person couldn't do that, but since Ara existed on five hours sleep, he put his free time to use by reading. He kept a steady stream of information flowing to his computer-like mind.

Ara brought this wealth of knowledge into our meetings and led us in discussions ranging from outer space to life after death. Politics was a favorite subject, especially during the Watergate proceedings. He was anti-Nixon before any of the Watergate information broke. He felt that there was something that didn't ring true about the man and predicted his downfall. He read every line the papers carried about the Watergate proceedings, as he had years earlier with the Sam Sheppard trial and later with the Patty Hearst trial.

Ara never imposed his political philosophies on anyone. He felt that it was a personal issue, as were religion and income. But in the confines of our staff room we talked about the politicians he admired and why. He wouldn't actively endorse candidates and in one instance castigated a politician for involving him without his consent. While driving home one evening he spotted a billboard reading, "Ruckleshaus is difficult to say, but so is Parseghian." He realized that the candidate didn't design publicity slogans, and it wasn't that he didn't support him but he just wouldn't want his name tied into any campaign.

Whenever Ara returned from vacations or speaking appearances he was armed with new discussion material. He was appalled by the poverty he had witnessed during a trip to Jamaica. One youngster, emaciated and dressed in rags, ran behind Ara's taxi for blocks, hoping to keep pace to plead for a handout. Ara compared that to the prosperity he had seen in his other travels, and it saddened him.

In the fall we didn't have time for anything but football strategy. People couldn't comprehend our 7:00 a.m. to 10:00 p.m. schedule, wondering what we could possibly cover in those meetings. What they didn't realize was that two hours of practice took another eight or nine of preparation. If we hadn't viewed film of our opponent repeatedly to discover tendencies, and then if we hadn't discussed what we could best do with our personnel to combat them, practicing would have been a waste of time. Everything we did on the field had a purpose and was an outgrowth of our meetings.

Ara made very few decisions over the years that hadn't been covered one way or another in our meetings. Every phase of the offensive and defensive game plan was thrashed out. Ara expected us to contribute, even if the idea was eventually discarded. If one of us had a suggestion it was picked apart by the rest of the staff. Those without "holes" were utilized. Ara's ideas were also fair game for discussion, and we were free to make comments. With his or anyone else's concepts you better have had some sound thoughts before criticizing. Ara could tear you apart instantly if you didn't.

Sometimes that hurt and you'd feel like telling him what he could do with his arguments. On those occasions he would be the topic of our luncheon conversations, and I'm sure his ears must have been burning back in his office. He realized we had to blow off steam amongst ourselves, and as long as it stayed there he didn't object. His greatest demand to us was loyalty. He exploded at the first hint of disloyalty. "Look," he would shout after summoning the offender behind closed doors, "this is the way it's going to be and if you don't like it you're free to leave."

Lack of effort was another of his peeves. He had no use for a player who gave less than 100 percent. And when you analyze his request of them, there really was no reason for a player to drag. He had a term called the "Great Interval." The interval was effort, execution and endurance. His premise was that each play of a football game lasts an average of 3.5 seconds and there are approximately 80 offensive and defensive plays in a game.

This figures out to about five minutes of action. So he put it to the players: "Can you give Our Lady of Notre Dame five minutes of your effort, execution and endurance today?" From that viewpoint who could explain lethargy?

For all his organizational skills, there was one thing that bothered us about Ara's decision making. While we wanted to choose an alternative and get it over with, Ara procrastinated. That upset me so much at one point I thought he didn't know how to make decisions. I kept tormenting him about an issue day after day, and finally he let me have it. "Would you quit pestering me about that. I'll let you know when I'm ready. We don't have to make a decision for two days yet. In that time several things could develop that will affect our choice." He could make decisions all right, and one of them was not to decide anything until he had all the "late scratches."

One of our toughest decisions in 1971 staff meetings was whom to start at quarterback. There were four candidates. Pat Steenberge was a good field leader and a talented runner who was best-suited for option football. Bill Etter was a bonus because one year earlier doctors had told him to give up football, fearing he had developed an aneurysm. We were delighted when he got clearance to rejoin us, since he was a quarterback in the mold of Joe Theismann. Still, he had been away from the game for a year, and timing is difficult to recover. Cliff Brown had a great arm with as quick a release as anyone we've ever had. He suffered from lack of experience and resulting mechanical errors. Jim Bulger was the tallest candidate and could throw even farther than Brown. He lacked accuracy and the refinement of footwork.

Ara selected Steenberge to start the opener against Northwestern. Fortunately, we were able to rotate the quarterbacks and get them all in. None of them sparkled though the score, 50-7 in our favor, wouldn't indicate that.

Steenberge was again the choice the next week in West Lafayette, Indiana, against Purdue. The field was a swamp, but a record crowd of over 69,000 sat through a constant, cold rain and watched two impotent offenses slosh it out. Purdue went ahead 7-0 on a 26-yard screen pass 26:20 into the game. With three minutes to play and our offense totally powerless it looked as though we would suffer the second shutout of Ara's

198

The 1971 quarterback candidates—Pat Steenberge (11), Jim Bulger (4), Cliff Brown (8) and Bill Etter (2).

era.

Then our defense, using a punt rush designed by George Kelly, Paul Shoults and Joe Yonto, came through. Purdue was forced to punt from its own end zone, and Clarence Ellis, aided by a bobble on the snap, screamed in and batted the ball down. Defensive end Fred Swendsen fell on it for a touchdown, leaving Ara with another crucial 1971 decision.

Of course, he wouldn't have to contemplate long. After all, wasn't he the guy who plays for ties? All he had to do was call Bob Thomas, our kicking specialist, and he would even the score.

Ara never even considered that. His concern was which two-point conversion play to select, having prepared several. Ara picked a trick play which we later termed the "Genuflect Play." Steenberge was supposed to roll out to his right and fake a sweep. At the other end of the line tight end Mike Creaney had to be an actor and athlete. His role demanded that he attempt to block the defensive end but fall to one knee (thus the title), seeming to miss his assignment. With the defensive end charging toward the quarterback, Creaney would then get up and become a receiver.

We couldn't have coached the Boilermakers to react to the play any better, but that put all the pressure on Steenberge. He had to cope with sloppy footing, a slippery ball and a defender bent on playing in the mud with him as his toy. Pat barely got the ball off, more in the style of a shot put than a spiral. Creaney gave it a bear hug, and we had an 8-7 victory.

Steenberge hadn't been effective, but nobody could have been in those climatic conditions. He had pulled a hamstring muscle late in the game and didn't report it. The doctors later advised him to stay off the leg for several days but he feared that, with the quarterback race as tight as it was, he who faltered even for a day might never recover the starting position. So he continued to practice and was hobbled all year.

Steenberge's injury gave Etter his chance against Michigan State. Bill didn't do anything fancy against the Spartans, but he completed 10 of 16 passes with only one interception and moved our rushing attack well. We won 14-2, and prepared for Miami, thinking we had the quarterback issue settled.

With fullback Andy Huff and halfbacks Ed Gulyas and Darryll Dewan grinding out the yardage under Etter's guidance, we were feeling pretty good. Then, early in the second quarter Etter was tackled on the knee, tearing cartilage and ending his comeback effort. Bill was a quick-thinking quarterback all his teammates respected. Ara kidded him that he ran like a "wet noodle," but he never coached a player he respected more, either for his effort or intelligence. No one can imagine the mental anguish Bill experienced in battling back in the game doctors at one time told him to forget.

An injury to a quarterback always throws things into a frenzy on the sidelines but especially so this season when the situation was unsettled. I immediately shouted for Steenberge, but Ara overruled me. He had witnessed Steenberge's condition in practice all week and chose instead a healthy inexperienced sophomore, Cliff Brown. Cliff made some mistakes that night, but he won the game for us. Aided by our starting backs plus John Cieszkowski and Larry Parker, excellent line play and our

200

Pat Steenberge throws the pass on the famous "Genuflect Play."

stingy defense, we won, 17-0.

Cliff Brown was a self-taught athlete of amazing physical ability. Everything he did came naturally to him. More than once I saw him send the ball through the uprights on a *kickoff*. Just as frequently, as a sophomore he dribbled his kickoffs along the ground. He had trouble harnessing his skills because he had formed habits difficult to break. His greatest flaw was overlooking the open receiver. If Cliff decided to throw to a particular receiver he was going to, even if that man was covered while others weren't. We drilled him against that at practice, and eventually he made progress. Given the time to develop we knew Cliff would smooth out.

No one had more to swallow during a college career than Cliff Brown. He believed in himself and rightly so. As the first black quarterback at Notre Dame he had broken a difficult barrier. Ara used to say, "Quarterbacks and head coaches get too much credit and too much blame." That position did cast him in the limelight. I could hear the shouts of the fans when things were going wrong for Cliff. "Are they forcing you guys to play a black quarterback?" "Get that nigger out of there!"

Cliff heard the abuse, too. It hurt him. It made him defensive. He had two elements working against him—he was inexperienced, so he was going to make mistakes, and he was

201

the black barrier-breaker at his position. Reporters might have thought him abrasive his sophomore year. He wasn't used to dealing with the press and after coming off the field from a so-so performance, booed along the way by his own fans, there were a lot of emotions working on him.

Cliff made more personal development from 1971 on then any player I've ever coached. His sophomore season certainly had its trials, but 1972 brought a new conflict. Freshman Tom Clements came along the next spring and fit into our system perfectly. It was obvious Cliff would have to improve rapidly to regain the starting job for his junior year. That realization was a turning point in his life. He could have been sullen or he could have quit, but some counseling from his brother and Ara prevented that. His brother witnessed Clements' impressive performance during the spring game. He admitted that Tom was a super athlete, well-qualified for his position and passed his observations along to Cliff. When we picked Tom that fall, Ara pulled Cliff aside and explained his reasoning. He asked Cliff to continue his dedication at practice because we might need him at any time. He accepted that and matured in the process. Clements never did need spelling but Cliff pulled for him on the sidelines in every game. It earned him our respect.

Ara was touchy about the quarterback comments throughout the 1971 season. The remarks of writers and fans who couldn't possibly know as much about the ability and faults of our players annoyed him. Did they imagine he wasn't playing the best player available? Were they suggesting he wasn't a capable judge of talent? Both interpretations upset him.

The defense earned its second shutout and Bob Thomas booted three field goals to highlight our 16-0 win over North Carolina. Brown did throw a touchdown pass to Gatewood in the fourth quarter, Tom's first TD reception of the year.

It wasn't so much the inability of our offense that cost us against Southern Cal the next week as it was the footwork of the Trojans, especially wide receiver Edesel Garrison. With his 4.5 speed we just didn't have anyone to keep up with him. He stung us for touchdown receptions of 31 and 24 yards while setting up another with a 42-yard catch. Midway through the second quarter we were down 28-7, putting Cliff in a precarious situation, but from that point forward he performed admirably,

Bill Etter— the answer to our problem.

completing 10 of 27 for 134 yards and only one interception. We held the Trojans and scored once more ourselves for a 28-14 setback, our first of the season.

Successive wins over Navy, 21-0; Pittsburgh, 56-7; and Tulane, 21-7, brought us to 8-1 in time for "bowl week." This was the time invitations were extended to the nation's top teams, giving them a chance to consider. Policies differed from school to school. Some institutions gave the proposal to their athletic board, and that body alone made the decision. Other schools, including Notre Dame, allowed the players to voice their opinions. In the past that had been no problem, but like everything else, there's always a first time.

Ara's procedure was exactly the same as it had been for the two Cotton Bowl bids. The Gator Bowl, commonly regarded as the fifth most prestigious of the postseason matchups, wanted us to meet either Penn State or Georgia, probably State. The Nittany Lions were having the same kind of year we were and eventually wound up with a fifth-place national ranking. Both schools had been trying to arrange a game for years. The rivalry was natural since Penn State had a similar academic philosophy, was our prime competitor for student-athletes in Pennsylvania, and was a perennially strong independent. The coaches were anxious to see the game booked.

Unfortunately, the players weren't. Ara outlined the situation as he knew it. He told them the date of the game, the tentative practice schedule, the social events planned at the Jacksonville, Florida, site and the rewards he would try to gain for them from the school.

For the previous bowl games the players asked questions after Ara made his presentation, then took a written vote, signing their names. Ara allowed all the players to ballot, even those who wouldn't suit up. He felt that was their right. He wanted all of them to make suggestions or elaborate why they might be against the game. That way he could tell if a dissident reserve who wasn't going to be a factor in the bowl game was

The General—flanked by lieutenants Wally Moore, Joe Yonto, George Kelly, Brian Boulac, Paul Shoults and Tom Pagna.

influencing the rest of the team.

Captains Tom Gatewood and Walt Patulski, at the urging of some of their teammates, requested that the coaching staff leave the meeting room and this year the ballots not be signed. That should have tipped us to the unpleasantness ahead, but Ara consented.

Very few players wanted to attend the bowl. They all had their reasons, some valid but others purely selfish. Most of them felt we weren't good enough to compete. That isn't the type of confidence on which the legendary Notre Dame tradition had been built, but it was sincere appraisal. Those who had faith in our ability figured an appearance in the Gator Bowl couldn't enhance our national position. Others didn't want the season extended an extra month, and some already had commitments for the holidays.

After we left it didn't take long for the various anti-bowl expressions to surface. One of the reserve players stood up and blasted Ara for making promises he had "no intention of keeping." One of the blacks, referring to a story circulated after our last Cotton Bowl Game that the school hadn't turned over as much of the bowl receipts as promised to the minority scholarship fund, said he wouldn't participate regardless of the vote's outcome. He said that the school was deceiving minority students. What he and the journalist who wrote the story failed to realize was that transporting a team and official party and lodging them in the manner the players expected required thousands of dollars—more than they could possibly imagine.

Regardless, this emotion prevailed, and the bid was rejected by a large margin. The next morning some of the players came to see Ara, alarmed by what had transpired the night before. These players, regulars who had the most to win or lose by playing, had voted against the bowl but reconsidered, shocked by what they had heard. They requested another vote.

The vote was retaken that night, but the statements from the previous meeting influenced the prep players and their ballots upheld the first decision.

Ara was deeply hurt by what had taken place. He was adamant about letting the players make the choice, however. "You never want to take a team to a bowl game if it doesn't want to play," he stressed. "That would be a disaster." Still, he

Andy Huff fought off injuries throughout his career to become a steady performer.

couldn't comprehend why they wouldn't want to go. Those who made the Cotton Bowl trips, and there were many left on the team, knew that Ara had arranged first-rate accommodations. Beyond the decision was the insubordination of the two outspoken players. Ara didn't display his grief, but then Ara never burdened others with his problems. The closest he came to revealing his feelings was to ask rhetorically, "After they leave here do you think they'll regret passing up this opportunity?"

This bowl vote was similar to all others in one regard—it distracted the team from thinking about the regular season. Ara was more concerned about our remaining game with LSU than for any previous encounter. Rightfully so! We had to prepare a squad splintered psychologically and wounded physically. We were so banged up at fullback with John Cieszkowski out for the year and Andy Huff limping, we had to give middle linebacker Gary Potempa a crash course. Facing us was a team vengeful after a 3-0 loss to us in 1970. We had to play at night on national television in Tiger Stadium amid the cheers of "Go to hell, Notre Dame, go to hell!"

They put it to us from beginning to end. Quarterback Bert Jones burned us on two long touchdown passes, and in our state we couldn't catch up. After 60 minutes it was LSU 28, ND 6.

The *season of decisions* was over. We finished 8 and 2—out of the Top 10 for the first time since Ara came to Notre Dame. The events of the year deeply affected Ara and contributed to the most significant *decision* he was to make in 1974.

Cliff Brown (8) lost his quarterback job to Tom Clements (2) but won something more valuable.

1972 -
A Black
And Blue Orange

"I told you what could happen, but you just wouldn't make yourselves believe me," Ara said softly to the players. The look of disgust streaming from his eyes did his shouting for him. "That was a good football team but we're better. Because we didn't take them seriously enough, they beat us. The loss hurts, but if you're ready to work from here out we can still come out on top."

There's no way we should have lost to Missouri in 1972. It was our fifth game, and we were undefeated, having beaten Northwestern, 37-0; Purdue, 35-14; Michigan State, 16-0; and Pittsburgh, 42-16. The Tigers were 2-3 and were coming off a humiliating 62-0 loss to Nebraska.

Ara pleaded with the team that week during practice to regard Missouri as a very real threat to our National Championship aspirations. He knew that the Tigers had excellent speed and a sharp quarterback named John Cherry. He knew that even though we would be playing on our home field before vocal supporters, every team gets up for Notre Dame and underrating Missouri could be disastrous. He also knew that teams embarrassed by a loss have something to prove their next time out. But we still shouldn't have lost.

No sooner had the Tigers taken a 24-14 lead and with it our game plan, than a cold mist moved over the stadium, making comeback efforts all the more difficult. They wouldn't have held that 10-point margin if it hadn't been for an oversight by the officials, which ultimately cost us the game. It was fourth down with one yard to go for a Missouri touchdown. Cherry handed off to his fullback Don Johnson, who bulled up the middle but left the ball back in the starting block. Slow motion film captured the scene for posterity, but only posterity and our defensive players knew that Johnson fumbled as he started his dive into the end zone. Our players had been sprawling over the ball at the one-yard line and protested the call vehemently. But the officials refused to yield.

Ara had seen some hellish calls during his time, pro and con, but rarely would he ever comment about them publicly. Ara developed a psychology about officiating. In discussions about that subject he said that too many coaches made the mistake of being intimidated by officials. Ara wasn't one for checking the officials' schedule before the season and moaning because we had one individual or another. He would examine the list because some officials call a tighter game than others. For instance, technically, holding could be called against the offensive linemen on every play. Ara wanted to forewarn the team if we had a crew prone to strict interpretation.

The officials always came into the locker room before the game to introduce themselves, though Ara had known most of them already. Generally there were two types—the ones who strutted in arrogantly, insisting that they were running things and we had better cooperate, and the low-keyed guys who were cordial and merely asked for a clean game. The former group was usually composed of the insecure, mistake-prone officials. The latter tended to be more established officials confident of their abilities.

When Ara badgered officials, and he did it more than once in his era, it was normally because they refused to explain their rulings to him, an obligation on their part. One year in Atlanta Ara got into it with a southern official who turned a deaf ear to such a request. He was standing directly in front of our bench and after repeated requests by Ara had drawn no response, he snapped at the official, "What the hell's your problem? Are you on their payroll?" The man in the striped shirt halted play and turned to Ara, calling him every vulgar name in the book. On the way to the dressing room at the half Ara chased after him

Ara developed a psychology with officials.

while some of us followed behind to restrain him. "You're one gutless bastard," Ara hollered. "You knew I couldn't get back at you out there. There ought to be a way to penalize officials, too."

Ara had always lectured the team against penalties, but during his last season he picked up a 30-yarder in one game. There again the referee had ignored Ara's plea for a clarification of a ruling. It was vital that he know the interpretation because the penalty assessed was based on our standard offensive back-field motion. It could have affected every play. The official refused to come over to Ara to discuss it so Ara charged beyond the "Gridiron Wall," the 30-yard restricted area for each team, and went instead to him. That called for an automatic 15-yard penalty. Since Ara had every right for an explanation of the pre-vious ruling, he felt he was entitled to violate the rules, too, until he got what he was after. When Ara saw the flag thrown he erupted. His vocabulary is by no means limited, and he used most of it before the ref threw the next yellow flag.

The next day, as we were reviewing our latest victory, George Kelly felt enough courage to break the ice at our staff meetings. "You know, Coach, you aren't worth 30 yards to this team," he jabbed, drawing on the same line Ara used with the players.

Ara was convinced officials could be swayed, just by virtue of human nature. He always made some comment to them when a close call went the other way. He realized that nothing would be done about that particular decision, but arguing might give them second thoughts, inducing them to see a future call our way.

One time a referee signalled for a first down measurement right in front of our bench. It was a fourth down play at a critical point in the game. The tip of the ball was so close to the chain that the official had to kneel to study it. Ara bent over behind him insisting, "Aw hell, Herb, anybody can see that's good. There's no question that's a first down." I'm not so sure it was, but ol' Herb climbed up on his feet and motioned immediately for a first down.

The funniest incident we were ever involved in was during a Purdue game at our stadium. Jerry Markbreit was the official. We were down on the Purdue one-yard line with time running out in the first half. Tom Clements was signalling for a time out, but none of the officials saw him. So he instinctively lined up the team and threw quickly out of bounds to stop the clock. Unfortunately, it had been fourth down so Purdue should have taken possession, but for some reason that didn't register with the officiating crew. They had lost track of the down situation. So Markbreit ran over to our bench where he had seen a phone, thinking it was a direct hookup to the press box. We knew otherwise, however. It was really an outside line. The game had been stopped for all this, and we listened sheepishly as he sought to solve the problem. He picked up the phone and grumbled, "What down is it? Down...Don't you know what a *down* is?" Seconds later he discovered he had been dealing with a telephone operator, not a press box statistician, and stormed over to Ara. "You're never going to pull that on me again," Markbreit raved and quickly ran back onto the field. Ara howled from then until halftime, aided by the fact that we were up by a large margin.

Sometimes Ara had to be restrained when an official refused to reply to him.

He didn't find anything amusing against Missouri in 1972. The Tigers went ahead 30-14 with 10 minutes to play before we started to come alive. Clements directed us to touchdowns on 70- and 80-yard drives, climaxed by his 13-yard keeper for the first score and a 12-yard run by Andy Huff on the second. But after we got the ball back with 2:26 left, Tom threw an interception and our hopes faded.

"This was a tremendous victory for us, our biggest since I've been coach at Missouri," Al Onofrio admitted after the game. "We played a great Notre Dame team which was demonstrated by their ability to come back in the fourth quarter. We played the best possible game we could after dedication all week in practice. You just never know what will happen in this

212

game."

"This was a very disappointing loss for us," Ara was telling the writers over in our dressing room. "We failed to control the line of scrimmage. A combination of our mistakes and Missouri's lack of mistakes brought about the final score. Mistakes are part of the game and we certainly made our share today. It was obvious that Missouri was very well prepared. In addition they executed almost perfectly."

Our fans searched for reasons behind this upset. Surely it must have been the loss of freshman sensation Steve Niehaus at defensive tackle. He had been hurt in a freak accident during preparation for Missouri after playing incredibly through the first four games. He had been pursuing a runner during drills and stopped suddenly, firmly implanting his foot. Coincidentally, another player went hurling against Niehaus, jarring his leg and forcing it in the opposite direction. Something had to give, and it turned out to be Niehaus' knee. He had torn ligaments, and while immediate surgery made his leg stronger than before, it cost him the remainder of the season.

Niehaus and his classmates were the first freshmen eligible for varsity competition under new NCAA regulations. We hadn't been counting on any of them to step right in and start, but we were hopeful they might be able to give us some immediate reserve strength. Anything beyond that would be a bonus.

We had seen Niehaus play in a high school all-star game that summer, and his quickness despite his 6-5, 265-pound frame impressed us. Once he showed up for fall practice it was just a matter of days before he moved into the number-one spot at tackle. He was starting for us in our opener against Northwestern at the age of 17. Physically he was mature beyond his years. Emotional maturity was difficult to gauge because Steve was so very quiet.

His personality did not waver during his four-year stay. He remained reserved through the good times and bad. He worked tirelessly to regain his strength and agility before the start of the 1973 season. But then, once more after four games ironically, he tore ligaments playing against Rice and had to face surgery on the other knee. Once more he would have to endure pain and push himself when it would be so much easier to quit. His

213

spirits were at an all-time low, but he fought through it. When Steve returned for the 1974 season it was as though he had never missed a day. Ara asked him to move to defensive end, a switch he inwardly dreaded but one he made without complaint because of our weakness there. He played sensationally, but had he remained at his natural position he probably would have been named All-American his junior year. The acclaim finally caught up with him the next season when he became a consensus All-American and the second pick in the National Football League draft.

Niehaus' loss hurt, but that alone didn't cost us the Missouri game or any other. The players responded to Ara's petition for renewed dedication, and we knocked off our next three opponents. The first was a shutout victory over TCU, 21-0. Another freshman excited the fans in that game, halfback Art Best, as he broke away on a 57-yard touchdown run. On his first play for Notre Dame against Pittsburgh two games earlier he had scored on a 56-yard run.

Gary Diminick fielded the opening kickoff against Navy at the 16, and he was one of many Notre Dame players to reach the end zone as we jumped off to a 35-0 halftime lead. That gave us a chance to use our subs who in turn gave Navy a chance to score 23 second half points. We held on for a 42-23 win.

Tom Clements had been nearly flawless that day. From the spring of his freshman year on there was little doubt Tom would be our quarterback, and one of our better ones at that. Picking Ara's top quarterback at Notre Dame would be difficult. You'd be speaking of John Huarte, Bill Zloch, Coley O'Brien, Terry Hanratty, Joe Theismann, Bill Etter and Clements, and we were delighted with all of them. Huarte probably had the fewest physical tools but got the most out of the skills he did possess. He was an adequate runner and accurate passer. He ran our team well because he understood our offensive concepts. This was also true of Zloch, O'Brien, and Etter.

Hanratty was our strongest passer and surprisingly was faster afoot than wiry Theismann. Theismann combined all the elements you'd like to see in a quarterback—he had a slingshot

Ara knew what would happen if the team did not take an opponent seriously.

arm, could escape the rush like nobody who had ever played for or against us and had total faith in himself. Clements was a sensational runner and ball handler. He rivaled Theismann as a field leader.

A 21-7 win over Air Force brought us to 7-1, and despite the setback to Missouri the Orange Bowl officials invited us to their New Year's night party, contingent upon beating Miami. When we scored our first touchdown, fans began pelting the field with oranges. At least they had enough sense to wait until action stopped then, but after our next score one of them didn't. Brian Doherty was awaiting the snap for the extra point try by Bob Thomas. Just as the center sent him the ball a snowball from out of the stands shattered in front of Doherty, breaking his concentration. He bobbled the ball, and we missed the extra point.

That seemed insignificant after we scored another touchdown and pulled ahead 20-3 to start the fourth quarter. Then Miami's quarterback, Ed Carney, started passing with great accuracy and put together two scoring drives. Our lead had dwindled to 20-17 with 3:30 to play. All of a sudden that missed extra point looked mighty big.

Miami kicked off, and we were aiming for one first down that would run out the clock. Not wanting to risk putting the ball in the air, Ara had Tom fake a rollout pass on third and six. He got a good block from Andy Huff, stepped high over a pileup and had the first down easily until the ball got plunked free by a defender's helmet. Miami recovered on our 34 and wound up attempting a 46-yard field goal. It went wide to the right, and so ended their *snowball's chance.*

Alabama and Southern Cal were the only teams left in the undefeated ranks. Our chance to repay an old debt to the Trojans was upcoming.

But a sophomore running back named Anthony Davis had something to say about that. He put on one of the greatest shows in college football history—which even included choreography after each act. He started the game by stunning us, and after we clawed back to within range he delivered the knockout punch.

Gary Diminick—a record-setting kickoff return man.

217

Tom Clements understood our system...and had the talent to put it into action.

Davis ran back the opening kick for a 97-yard touchdown and set the tone for the entire game. We slugged it out and netted a 45-yard Bob Thomas field goal but then made things easy for the Trojans as we always seemed to do. Our defensive back Reggie Barnett was covering USC's fleet receiver Lynn Swann and bumped him in the end zone. The interference call advanced the ball 40 yards to our one. Scoring from there was easy, and on the first play of the next series we made it almost as simple when sophomore halfback Eric Penick fumbled on our nine. Penick had been a successful runner for us in his first varsity season, gaining 727 yards, but he was fumble-prone. He didn't come to Notre Dame with much style. He was a big, fast sprinter, and in high school he not only ran over people but he did it in a hurry. His biggest fault was holding the ball away from his body when he ran, leaving it unprotected. The hughest hulk in the world doesn't stand a chance of keeping the ball that way if a defender merely taps it.

Clements connected on four passes in our next drive, the longest a 36-yarder to halfback Gary Diminick, to push the halftime score to 19-10. Tom threw an interception to open the second half, and the Trojans had another assist from us on a touchdown.

A 36-yard pass to Mike Creaney and one of 20 yards to Diminick got us going again. We took it all the way down to the USC one where Art Best fumbled. Even that didn't discourage us. When we got the ball back Clements threw an 11-yard touchdown pass to Diminick and then a 10-yarder to Creaney, and we were within two. That's when Davis did his most damaging work of the day. Cliff Brown kicked off to him on the four, and he ran the length of the field, breaking two tackles along the way.

Our players let the "what-more-do-we-have-to-do attitude" control them the rest of the way. We couldn't click on anything we tried. Clements threw another interception three plays later, and of course USC capitalized on it. Davis went the final eight yards for his sixth touchdown of the day. Oh, how his little dance in the end zone after each score sickened us.

The Trojans pushed across one more touchdown, making the final, 45-23.

"USC has had a lot of good football teams in the past, but this is probably the best balanced team they've ever had," Ara exclaimed to the press. "Davis' two kickoff returns plus the errors in the game really killed us. Fumbles, interceptions, interference calls—you can't make those mistakes against a team like USC. Just take the two returns, the interference call and the fumble at the nine, add it together and you get 28 points. You just can't give that away.

"When we fell behind we had to throw out our game plan. Before we knew it the score was 19-3 after key errors. Then we moved up to 19-10 and another interception turned things around. We moved up again to 25-23 and then came the kickoff return. No question about it, that was the turning point of the game."

John McKay justifiably declared, "I've never seen a greater day by an individual than Anthony Davis' performance today."

Davis was engulfed by the press corps, adding further insult to our wounded pride. "Notre Dame sent me letters trying to recruit me, but I just turned them down," he crowed. "Notre Dame was big but didn't hit as hard as Washington did." We would arrange to hit him harder next season.

Any thoughts of next season had to be delayed because of one last test—Nebraska in the Orange Bowl. Head coach Bob Devaney announced that this would be his last game with the Cornhuskers, and running back Johnny Rodgers was the newly-crowned Heisman Trophy winner. This would be their opportunity to go out in style.

Our players relaxed after the Southern Cal game, thinking they could get back in the groove when practices began again. When we did reassemble we practiced efficiently. Our strategy was sound, but we did not perform and the result was the most lopsided defeat during Ara's era, 40-6. We weren't in the game for an instant as it turned out. I think we all wished we could have left at the half. We were humiliated—not by the score, not by the loss, but by the way we performed. We were not Notre Dame that night.

The players were trying, but ultimately the holiday atmosphere of Miami made the difference. They were adhering to our curfew rules, but only later did we discover that friends from school who needed a place to stay used their rooms as a

220

Ara works the players hard in the heat of Miami.

base of operations. Any time was party time for them, and that had its effect on the team.

Physically we were hurting by then and couldn't match Nebraska's skill, speed and depth. The National Championship wasn't an issue so our players didn't have much incentive. Added to that was a bit of controversy. The word got out in the press box that we weren't starting Eric Penick for disciplinary reasons. Penick and Art Best had sneaked onto an Orange Bowl float the night before and joined with the other performers aboard in waving flags and bouncing balls. It was the sort of spur-of-the-moment decision both players were prone to make, failing to regard the consequences. Ara wasn't happy about that, but he had decided weeks before not to start Penick. Eric was excitable so Ara planned to insert him when the time was right. It was his fumbling problem, not his float participation that kept him out of the lineup. But as far as the millions of viewers at home were aware, old Notre Dame was having attitude problems again.

Everything went wrong for us that night. We had interceptions, missed passes, fumbles and breakdowns on offense. Defensively we were dismal. Johnny Rodgers was all he had been built up to be, and we got waxed.

The ever-present post-defeat remarks were there. "The team probably went to a big party before the game." "Devaney is a genius." "I told you Parseghian couldn't win the big ones."

Ara resented the latter statement which became a tag that followed him throughout his Notre Dame career, but he tried to consider the source of such remarks. Every game we played was a big one, but for Ara's critics only the losses were significant. You had only to feel the fire emerging from the opponents' locker room week after week to realize who started it. All familiar phrases are diluted by time, so most sports fans weren't convinced by the statement that every team can make its season by beating Notre Dame.

Another popular dig related to that was "Notre Dame doesn't play anybody." Once again, the "nobodys" on our schedule had a way of blossoming by the motivation of meeting us. Beyond that, Ara's argument was logical and honest, though usually unconvincing to antagonists. He pointed out that schedules are prepared 10 to 12 years in advance and who's to say where the balance of power might be that far ahead of time. A columnist once researched the caliber of our current opponents at the time the games were originally booked and discovered that with the exception of one or two of our traditional rivals, all the teams were well-to-do when contracted.

Ara was too much a competitor to duck anyone. That was true in his private life while playing handball or golf, and it applied to football scheduling. He believed the saying that to be the best you have to play the best so he conferred with Athletic Director Moose Krause when the NCAA approved an eleventh game. He hoped to see Ohio State, Penn State, Michigan, Louisiana State and Alabama worked into the schedule, and in future years, because of his influence, all but the Buckeyes will be. He advocated a "wildcard" game to be set aside by each team as its eleventh date. The game couldn't be contracted until one year before, enabling teams to schedule the most competitive opponent. Athletic administrators were so anxious to have commitments in writing, however, that his plan wasn't feasible.

Typically, people overlooked that attempt and remembered something negative. Ara always got less credit than he

Johnny Rodgers was all he had been built up to be.

deserved principally because he was at Notre Dame. "A cheer-leader could coach the team at Notre Dame," a magazine reporter wrote. How wrong he was, but how well he captured the feeling that was so prevalent. There was no harder assign-ment than coaching at Notre Dame, and strategically Ara never faltered. We might have been out-psyched or out-personneled on occasion, but there wasn't a game we entered where Ara hadn't outlined the way to stop everything our opponent threw at us or penetrate every defense the competition displayed.

In 1972 we experienced three of the most stunning defeats in Notre Dame history. The Missouri loss was the biggest upset Ara ever suffered, Anthony Davis' performance in Southern Cal's victory magnified our setback for the world to mock and Nebraska thumped us more soundly than a Parseghian-coached Notre Dame team had ever known. The Missouri game in retrospect should have been a forewarning. We lost more than a game that day, we lost intensity and emotion.

Still, it's true that something good comes of everything. It would have been impossible to explain despondency half as well as our players now knew it. They were experiencing it on their own. After the three incredible losses we sustained, this group of players had nothing to brag about. That had been true after the 1971 season as well, but perhaps a new day was dawning. Maybe the urge for "individualism" was finally bowing to the benefits of team success. Whatever the motivation, these players considered the empty feeling of what had just taken place and sought to amend it in the future.

1973 -
From The
Ashes Of Disaster

Ara was much less visible the winter of 1973 than any postseason period in the past. It wasn't so much that he was hiding out of shame, but answering questions about the 1972 season only gouged deeper into his wounds. All progress being relative, his 8-3 record of 1972 was comparable in impact to his 0-9 record at Northwestern in 1957.

But Ara had matured in those 15 years. He didn't spend the winter chastising himself for omissions. He didn't drive the staff with increased frenzy. He didn't plot radical changes. None of that was necessary as it once had been when he was a younger coach.

By now he realized the uncontrollable factors of college football. He was sensible enough to see that once you have pushed yourself to the "fullest measure," there is nothing left to be done. Given the opportunity to replay the Missouri, Southern Cal and Nebraska games I don't know what he would have done differently. He wisely accepted that and merely approached the 1973 season with the same organization as ever.

That's not to say the sting wasn't there. He was more anxious than anyone to get on with 1973 and put the past where it belonged.

The students, too, seemed to be moving in a new direction. The years of counterculture had run their course. Maybe it was the Vietnam War ending or perhaps being *different* was a fad

Football fit in perfectly with the new Notre Dame look.

that had passed, but students now were only bothered by the age-old concerns of getting good grades, finding a job and who to date on Friday night.

Female students had been admitted to the University, and they brought with them a fresh spirit. Their male counterparts were a little better groomed and appeared more eager to join the world again. The Notre Dame tradition of racing to the window every time a girl walked in front of the dorm had ended. Coeds were becoming commonplace, and they were giving the school a different personality.

And for some reason, football fit in perfectly with this new look. The students were once again enchanted by the fall football pageantry. For the longtime Fighting Irish fans it was like the "good old days."

Our team typified this enthusiasm. We broke precedent by naming tri-captains—offensive captain Frank Pomarico, defensive captain Mike Townsend and team captain Dave Casper. They contrasted ethnically, intellectually and physically and gave us just the right combination of leadership. They offered something for everybody. Casper referred to the three as "the Italian, the black and the Wisconsin farmer."

Pomarico was a throwback to Larry DiNardo, our captain in 1970, and went to the same high school in Howard Beach, New York. He, too, had come from a strict Italian upbringing and refused to change with the times. He was one of the rare young men who truly believed that the clean-living, hard-working people of this world always reached their goals. There was a wholesomeness in that.

When Mike Townsend first came to school we felt he wouldn't be as capable a player as his older brother Willie, a split end. But by moving him from offense to the defensive secondary he used his height and tremendous leaping ability to become one of Notre Dame's greatest. He was named All-America that season and broke the school's career interception record. Nothing in the world could make Mike frown. His great sense of humor and sunny disposition kept his teammates loose.

Casper was extremely intelligent but was blase about life almost to the point of being discourteous, though I don't think he intended to be. He was one of the most talented players ever to wear the Notre Dame uniform. He had size, speed and unwavering determination. Since we had a qualified tight end in Mike Creaney Casper's first three seasons, "The Ghost" played at offensive tackle. With Creaney's graduation we moved Casper to end, adding receiving to his previous list of accomplishments. By his own admission there were other things in life as important to him as football, but since the sport was occupying him at the moment he wanted to do it better than anyone. He, too, was named All-America as a senior.

This blend went deeper than just the captains. There were no superstars on our squad—guys we couldn't get along without. At every position we had people with something to prove. Center Mark Brenneman had missed the 1972 season with a back injury and played on the prep team his first two years. Tackles Steve Sylvester and Steve Neece and split end Pete Demmerle fell into the same category. Guard Gerry DiNardo would be a second-year starter, but he had yet to move out from the shadow of his brother Larry. Fullback Wayne Bullock was a varsity newcomer, halfback Art Best had never been a starter and running mate Eric Penick wanted to lose the reputation of being a fumbler.

Defensively, those returning from 1972 wanted to make amends for our three losses. In those games they had allowed 115 points. Steve Niehaus was back to put his knee to the test. Jim Stock wanted to be more than just coach Mike Stock's "little brother" as a defensive end. Gary Potempa had been a journeyman linebacker his first three seasons, but by going to a middle linebacker system he became a key performer. Then there were the freshmen. Ross Browner and Willie Fry moved in immediately at defensive end as did Luther Bradley at strong safety. Big time football was brand new to them, and they wanted to make an impression.

We had two other players who made significant contributions in punter-holder Brian Doherty and kicker Bob Thomas. They emerged as producers–directors of our weekly cheers which were once again as inspired as in our early years and now even more artistic. Unlike most specialists who go off on their own in the *North pasture* these two were an integral part of the team. They were psyche artists who kept their teammates alive and Ara smiling. Thomas and Ara challenged one another to field goal contests nearly every day before practice. By the end of the season Ara had run up a debt of 1,329 milkshakes, and knowing Bob he's probably still collecting.

We lost three players in our first fall scrimmage. Frank Pomarico was the only starter, and he'd be out for five weeks. Ara halted that practice session early. "What did we do wrong?" he mused while getting undressed. "We have to scrimmage sometime!"

We survived it and persevered. Those players in casts and others with minor bruises came to practice everyday and watched from the sidelines. Their interest and enthusiasm were still there. Ara began to pick up the pace with the coaching staff. Now that he was into the season he drove himself and us. Our staff included three new coaches. Brian Boulac and Bill Hickey, both alumni, had joined us in 1971, and Greg Blache, a graduate assistant the past two years, had been added fulltime in 1973.

Our opener with Northwestern didn't arrive any too soon. Nine months is a long time to wait to erase a bad dream.

Freshman Ross Browner blocks a punt in his first Notre Dame game.

Unfortunately for John Pont, a player on Ara's first Miami team, the Wildcats had to bear the brunt. Not that we were trying to run up the score, but this was a stored emotion whose time had come. Our defense was awesome and our offense fleet. For the first time in Ara's coaching career we had speed—that's right, speed—in the backfield. There were Best, Penick, Clements, Bullock, Gary Diminick, Al Samuel, Ron Goodman, Russ Kornman and, the fastest of all, a freshman who had run the 100 in 9.5 seconds in high school, Al Hunter. All of them had their chance as we passed for 200 yards and rushed 273, and Northwestern fell, 44-0.

But happiness could never last long for us. No sooner had we come into the locker room after the game than we heard the news that Tom Clements' 14-year-old sister, Alice, had died. She had been walking along a highway at sunset the night before when a car hit her, hurling her 100 feet in the air. Tom played the game knowing she was in a coma in critical condition. A priest sent word to Dr. Harry Clements in the stadium before the game that Alice had passed away, but Tom's father decided to withhold the information from him until afterward. They left immediately for their McKees Rocks, Pennsylvania, home.

George Kelly and I represented the staff at the funeral. It would take something that serious for any of us to miss practice. We worried about Tom, thinking that this tragedy might affect him so deeply he couldn't go on. Cliff Brown took over at quarterback Monday and Tuesday, but even though we told Tom to take the week off he returned Wednesday and was his same poised, expressionless self. Inside, football had to be the least important thing in the world at this time, but he didn't show it. Only once did I detect a crack in his passive exterior. We were going over the game plan his first night back, and I saw him gaze into the distance—his thoughts a long way off. Tom's family was a close group. They were deep and loved in a way that makes family something special.

Tom had a brother and sister who were lawyers and another brother who was a doctor, but Tom was destined to leave his mark in the world of athletics. He was a two-sport star in high school and had his pick of any college in the nation to play either football or basketball. He was sensible enough even at that age to realize he couldn't continue to be outstanding in both sports, and he thought his greatest potential was in football.

To use a cliche, Tom truly did have ice water in his veins. He never lost his composure. He had a quiet confidence about himself and was anything but showy. It wasn't his style to yell at others for their errors, though occasionally he'd rebuke himself. His mind was a steel trap, and anything he heard registered. He took criticism well, but if it didn't make sense to him he'd ask for an explanation. He worked on any shortcomings we brought to his attention, and gradually we were able to expand our offensive capabilities because of his total grasp of our system. Tom may have been quiet, but because of the respect his teammates held for him he was a true leader.

Art Best rushed for 125 yards against Purdue, including 65 on our first offensive play, and we beat the Boilermakers on

Football had to be the least important thing in the world after Tom Clements' sister's death.

their field, 20-7. Michigan State startled us the next week. Leading 14-3 in the fourth quarter Clements threw an inopportune interception at our 15-yard line and the Spartans carried it in for the score. Our defense was immovable the next 13:56, and we clung to the 14-10 margin.

Rice coach Al Conover was as much a showman as a strategist, and he decided that the way to stay with Notre Dame was through the power of prayer. So he invited 80 priests to be his sideline guests for our game. Only a few were *traitors* to the Notre Dame cause, and a few just weren't enough. We slugged out a 28-0 win. It cost us Steve Niehaus who suffered his second knee injury.

Army made the mistake of scoring first after we had

Even all this "prayer power" did not help Rice.

played listlessly most of the opening quarter. The Cadets' 3-0 lead jarred us into action, and we didn't stop until 62 points later. Ara tried to hold the score down and even asked our reserves to fall to the ground at one point. Freshman Tim Simon fielded a punt on our 28-yard line with minutes to play and found enough defensive holes to score a 72-yard touchdown. Ara was upset, but how do you scold a freshman for succeeding at what he had been trained to do? Ara sympathized with Army coach Tom Cahill. Only a few years prior he had been coach of the year, but now the service academies were having their troubles.

We were 5-0 and ready to make real restitution for 1972. Southern Cal was coming to town with a 23-game winning streak, the longest in the nation. The Trojans had tied Oklahoma 7-7 in their third game this year and UCLA by the same score in 1971, but were winners 21 other times, starting with a 28-14 victory in our stadium in 1971.

Each year before the ND-USC matchup some writer would unearth a quotation said to have been made by Southern Cal coach John McKay. Though he denies it he supposedly vowed

232

after our 51-0 rout at Los Angeles in 1966 never to lose to Notre Dame again. If he did say that he was a man of his word because we had been unsuccessful against the Trojans since then in six tries.

Insults from the USC team made losing all the more painful. Ara had always trained our players to be gracious in victory or defeat, but the Trojan players had a way of twisting the sword by their verbal assaults. They often demeaned our efforts even though they were usually vastly superior in strength.

This year our personnel was about even, and we were ready to return all past injustices. The campus was ablaze with anticipation. Classes might just as well have been cancelled because the students were thinking only about one thing—beating USC. Some enterprising student came up with a picture of Anthony Davis doing his end zone dance and had hundreds of reproductions made. They were taped to the sidewalks around campus so the whole student body could literally walk

The students had a chance to walk on this image of Anthony Davis.

Davis was not the most popular guy on the block at Notre Dame.

all over "A.D." Every dorm was plastered with signs, and one hall hung Davis in effigy.

Back in 1966 I thought I had witnessed the ultimate in student involvement before the fabled Michigan State game, but that couldn't compare with this delirium. Nightly pep rallies were back in vogue, and for the first time since our arrival at Notre Dame the band marched out to play for us at practice. Southern Cal had a catchy fight song of its own, and our players kept it going constantly in the locker room that week. The

Clobber Board was loaded with statements from USC players—they were plentiful. That picture of Anthony Davis was placed in the locker of every defensive player.

We were ready! Purely on the basis of talent it was feasible, but in reality there was no way Southern Cal could have beaten us. I have never seen our team with a better frame of mind. They weren't the crazy, berserk type of "up," but totally convinced that their mission was one of destiny.

And the first time the Trojans handled the ball they probably sensed that, too. Quarterback Pat Haden threw a screen pass to Lynn Swann, and freshman Luther Bradley smacked him so hard the ball popped free and Swann's helmet fell off. We took a 13-7 lead and the momentum into the locker room at halftime.

Then came the biggest play of the game, on our first offensive series of the second half. Eric Penick took a handoff around left end and lugged it 85 yards for a touchdown. Only in the sense that all plays executed to perfection are capable of going all the way could this be considered a breakaway play. But every player did carry out his assignment, and Penick was able to score. Bullock faked well to freeze USC's linebackers; Casper made a great block and Best sealed off the defensive end; Pomarico and DiNardo turned the corner, guiding Penick into the open. He broke one tackle and was on his way. It couldn't have come at a better time.

The celebration in the end zone delayed play for several minutes. Penick's teammates swarmed him as did hundreds of fans from out of the stands. The Trojans scored one more touchdown, but Bob Thomas kicked his third field goal of the day to give us a 23-14 keepsake.

Our defense limited Davis to 55 yards in 19 carries, and he didn't have one pass reception. As a team we outrushed the Trojans 316 to 68.

Ara had been waiting six long years to meet the press after a USC game.

"We are delighted to have this game ball," he began. "Because Southern Cal's 23-game streak began here at Notre Dame I think it is appropriate it has ended here as well. Southern Cal played great football during that streak and they did so today, but our kids put forth a tremendous effort and deserved

Eric Penick's 85-yard touchdown run.

to win. They were up all week and they remembered last year's 45 points by Southern Cal and six touchdowns by Anthony Davis.

"We did not key on Davis. In fact, I was most concerned about Southern Cal's passing attack. It brings such big rewards quickly, just like it did in the third quarter when they got a touchdown a minute or so after Penick's long run."

Credit again came grudgingly from the Trojan dressing room.

"Notre Dame won the game," said McKay matter-of-factly. "That's it. They outplayed us which is the name of the game. They didn't do anything we didn't expect.

"We were hurt when defensive tackle Art Riley lost his contacts and couldn't play after the first series or two. He couldn't see well enough to play without them although he tried for awhile.

"One thing that upsets me is that I never made a statement that we would never lose to Notre Dame again. I don't make vows."

Anthony Davis refused to compliment our performance.

"With the poor field position we had, a lot of things can happen and they did," he said. "I don't think they are as strong inside as they were last year. Notre Dame would have its hands full against Oklahoma, and Arkansas was the toughest hitting team we played this year. Tim Rudnick (defensive back) talked to me through the entire game and that's because he'll never forget me from last year."

Back in our dressing room Eric Penick added the ultimate squelch to the day. A reporter asked him why he didn't dance after his long touchdown run. "This is Notre Dame," he replied, "we're not hot dogs."

The next day all the assistant coaches arranged to get to the office well ahead of Ara. When he arrived we all stood and applauded him. He was touched by the act, treasuring such appreciation by his contemporaries. "Thank you for this tribute," he beamed. "We're only halfway home, though, so let's go to work!"

Despite our showing against USC, Ohio State, Michigan, LSU, Alabama, Oklahoma and Penn State were all ranked ahead of us. "The polls will take care of themselves," Ara told the

Notre Dame fans had six years of emotion saved up for a win over the Trojans.

squad, "so long as we continue to win."

The team matured visibly after that game. The players weren't arrogant, but they sensed that it would require a great effort to overcome anything they had their minds set on. That's exactly what Ara feared most. The Southern Cal game peaked our emotion, and a psychological letdown was only natural. The team had been working hard enough in its preparation for Navy, it had been attentive, but it had also been awfully relaxed.

When the whistle blew against Navy all our players showed up—physically and emotionally. We won handily, 44-7.

Pittsburgh's new head coach Johnny Majors promised the Panther fans to knock off one of the two remaining powers left on the schedule. That meant either Penn State or us. Majors had recruited 80 players that winter, trying to beat the 30-player limit imposed by the NCAA for the next year.

Tom Clements was going to have a chance to display his talent in his home town. He had been looking forward to it until the Thursday before the game. During practice he pulled up short on a routine play, and the ς, jck jerking motion tore a stomach muscle.

Ara had a lot of faith in Cliff Brown, but our offense with Tom gave us a four-back running attack. Cliff could throw the ball with anyone, but we were more effective as a running team. The morning of the game Tom claimed he felt well enough to play, though admittedly a little sore.

Tony Dorsett had been the most talked-about freshman running back in the nation that season. He was Pitt's answer to Anthony Davis. He was impressive against us, rushing for 209 yards—the most ever by a Notre Dame opponent. But he failed in one category—scoring. We had a running back of our own who really did a better job. Fullback Wayne Bullock was magnificent when we needed his help the most. He carried 27 times for 167 yards and scored all four of our touchdowns. Clements couldn't pass with his injury, and he tried only four times.

Fullback Wayne Bullock (30) was the most productive runner on the field against Pittsburgh.

Thanks to Bullock and our other backs, not to mention seven Panther turnovers, we won, 31-10.

Air Force was our Thanksgiving Day opponent. The game had been switched to that date to accommodate ABC television. Viewers certainly weren't treated to a see-saw game, as three early Falcon turnovers enabled us to jump ahead 28-0 in the first quarter. With reserves playing the second half we wound up 48-15 victors.

That left just one regular season game to be played. A win would give Ara his first perfect record at Notre Dame and only his second ever. His last Miami team went 9-0 in 1955. No Notre Dame team had done it since Frank Leahy's 1949 squad won the National Championship with a 10-0-0 record. Miami of Florida would be a difficult obstacle. The Hurricanes had beaten Texas in their opener and tested Oklahoma before falling, 24-19.

We headed for the heat and humidity of Florida and walked into the same locker room at the Orange Bowl Stadium we had been in 11 months earlier to play Nebraska. All the images of that horrendous night came to mind, but the players wanted this too desperately to be bothered by deja vu.

We scored quickly the first time we had the ball. Our only miscue all night was on our second possession deep in our territory. Clements kept the ball too long and fired an option pitch behind Penick. Miami recovered at the 14. Our defense was bent on a shutout and stopped the Hurricanes at the 10. From that point forward we played our best game of the year. Center Mark Brenneman handled All-American middle guard Tony Cristiani, and offensive tackle Steve Neece did his job against All-American tackle Rubin Carter. Our performance was reflected by beating a good team on its home field, 44-0.

The media asked Ara if this was his best team.

"Well, no other team has gone 10-0-0 but I'll wait and see," he answered.

They wondered if the 44-0 score surprised him.

"Nothing surprises me about football any more!"

How about "Bear" Bryant?

"What about Bear?"

Could Notre Dame beat Alabama in the upcoming Sugar Bowl?

Gary Potempa became a key player in our new middle line-backer system.

"Hell, I don't know," he said, "that's a month off. Let me enjoy this one at least for tonight. If you have no more questions I'm awfully tired. I just want to go to the hotel and have a quiet drink with my wife."

As usual, the day after our last game was a holiday for us. For once we had a chance to enjoy it, but Mike Stock and I used the time to visit a young Notre Dame fan in the hospital. The "George Cunningham Story" had filled the local papers the week before the Miami game. George was injured in the last football game of his high school career, leaving him paralyzed from the neck down. He was under intensive care in a Ft. Lauderdale hospital, mounted on a table-like bed elevated at the top.

George couldn't speak, but he blinked his eyes once for "yes" and twice for "no." His mother was delighted to see us. "We knew someone from Notre Dame would come!" she exclaimed. She crouched over close to George to read his lips. "He says you should have been National Champs in 1964." She looked back at her son whose lifelong dream it had been to attend Notre Dame. "He thinks you'll beat Alabama, but it'll be

242

close."

We left the hospitable praying for the miracle necessary for his recovery and hoping our young friend turned out to be a prophet.

Bear Bryant must have been confident his Crimson Tide team could whip us in a postseason game. Even before bowl invitations were extended, he announced that his players wanted to attend the Sugar Bowl and they hoped their opponent would be Notre Dame. Bear rated his team the best he had ever coached and termed our meeting the "singly most important game the South has ever played." If we had ambitions of going elsewhere, we couldn't disregard this challenge. So the Sugar Bowl it was.

Since renewing our bowl involvement this was the first time the National Championship was at stake for the winner. Refreshingly, that gave our players a completely different attitude toward the preparation for the game. Their vote this time was unanimous and didn't carry with it any contingencies. They just wanted to play and win. On their own they decided to stay on campus to practice instead of going home for Christmas. So we worked as hard as possible in our snowy clime and left for New Orleans four days before the game.

We headquartered at the Marriott Hotel on the perimeter of the French Quarter. The distractions of Miami Beach were nothing compared to this. New Orleans natives claimed that the excitement generated by the rabid Notre Dame and Alabama fans rivaled the magic of Mardi Gras. The French Quarter is the focal point for all visitors to New Orleans, and the thousands of fans from both teams isolated into one area produced the best possible bowl enthusiasm. Certainly there are no more vocal supporters than those of Notre Dame and Alabama, and it was amusing to see them passing each other in the Quarter shouting "Go Irish!" and "Rolllllllllll TIDE!" But they did it respectfully, not violently.

The Quarter tempted our players with every imprudent product going. It featured block after block of bars and strip joints—just the things to take their minds off the game. Ara didn't preach to them about their obligations. He painted our objective and the dedication it would take to achieve it and let them guide themselves. Nothing more was needed with this group because it was dead serious about the purpose of this trip. To a man they said, "I don't know what everybody else is going to do, but I'm going to get my rest and play it safe *before* this game." Their friends from school would have to find other accommodations this time.

We had purchased special blue and gold shoes for this game and didn't discover until after we had them that they would be inefficient if it rained on the Tulane Stadium polyturf. We checked with both the New Orleans Saints and Tulane, and they recommended a rubber-soled shoe with nearly 90 pinpointed spikes. Unfortunately, the company in Canada that produced them had been on strike for four months. The Saints' players owned their shoes, and Tulane had already turned over its surplus to Alabama. Tulane was playing in the Bluebonnet Bowl in Houston the night before our game and promised to get us the shoes its players wore the next morning.

So we practiced for three days with our pretty but slippery blue and gold shoes. Alabama had its workouts in the morning, and ours were at 2:00 p.m. Naturally the weather turned sour when we took the field, but to this team even that was a blessing. Ara had them lined up in the end zone for calisthenics when the rains came in torrents. The surface couldn't drain fast enough, and shallow lakes were forming all over. Instead of fleeing to shelter, the players reverted to their childhood days and stomped and splashed in the puddles. The bolder ones got a running start and belly-whopped into the water pools, sliding for yards and kicking up the moisture. Others were having water fights. When the rain subsided and they were all thoroughly soaked, Ara reassembled them, fractured by what had just happened. Their spirits were high for the work ahead.

One of the plays we rehearsed that day was a new kickoff return formation. In it our five linemen were responsible for blocking the first five Alabama defenders down the field. Behind these men were two tight ends and two fullbacks, whose job it was to form a semicircle with one of our deep backs. The other halfback would field the ball and set this second wave of blockers in motion by yelling, "Go!" If properly timed this inner wall would guide the return man far enough downfield to find an opening.

This play had become a joke that week because Ara kept

244

State pride was at stake as Congressman John Brademas (right) wagers an autographed football with his Alabama counterpart.

harping on all of them, "Don't forget to yell 'Go.'"

"Hey, Al (Hunter)," he persisted, "don't forget to yell 'Go.'"

"Gary," he began.

"Yeah, I know, Coach," Diminick interrupted, "yell 'Go.'"

Comparing individual games in Ara's era is impossible. At the time each seemed to be the most vital. If he had to single out one game would he choose a win over Woody Hayes and Ohio State when he was at Northwestern? Or how about the times a victory late in the season could have put his Wildcat teams in the Rose Bowl? What about the 1964 or 1970 Southern Cal games that would have given him National Championships? Or the 1966 Michigan State game? Those were all key games in his career, but now they were only memories. Alabama was the competition at hand, and no game in the past could have been more important. We were all proportionately nervous.

On the way to the team bus I spotted my mother among the mass of bodies on watch in the hotel lobby. I struggled to get over to her for a good luck kiss, and as I did she whispered in my ear. "Tom, does Parseghian have a little something up his sleeve?" Her comment was exactly what I needed at that point. I chuckled and answered her as best I could. "For once in my life, Mom, I really hope he does!"

We took the field for our pregame warmups complete with our borrowed Tulane shoes. It had rained much of the day and evening, and overhead the lightning was freely crackling. Ara put the team through a few timing drills but fearing the lightning soon whistled them into the locker room. By the time the bands and guest performers had cleared the field for our return, the storm had ended.

Hunter and Diminick were set to receive the opening kick, but Alabama crossed us by sending the ball out of the end zone. Both teams felt each other out the first two series, but Ara opened things up on our third possession. Clements hit Pete Demmerle on three run-action passes of 59 yards that set up Wayne Bullock's one-yard touchdown plunge. A bad center snap cost us the point after, and we led, 6-0. As the first quarter ended, our defense had held the Crimson Tide to one net yard.

The second quarter was a different story. Alabama

246

The Sugar Bowl Queen parades on a giant mockup of the game's trophy.

evidently solved our defensive look and also stymied our offense. Quarterback Gary Rutledge kept the Tide on the ground from its wishbone formation and put his team ahead with a seven-play drive.

Now 'Bama had to kick to us again, this time into the wind. The kick was high, and Al Hunter fielded it on our seven. Mark Brenneman threw his body as did his four linemates. Robin Weber, Dave Casper, Wayne Bullock, Art Best and Gary Diminick set up Hunter's escort. Al aimed for the middle, saw running room to his right at about the 40 and left the nest to strike out on his own. His feet were flying, and the Alabama defenders followed in vain. The whole team, Ara and all the coaches included, left the sidelines to celebrate in the end zone. It cost us 15 yards for delay of game, but it was worth it.

Ara composed himself and carefully considered his course of action. We were ahead 12-7, and he wanted to make up for the missed point on our first touchdown. He called for a pass play to Casper who wound up being covered, but the ever-thinking Pete Demmerle adjusted his course and Clements lofted the ball over the fingertips of an Alabama safety.

Alabama came up with a 39-yard field goal to cut our half-time lead to 14-10. Ara was most concerned about our defense during the intermission break. He huddled with Paul Shoults, George Kelly and Joe Yonto and decided to use our defenses on a rotating basis. He challenged the Tide to solve each one, and about the time it had he would switch to another.

He reminded the team of only one thing. "We're one half away from the National Championship," he shouted.

The first defense we threw at the Alabama players hardly baffled them. In 11 plays Rutledge directed his teammates on a 93-yard scoring drive for a 17-14 edge. With alternate quarter-back Richard Todd in the game, running back Willie Shelby fumbled after a scorching tackle by linebacker Greg Collins. His partner, linebacker Drew Mahalic, grabbed the ball before it hit the ground and returned it eight yards to the 'Bama 12.

Eric Penick called on all his elusive cuts and behind two blocks by Casper weaved his way into the end zone for a 12-yard score. Thomas made it 21-17, a lead we carried into the fourth quarter.

We traded turnovers within a matter of seconds, but after Wayne Bullock fumbled for the third miscue of the final period the Tide really did *roll*. On a third and seven situation the Bear replaced Rutledge, his top passing quarterback, with Todd, his top running quarterback. We sensed a smoke screen, figuring Alabama would pass even with Todd in the game, and decided to send a seven-man blitz. Bear was counting on Ara to use his noggin, and a blitz was just what he wanted. Todd handed off to halfback Mike Stock, no relation to our Mike Stock the coach or his defensive end brother Jim, and Todd circled around to his left and down the sideline unnoticed. Stock

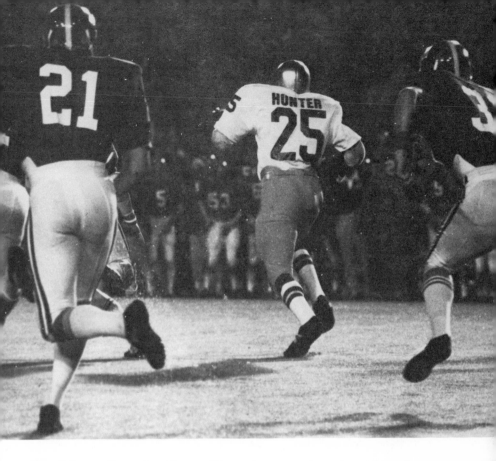

The "Hunter" is the "hunted" on his record-setting 93-yard kickoff return.

threw him the ball and he had no trouble scoring. It was a brilliant call. Their talented place kicker, Bill Davis, failed to convert when his holder juggled the snap. We trailed, 23-21, with 9:33 to play.

Clements then went to work. Starting on our own 19-yard line Tom moved us to the 46 on five straight rushes. On third and one he faked to Bullock and threw a high "hope" toward Casper. Dave was covered by two Alabama defenders but spotted the throw and broke from the crowd, out-rebounding the Tide backs for the reception. That got us to the Alabama 15. We drove as far as the two before stalling on fourth down. That left it all up to Bob Thomas. His 19-yard field goal could put us up, 24-23. It wasn't one of Bob's better efforts—it wasn't strong or long or even straight, but it was good by a couple of feet, and we were ahead.

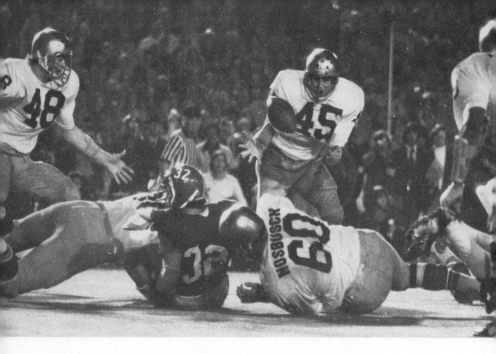

Drew Mahalic makes a timely mid-air recovery.

When Thomas came to the sidelines Ara grabbed him. "That was a little close, don't you think?"

Typically cocky, Thomas quipped, "I was thinking on the way out that if I stuck it right down the pipe nobody would ever remember it. This way they'll be talking about it for years!"

We weren't out of danger yet. Ross Browner had pinned Rutledge for negative yardage, and the Tide faced a fourth and 19 situation with just over three minutes left. Bear called for a punt, and with Browner coming full steam he jarred the punter and drew a penalty. Greg Gantt's punt had carried all the way down to our one-yard line. That left Bear with a difficult decision and one he was criticized for by those who really didn't understand collegiate rules. Contrary to popular belief, roughing the kicker is not an automatic first down in college football. It is a 15-yard penalty, and Bear had to choose between risking a fourth and four attempt or letting his defense pressure us from our one. He picked the latter and rightfully so.

Then on third and six Ara had his day of reckoning. Alabama stopped the clock with 2:12 left, giving Clements a chance to come to the sideline.

"I know it's risky, but let's go with a long cadence," I

suggested.

"Great idea," he replied. "Tom, take a long count and set up a run-action pass to Casper."

For the first time ever, Clements displayed an emotion—surprise. He nodded, though, and ran back on the field. "Are you sure that's what you want to do, Ara?" I asked. "Did I hear you right?"

"Hell yes you did," he snapped. "It's a good call. If they jump we'll get an easy five yards. If they don't then the rush

Bob Thomas connects on a field goal people will remember.

shouldn't be much and we ought to be able to get the ball away."

The teams were at the line of scrimmage now, and I was praying Alabama would jump. A fumble, an interception, a safety—all those were very real possibilities in a passing situation at the five, and any of them would mean the game. My angle was blocked, but I heard someone shout, "Damn it! Casper moved too soon!" That cost us half the distance to the goal and pushed us back to the two. Clements looked toward Ara who signalled for the same play.

Casper was our intended receiver, but Ara had inserted a second tight end, Robin Weber, to disguise our pass plans. With the snap the Alabama secondary converged on Casper, leaving Weber virtually free. He was running a deep pattern toward the Alabama sideline. Meanwhile in the end zone, Clements was fortunate to get the pass off. Two of our players had missed blocks, and an Alabama tackle who should have been on the ground by now lunged toward Tom and barely missed his pass. Weber did some stretching of his own, and after juggling the ball momentarily he cradled it for his first Notre Dame reception—a 35-yard gain. Now we had breathing room, and with an additional first down we ran out the clock.

With one clutch call that would make national headlines, Ara went a long way toward removing the label his enemies insisted on sticking him with ever since the 1966 MSU tie. This wasn't any better than scores of other plays he had come up with in pressure situations, but it would become the most publicized.

We practically floated back to our small dressing room. I couldn't help noting the contrast between the two teams as we merged through the same tunnel. The Alabama players looked at ours, envious perhaps of our elation, but proud nonetheless of their performance. Both teams developed the utmost respect for one another in our first meeting.

Our locker room scene was the greatest ever. The players and coaches embraced emotionally. Pepsi took the place of champagne for our toasts and baptisms. The managers battled to keep visitors out, but gradually the players' relatives and University officials made their way in, further congesting our quarters.

252

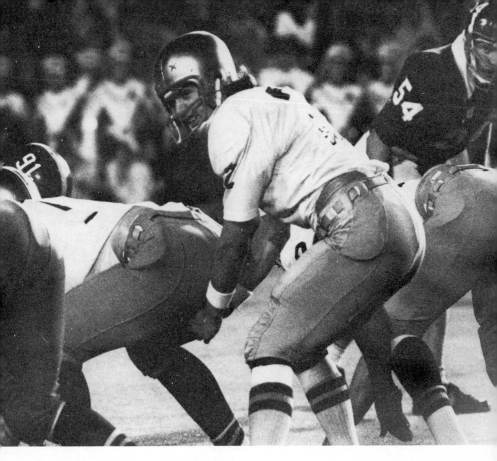

How we hoped Alabama would jump.

Ara had not yet arrived, being detained for postgame presentations. After he managed to pick his way through the throng outside, the team erupted once more and hoisted him on their shoulders to the center of the room.

"They gave us two things out there," he screeched in a -hoarse voice. "One is the Sugar Bowl trophy!" We cheered that for several minutes and then he continued. "Two is the MacArthur Bowl, symbolic of the National...Championship!" With that we were given a visual description of the word "bedlam." It continued for nearly an hour.

The press was now admitted, making conditions tighter than before. The heat from our expenditure in the game and from the affinity of people in our locker room made showering futile. But who cared.

"The pass from Clements to Weber with seconds to go was

The locker room scene was the greatest ever.

the key to the win," Ara explained to the media. "It was a win or punt situation. If we hadn't made the first down Alabama would surely have been in field goal position with us punting from our end zone.

"I definitely feel we're the National Champions. We beat the leading scoring team in the nation. They are an excellently disciplined team. We beat a great football team and they lost to a great football team."

A tall man in a black and white hound's tooth hat came through the doorway. The players made a path for the Bear as he headed for Ara. He congratulated Ara and then asked, "Where is *Mark* Clements? I want to shake his hand."

We didn't get a phone call from the President as so many other National Championship teams had in the past. It didn't matter. Nothing could have increased our utter jubilation. In one's lifetime there aren't more than a handful of moments like this.

By the time Ara boarded the team bus everyone else was seated or clogged in the aisleway. The players' girl friends, wives and parents had joined them for the ride back to the hotel. I was seated near Ara as Al Hunter made his way up front. He had raised his voice over others to get his message across. "You know, Coach," he confessed in his bashful manner, "I forgot to yell 'Go.'" Ara burst out laughing and continued to chuckle the

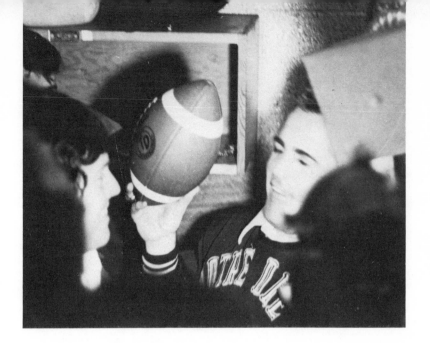

Ara displays the game ball and trophy.

rest of the way back.

The bus ride passed quickly. Naturally the joy of our present accomplishment enveloped us. But with the loss of only five seniors to graduation we were dreaming about doing all this again next year.

1974 -
Heroes Sometimes Cry

Notre Dame was the place to be during the winter of 1974. Three weeks after we had beaten Alabama to win the National Championship, the Fighting Irish basketball team snapped UCLA's 88-game winning streak and the hockey team knocked off top-ranked Michigan Tech, all in the same weekend. The local Chamber of Commerce had prearranged to hold a "Salute to the Champions" ceremony that Sunday in the Athletic and Convocation Center. The emotion couldn't have been greater for that event, and with the majority of our football recruits making their visit that weekend we didn't have to do much convincing.

Ara's speaking requests soared, and every organization in the area wanted to pay tribute to him and the team. The most impressive of these banquets was the Ara Parseghian Testimonial, held in the ACC arena following our spring game. Over 1,100 supporters showed up to toast Ara for 10 years of accomplishment at Notre Dame. All the speakers held various associations with him, but they all had words of praise.

"There is a clause in the alumni constitution that permits us to award honorary membership," noted William K. McGowan, Jr., president of the Alumni Association. "It's something we have never taken advantage of before tonight. Ara Parseghian is the first honorary Notre Dame alumnus. When I told him about it a few days ago, he thought it was great but wanted

Ara's mother and Katie join him at his Notre Dame testimonial.

to know why it took most people four years to get the sheep-skin and him 10!"

"There are many reasons I am proud to represent the Third District in Congress; mostly because two of the top leaders in the country are in my district—Father Ted Hesburgh and Ara Parseghian," Congressman John Brademas cited. "As the stadium cheers die down years from now, the goals of excellence that Ara has stood for will still exist. He has headed drives for the afflicted and donated not only money but his time. He is dedicated not only as a family man, but also to the family of man. He is a man not only in this championship season, but is a man for all seasons."

"We have asked you so many times to bring home victories

257

for us and never before really thanked you for all the times you did," said Pat McLaughlin, student body president. "Tonight we thank you not only for the 85 victories, but more for the sportsmanship you have nurtured and the class you have shown on and off the field. We thought about giving you an umbrella for those times when you can't stop the rain, but what we decided to do was give you our support for 10 more years."

"I've known Ara for 34 years as a coach and player, and he comes as close to being perfect as any man I've ever known," praised Purdue coach Alex Agase, Ara's Cleveland Browns teammate and assistant coach at Northwestern. "I owe him more than I'll ever be able to repay. When he got the coach of the year award from *Football News*, I wrote to tell him how happy I was to see him honored for something I've known for a long time."

"Being part of Notre Dame is being part of a tradition much bigger than any one man, one team or one season," declared Jim Lynch, team captain in 1966 and now a member of the Kansas City Chiefs. "But Ara embodies that quality which will always describe Notre Dame—class. Under him I learned how to win and how to lose. Ara is, very simply, the finest man I have ever been associated with."

Then Ara had his turn at the podium. "I've sat here and listened to all the kind things that have been said tonight and I'm honored, pleased, embarrassed, appreciative, apprehensive and thankful," he began. "I'm honored by all my friends who have travelled so far to be here. I'm pleased to have the members of my family in attendance. I'm embarrassed because I am the focus of attention and I've always preached the importance of teamwork. Success is always based on that.

"I'm appreciative to my staff members who have worked so hard. I'm apprehensive because at the other end of the dais is an opponent, a friend but an opponent (Alex Agase—who would turn out to be a *dreaded* opponent). We will not be successful in 1974 because of what we did in 1973. We're well aware that an even greater determination will be needed. And I'm thankful because the opportunity Notre Dame has given me has been a wonderful experience. I don't know if I can handle another decade, but I'd like to take one year at a time."

One year at a time! I don't think Ara intended to forewarn

anyone that evening, but he was expressing a very real concern—the day was approaching when all this would have to end. Resignation was on Ara's mind in the months after the Sugar Bowl win. He asked himself "Where do I go from here? How can I improve? Achieving success is not nearly as difficult as repeating it. I've been a head coach for 24 years and there's very little in football I haven't experienced." But walking away from the Notre Dame job isn't a decision that is lightly made, and the demands of the 1974 season caught up with him before he had a chance to reflect.

The summer months had always given Ara ample opportunity to court his second love—golf. The hectic lifestyle demanded by the season and the recruiting period that followed gave way to the leisure period that everyone, including Ara, must have. He was preparing for a treasured getaway with his family when a phone call brought word of a calamity involving six of our black players.

The players, all sophomores-to-be enrolled in the Notre Dame summer session, had a girl in a dormitory room after hours. She was there of her own volition, but later decided to call the police and charge our players with rape. Though the authorities were contacted, she never did file a formal complaint. That made no difference, however, because the story was out. A violation of University rules had taken place, and school officials were forced to act.

A formal hearing was held, and the Notre Dame administrators initially planned to expel the players. That *sentence* seemed unnecessarily harsh to Ara. He didn't contend the players were in the right, but he did feel their offense was being exaggerated by some. He proposed that the players be allowed to complete their education but be restricted from playing football for at least one year. If after that time they proved to be remorseful their athletic participation could be reviewed. The school officials eventually settled on suspending them for one year with the possibility, not a guarantee, of readmission.

As had been University policy, the names of the players and their offense would not be made public. But by the time the school made the simplistic announcement that "Six students had been suspended for a violation of University policy," the whole world knew who the six were, that they

259

were football players and that they had been involved in some sort of sexual activity. The *South Bend Tribune* carried a story pointing out that no formal charge had been made by the girl, and the wire services used information from that account to augment the University statement. But the sensationalists around the country had their day. A Los Angeles newspaper used the headline "Rape at ND" even though the story it carried pointed out that rape charges weren't filed. The New York *Daily News* headed its writeup with "Sex Scandal Ousts Six Notre Dame Gridders." It made little difference that both stories clarified the facts. Many readers didn't go beyond the headlines, and even if they did it was with prejudgment. Ara's greatest fear was materializing—insensitive editors were going to magnify the offense and mark these young men for life.

Ara had always worried about the actions of every staff and team member. It was more than just pride with him that no blemish, no tragic episode, no defamation to Notre Dame would ever result from anything he was connected with, but now he wore the look of anguish. It went beyond the great loss of talent that would weaken us. Five of the six would play key roles. We could always field a team, but what of these young men who had been part of us? Do they face the public for the rest of their lives stigmatized? Do they transfer schools, change their names? They made a mistake, but they had been respectful, cooperative, dedicated student-athletes.

Right away the vultures from other schools attempted to lure the players away. They all made the same pitch—since you have to sit out a year anyway, why not transfer to our school and start anew. That had to be a temptation because the players had no way of knowing what brand would mark them when they returned to Notre Dame or even if they could return. Five of them accepted that because of their devotion to Ara. The sixth took the opportunity to move to a school where he stood a better chance of playing.

Even before this matter had been resolved Ara was informed of two other mishaps. Tim Simon, a speedy defensive back slated to be our top punt returner, had his eye poked in a strange backyard accident. Though doctors wouldn't know the extent of the damage for several weeks, they were certain Tim would be at least partially blinded.

Days later Ara learned that Steve Quehl, a journeyman at tight end and tackle who was finally scheduled to be a starter, was seriously injured in an explosion. He had been driving a truck when the transmission blew up. Somehow he had enough composure to leap from the moving vehicle before the second explosion that surely would have killed him. His leg was broken in 10 places, and physicians feared he would always limp. Steve wouldn't accept that and drove himself hard enough to return for the 1975 season.

In our first 1974 fall scrimmage Bob Zanot, another defensive back and punt return specialist, suffered a knee injury and was lost for the season. Halfback Eric Penick had broken his ankle in spring practice, and we knew he wouldn't be available until late in the year if at all. That brought our total loss of personnel before our first game to 10 players—nine of them vital performers. If ever a team with spirit, talent and momentum was going to carry over from the year before, this had figured to be one. Now that was extremely questionable.

Ara was morose, less dynamic and energetic than I ever remembered. His hair flecked gray, almost suddenly. The wrinkles in his face were more prominent. He didn't seem as tall and lost the bounce in his step. He no longer laughed or clowned, and our staff meetings were all business. He was tired and stooped, almost totally preoccupied. Where his radiant eyes formerly pierced your mind, they now drifted in a distant gaze.

The staff was wary of the troubles facing us, but apparently our collective feelings couldn't match Ara's. He was deeply hurt, and he carried the burden. We speculated that his daughter Karan had taken a turn for the worse or that he was concerned with preparations for her upcoming wedding date. Rescheduling of our late-season game with Georgia Tech to September 9 would mean advancing fall practice. It would also mean opening the season two days after Karan's wedding.

Kris Parseghian had married one of Ara's former players, Jim Humbert. During that ceremony Karan developed a relationship with one of the other members of the wedding party, Jim Burke, a Notre Dame graduate studying to be a lawyer. They started dating and finally set a wedding date. Karan tried to pick a time that wouldn't inconvenience Ara, and September 7 would have been perfect if the Tech game hadn't been changed.

Naturally Ara's thoughts were on Karan. She desperately wanted to walk solidly down the aisle on her own, with her dad at her side giving her away in matrimony. When the day came, Ara slowly marched his daughter toward the altar of Notre Dame's Sacred Heart Church. Karan's coal black hair, partially veiled, was much darker than her father's, but their faces radiated the same glow. Later at the reception in the ACC, Ara blocked out his troubles and played his usual role as host. He mingled and danced and reveled at the happiness of his daughter.

Then just one day later he boarded a plane with the rest of us and flew to Atlanta to meet Georgia Tech. He carried concern for his daughter but now had to force himself to think about the game. The team, less than it might have been, was spurred by the adversity of the preseason. When someone screamed on the way to the field, "Remember, we're still the National Champs," starting center Mark Brennemen added, "You bet your sweet ass we are and we're gonna play like it!" The attending chaplain winced at the remark but understood that this was *battle*. This pride earned us a 31-7 win over a capable Yellow Jacket team.

The 49-3 score the next week against Northwestern was misleading. We played lethargically in the first half, and Ara pounced on the team in the locker room with us leading, 14-3. "You can't go through the motions and expect to win," he ranted. "We don't have to change one damn play this half, just go after them and execute!"

More bad news came while preparing for Purdue. Ed Smothers, a good friend of Ara's and an honorary staff member, died of a heart attack. Ed and his wife Madeline acted as surrogate "dad and mom" for black athletes attending Notre Dame. Their home and hearts were always open, and the exercise of feeding, allowing phone calls, writing families and visiting recruits must have pinched their meager budget. The black population at Notre Dame was small and relatively new, and the Smothers were rewarded knowing they were aiding young men in the adjustment to this environment. The events of the summer saddened them and involved them more than ever.

Pupil Alex Agase was finally successful against his teacher.

It seems all things come in groups of three. Ara's personal friend, an Armenian carpet dealer from Chicago, Carnig Manasian, had died of a heart attack that past summer. After the Purdue game another friend, the famed voice of Notre Dame, Van Patrick, succumbed to cancer.

Playing in Notre Dame Stadium as decided underdogs, the Purdue Boilermakers put 21 points on the board with less than eight minutes elapsed. Before the first quarter ended they had us down, 24-0, capitalizing on a fumble recovery, a pass interception and a 52-yard breakaway by Pete Gross. We edged ever closer the rest of the way, but the game ended with us on the short end, 31-20. Alex Agase's players won only three more that year, but they had dethroned the National Champions.

Since mistakes cost us the Purdue game, Ara planned to play conservatively against Michigan State in East Lansing. If we were going to lose again, it would have to be by Spartan merit rather than Irish gifts. That strategy got us a 19-14 win, though it might have put the fans to sleep. Still, we knew we had beaten a powerful team as the Spartans proved later in the year by upsetting Ohio State.

Then followed our worst and best performances of the year. All three resulted in victories. We got by Rice, 10-3, playing listlessly again. Stripped of offensive backfield speed by our off-season mishaps our attack consisted essentially of fullback Wayne Bullock rushing and Tom Clements passing to split end Pete Demmerle. Opposing teams were catching on and structuring their defenses to blunt our strengths. Army couldn't match us, however, and we shut out the Cadets, 48-0. The next week we came out in full force against Miami in a regionally televised game, 38-7.

That brought us to the game that produced the most critical decision of Ara's career. Offensively we moved the ball all over the field against Navy, but fumbled or threw an interception to stall each drive. Navy's defense, an excellent unit under head coach George Welsh, played its best game of the year, while Middie punter John Stufflebeem kept us pinned in our own territory with a 48-yard average on the day. Navy connected on two field goals and took a 6-0 lead into the fourth quarter. With 10 minutes to play Clements threw a six-yard touchdown pass to Demmerle, and freshman kicker Dave Reeve gave us the lead with his point after. Freshman safety Randy Harrison picked off a desperation pass attempt by the Middies and returned it for a 40-yard touchdown to insure our 14-6 win.

"It's a win, that's all that counts," Ara commented after the game. But it was one that he and Notre Dame paid a high price for. The pressure of this game encouraged him to hop off his merry-go-round and see where it was taking him. When we returned from Philadelphia after playing Navy, he called on his closest allies, Katie and his brother Jerry, and revealed his feelings. They talked into the night, and Ara resolved to resign from his Notre Dame post after the 1974 season.

His reasons were numerous. He didn't like what was happening to him. He had become Ara with a sleeping tablet or Ara with a blood pressure pill. The pressure from unusually close games, the quick deaths of close friends, the comments of

Mike Fanning (88) and Steve Niehaus (70), both eventually first-round pro draft choices, fulfill our reputation of being awesome.

critics and letters from anti-Notre Dame and anti-Catholic cynics, press innuendos, rumors of player dissension, the change in player attitudes, the suspension of the six players—the biblical Job hadn't had any more trials. To sit in the chair of Notre Dame's head coach for 11 years, to build winners, to drive men, to play in bowls, to recruit, to counsel, to raise funds for multiple sclerosis, to feel love and compassion and be all things to all people, to worry about family and its valued relationships—these concerns would drain any man, even Ara Parseghian. He had become an institution, a modern day Knute Rockne.

His decision was made, but he kept it secret. As close as I felt to Ara and as intimately as we worked on the sidelines, I never sensed his plans. Whenever we fell behind, his mind was sharper than ever.

His resolution must have been reinforced during and after our game with Pittsburgh. It was another contest we could have lost but pulled out in the fourth quarter, 14-10. Trailing 10-7 with eight minutes left, we took over on our own 45-yard line. Ara didn't panic in his play selection, nor did Clements in his execution. In 12 plays, only one a pass completion, Clements moved us 55 yards for a score. Tom wound up carrying it over for a three-yard touchdown with 2:49 left.

"Two weeks ago after Navy I told the team they were definitely causing my hair to turn gray," Ara quipped to the writers after the game. "Today I told them they were going to make me a replacement for Kojak.

"This is not the first time Notre Dame has fallen behind this year. It's not the first time we have come from behind and scored in the fourth quarter to win. I am very proud of our team and the way they came back to beat a darned good football team."

That left us with one more home game, the last, as it developed, in Ara's era. Pat DiNardo, father of Larry and Gerry, made a special request of Ara. The rugged Italian had always been enamored with Notre Dame, that's why he sent his two sons to play here. "I've been a cop for over 25 years and there isn't much I haven't witnessed, but the one thing I've always wanted to do is run through the tunnel to the field at Notre Dame Stadium." Ara consented, so we gave Mr. DiNardo a stocking cap and jacket and he took the field with the team, greeted along with us by the tumult of 59,000 fans. His dream fulfilled, he went to his seat in the stands, smiling all the way.

Air Force gave us too many first half turnovers, and we went up, 24-0. The reserves played the entire second half and got us a 38-0 final. Fullback Tom Parise had an outstanding day filling in for the injured Wayne Bullock. Parise gained 108 yards in 10 carries.

Halfback Art Best could have enhanced our offensive situation all season long. Few players ever brought more talent, or more trials, to Notre Dame. Two long touchdown runs as a freshman hurt him when he became an instant hero. Art wasn't malicious, but he was at the stage in his life where he didn't want anyone to have authority over him. He didn't want to be yelled at during practice or made an example of in any way. He

Time—the silent thief that took its toll of Ara.

thought that rules were for the other guys. If we had a meeting scheduled, he might show up and he might not. More often than not he was late when he did come. He had not been a hard worker in practice, but this season that attitude was carrying over into the games. Art had an alibi for everything—everybody was at fault but him.

Ara and I tried every approach we could think of with him—we treated him like a man, like a kid, we listened to all his excuses. Nothing seemed to work. Ara went farther than he had with any previous player, but he realized that Art's teammates could see what was going on and playing him over them would only destroy their morale.

Art Best—he brought talent and trials.

The ultimate offense came in the Navy game. Clements threw an interception after Art had been blocked to the ground. Rather than getting to his feet and trying to make a tackle, Art lay there and watched as the Navy defender ran by him. Up until then Ara had been much more lenient with Art than I prescribed, but that did it. We decided to take Art to Southern Cal, though he wouldn't start. Art showed up late for pregame calisthenics because he had to "make a phone call."

Art left Notre Dame the next year to complete his architecture degree and play football at Kent State. He married a girl he had been dating in South Bend and vowed to buckle down. I hope he does because once he realizes he won't always be 20, a gifted human being will finally have a chance to impress the world.

The Southern Cal game was one of the strangest in football annals. Some of the developments were all too familiar in this series, but others were unusual. We couldn't fail in the first half. We caught USC off guard with some run-action passes and pulled ahead 24-0 with less than a minute left in the half. For the first time since Ara came to Notre Dame we were scoring quickly against the Trojans. But our defense relaxed a little too soon. Quarterback Pat Haden completed several passes, the last one an eight-yard touchdown throw to Anthony Davis, and the Trojans took some life into their dressing room. They had cut our lead to 24-6.

As we headed for the tunnel I noticed Tom Clements limping. "It's just a little pull in the hamstring, Coach," he insisted. "I'll be all right." Only because Clements discounted the injury did Ara decide to keep playing him. "We've got to be careful what we call," Ara warned. "We can't expose him with the ball if he can't run to protect himself." Additionally, Wayne Bullock had pulled his Achilles tendon and would be incapacitated the rest of the day.

In the next 17 minutes we, the 84,000 fans in attendance and a national television audience would witness the most graphic exhibition of "momentum" in sports history. To this day Ara can't fully explain what happened, but in those 17 minutes the Trojans would score 49 points—almost at will. And it all began with their greatest catalyst—Anthony Davis. The brilliant back ran 102 yards on the second half kickoff behind

*There was no reason to feel alarm returning to the field for the
second half with the Trojans.*

great blocking.

Many of our seniors had been on the team the last time
Davis stunned us on a kickoff return in the Coliseum. They
thought back to his six touchdowns and the utter frustration of
that day. While they were reliving painful memories, the Trojans
were creating new ones. Their fans sensed their destiny, and the
noise in the stadium was incredible.

We had a chance to stem this emotion, but it had to be
done immediately. Without Bullock's ability to ramble or
Clements' passing threat, we went to the ground game. On our
first offensive attempt of the half we fell short of a first down

270

and punted to USC. Three plays later Davis took the ball in on a six-yard touchdown run, leaving the score at 24-19.

We desperately needed to sustain a drive and thought we were going to as Clements completed a pass to Pete Demmerle for what appeared to be a first down. But while still in the air Demmerle was crunched by a USC defender, and for one of the few times in his career he dropped the ball. USC recovered on our 31 and had another Anthony Davis score five plays later. Now we trailed, 27-24.

In short order it was Pat Haden to John McKay's son, J. K., for an 18-yard score after a 56-yard punt return by Marvin Cobb. USC 34, ND 24. Haden to McKay for a 44-yard touchdown. USC 41, ND 24. Haden to Shelton Diggs for a 16-yard score. USC 48, ND 24. Charles Phillips on a 58-yard interception return. USC 55, ND 24. We still had 13 minutes to play, but that's the way the game ended.

Ara was at a loss to account for this occurrence. There was no discernable difference in our approach to the second half. He reached for reasoning during his press conference.

"Yes, the momentum did shift on that kickoff return to Davis," he recounted. "Then we had the punt return, then the fumble and then.... They got good field position almost all the second half and didn't have to drive far for their touchdowns. We just didn't play football like we're capable of in the second half. We made too many mistakes. It was like two different ball games."

Still the media pressed him for an explanation, and though Ara repeated he didn't have one he did offer an observation.

"One problem is that we didn't have a good week of preparation. It was 20 degrees all week and we had to practice indoors almost all the time. The cold weather seems to thicken the blood or something. We've never had a good second half out here. I was worried about that factor all week long."

Some writers found that amusing. They mocked Ara in print for even hinting that "tired blood" led to our demise. That was bad enough, but writers and fans circulated their own theories for our downfall. The word spread that Art Best and Wayne Bullock had a fist fight in the locker room during halftime. As rumors go the principals in the fight changed in other versions, becoming Best and me or Best and Ara.

Wayne Bullock tried to come back in the second half but reinjured his leg.

A more serious story was being advanced by the media. A San Francisco writer claimed that the loss was the result of our black players folding up in the second half in order to disgrace Ara for his mishandling of the summer incident and for benching Art Best. According to the author, Wells Twombley, Best was the leader of our black militants. That alone proved how utterly ludicrous the argument was because Best is white. But since there have to be heinous circumstances behind every Notre Dame loss, Twombley's story gained credence. Ara was besieged with phone calls from reporters. He directed them to any black player they wished to talk to.

Amid all this Ara reviewed his decision to resign. The debacle at Southern Cal would be a terrible way to be remembered. That game almost convinced him to stay on. But his career had been too accomplished to be marred by one loss. Besides, he had one game left, a rematch with Alabama in the Orange Bowl. Ara discussed his feelings with Father Joyce and agreed to get back with him later in the week to make his commitment final.

Ara knew that he had several assistants worthy of the head job, and he hoped one of us would replace him. Without recommending any of us specifically he requested that we be interviewed and selected on our own merits. Even though he felt sure this appeal would be accepted, he still wanted to get the announcement out in the open so the athletic officials would have ample time to interview us and his successor could handle recruiting as he saw fit. We had scoured the nation for high school seniors, and after studying film and talking to contacts our list was drawn up and visiting dates established. Our initial response told us this could be one of our best recruiting years ever. But recruits are obviously interested in who the head coach is going to be, so Ara didn't want to hold the announcement until after the bowl.

On Saturday, December 14, Katie, Father Joyce, and Ara attended a party together in Elkhart, Indiana. They stopped off at Ara's house on the way back, and he and Father Joyce remained in the car to discuss Ara's final decision. Katie had been inside only briefly when she stormed down the driveway with a look of urgency about her.

"Mike just told me he heard a newscast saying that you are going to quit at Notre Dame," she reported.

Even before a release date had been set, Sid Hartman, a Minneapolis columnist, published a story that Saturday stating that Ara would resign as Notre Dame's head coach. How he got that information no one knows. Only Katie, Jerry, Father Joyce, Ara and, as he would soon discover, one other person knew. The story was now being circulated nationally. Ara did not want the staff to hear about this from anyone but him so these developments upset him. He and Father Joyce plotted their course of action.

Ara mentioned he wanted to call the staff together immediately, and he asked what the policy would be in selecting the new coach. Father Joyce told him his replacement

273

15:00

TOUCH DOWN

15:00

TROJANS BALL ON THE

DOWN YARDS TO

	1	2	3	4	T	TO LP
N.D.	14	10	0		24	
USC	0	6	35		41	

Ara still can't explain it.

had already been hired. It is only an observation on my part, but I believe Ara was crushed by that. All of us had brought something to the University and had not in any way sacrificed a principle in doing it. We had run an operation with class, dignity and success.

Ara contacted Athletic Director Moose Krause, a man he held the deepest respect for, and invited him to the house. When he arrived and Ara broke the news, Moose was shocked. He told Ara with complete sincerity that if he had any inclination toward the athletic director position he himself would step down immediately and let Ara take over.

Early Sunday morning Ara went about assembling the coaching staff. He called and asked us to meet in our conference room. We arrived within two or three minutes of each other, then Ara began. "I don't want to get melodramatic about this, men, but I've resigned from my job effective after the Orange Bowl," he said in a stage whisper. "This isn't something I've done in haste. I reached the decision after the Navy game and frequently reconsidered since then."

His words numbed us. We all sensed that something out of the ordinary was going to happen at this hastily-called conference. We had never met on Sundays after the regular season, and there was plenty of time for bowl preparation. He couldn't have told us anything that would have stung any harder.

I'm not ashamed that I was moved to tears, and so were others on the staff. Ara continued, saying he wanted to see the return of the six players who had been suspended and that he wanted each of us placed in jobs. He thanked us for our loyalty, effort and friendship.

"I had asked that some of you be considered to replace me but another man from the outside has been chosen," he added. "I am not permitted to divulge his name. I really don't know what else to say, guys."

Ara regretted that he couldn't get the team together. Exams had started, and many players had finished and gone home for a few days. Sports Information Directors Roger Valdiserri and Bob Best prepared the official announcement that afternoon, and by evening the whole country knew. Twenty-four hours later Dan Devine, general manager and coach of the Green Bay Packers and former athletic director and coach at Missouri, was publically named to succeed Ara. Monday night Ara appeared on ABC television at halftime of the Liberty Bowl game, and his appearance explained his logic for resigning. He was haggard looking, more drawn than I can ever recall. Two months of relaxation would cure that.

If failing health was his major concern, fans began to speculate why he hadn't sought a sabbatical leave. Professors took them, why couldn't Ara? Ara considered it, but because of his great sensitivity he had not requested it. He didn't think it

Reprinted courtesy of the *Chicago Tribune*.

"I came to ask for a blessing, Your Holiness, . . . Namely, talk Parseghian out of quitting."

would be fair to ask one of his assistants to recruit, organize and coach for a season, then make him step down. However, any of us would have gladly done it for Ara.

At a press conference on Tuesday, December 17, Ara stated that he would reevaluate his decision one year later and consider then whether or not to get back into football. He said since he regarded Notre Dame as the pinnacle of college football he would never again seek a job in the college ranks. Before he came to Notre Dame he had received three or four pro offers and then at least one a year after that. Surely there would be more to include in his deliberation.

I still couldn't believe that Ara was getting out. The young men he had coached made him come alive. He enjoyed helping them formulate life's principles. He also relished the staff meetings for the same reason. They gave him a chance to share with his assistants some of the knowledge he had gained, both in football and out. And along the way he learned from us, too.

Most of all Ara would miss the competition. He was never one to be sullen to his opponent in defeat. But no one worked harder to avoid losing. His life needed that sort of challenge—it drove him.

He wouldn't regret leaving his recruiting duties. That was the most thankless job. He was honest, but it frustrated him to see other schools that weren't. Unfortunately cheaters were a fact of life. Equally disappointing were the detractors who out of envy accused us of dishonesty or insisted that we always landed any player we went after.

For the first time ever, Ara resisted preparation for our game. He procrastinated scheduling our staff meetings, and even after we got into them he cut them short. His mind was far removed.

Letters poured in just days after his announcement. He couldn't help reminiscing. Former players, coaches, personal friends, alumni, fans and even enemies wrote words of encouragement. His thoughts of the bygone days distracted him from his last game.

"Please allow me to take these few moments to say a few things that I have felt for these last five years," wrote Dennis Gutowski, a player whose collegiate career had been ruined by an injury in his first varsity game. "As a starry-eyed high school senior I have to admit my greatest aspiration was to one day attend the University of Notre Dame. But more than that, I had a dream of playing football under the greatest football coach ever, Ara Parseghian.

"In those four extremely short years I had the breathtaking privilege of being a member of the team you coached. And I must say, you touched my life in such a way that no other person ever has. I came to Notre Dame with the greatest respect and admiration for Ara Parseghian the coach, and came away with magnified respect and admiration, and yes, even a love of Ara Parseghian the man.

"Coach, you have always stood for and lived all the things I cherished as good and worth living and dying for. Physical and mental excellence, comraderie and just honest-to-goodness caring about people radiate from you. After the Orange Bowl game in 1973 I had to be alone because I couldn't hold back my tears and I was too proud for anyone to see me. I would have given anything to turn back the hands of time to Evanston, September 21, 1971, and make that man miss me so I would've had two good legs in which to help Notre Dame beat Nebraska. But that wasn't the way the good Lord meant for it to be and it isn't my place to ask why.

"Allow one of your former players to say simply 'thank you' to the greatest coach a guy could ever hope to have."

Assistant coach Bill Hickey put his feelings in writing. "Coach, I cannot express in words how much I've appreciated working under you. Every day I had the privilege to serve under you I learned something. That in itself has made life very exciting for me. I came to Notre Dame with the goal of working for her, but with each working day the real inspiration was you. Your whole way of life has deeply influenced me. Not only your early and long working day, but your incredible knowledge of everything in our society from current and financial affairs to the political arena."

Ara even received notes from officials like Robert Hepler. "In the several years I had the opportunity to work with you, my respect for your approach to the game and for the way you regarded young men and officials, continued to grow. I sincerely hope you will be able to continue a close contact with athletics. Athletics deserve the fine and outstanding method by

Ara was so busy explaining his resignation he had little time for Orange Bowl preparation.

which you approach the game. I have always strongly felt that the country and world need athletics and only with the right kind of people leading the field can we hope to survive the struggle against all the other odds."

As the game drew nearer Ara began to get more active but not like before. He had made arrangements for the team to practice in Naples, Florida, and headquarter at the Marco Beach

Hotel, owned by the Deltona Corporation, a firm for which he did public relations work. He reasoned that our game plan could stay pretty much the same as last year because Alabama hadn't altered its style significantly.

The squad was physically scarred and still felt the psychological bruises of the Southern Cal game. Wayne Bullock sat out five of eight practice days with dysentery and influenza. Mark Brenneman suffered a hairline fracture of his ankle trying to keep in shape for the game, and it was doubtful his cast could be removed in time. Greg Collins needed stitches across both knee caps after falling from a motor bike. He, too, was doubtful. Kevin Nosbusch put off knee surgery to play this last game.

The practices were held in hot, humid weather, but the players were totally dedicated. During the heavy workouts Ara periodically strolled to the sidelines to chat with visitors. This was something he had never done before because he had wanted full knowledge and focus of everything that went on at practice. Now he didn't worry if he didn't catch every false move or breakdown. He didn't lash out at missed assignments.

After our pregame meal all the offensive coaches gathered their players together in one room. Ara had called for breakdown meetings and was suspicious when he found the whole group. We told him we were discussing kickoffs, and he bought it and left. All five of us knew what had to be said but waited for someone else to start it off. Sensing this I addressed the squad.

"Gentlemen," I said, "there aren't more than a half dozen people outside this room who think we can pull this game off. The writers pick us as 11-point underdogs. Your mothers and fathers, your friends and neighbors are all saying prayers that we won't be humiliated. They reflect what Southern Cal did to us a month ago. They are positive we've got black and white problems, that we are torn apart with internal problems, that we quit in the second half versus USC. Why should we bother to show up tonight?

"There is one very good reason. Ara Parseghian is too great and too humble a man to ask this team to win one for him. HE won't do it. I sure as hell am not too humble to ask you to dedicate yourselves to win this one for Ara. We've got to

A fitting way to go out.

execute and play our hearts out, but we can win!"

All of our doubtfuls saw action at least for whatever few plays they could muster. The game was emotional, electric and a labor of love by all the players and assistant coaches. Wayne Bullock scored a four-yard touchdown in the first quarter after Al Samuel recovered a punt at the Alabama 16. Mark McLane ran nine yards for a second quarter touchdown to put us up 13-0. Alabama kicked a field goal before the first half and added eight points with 3:13 to play. The Tide was rising again in the closing minute, but defensive back Reggie Barnett intercepted a Richard Todd pass and clinched the victory. That cost Alabama the National Championship and gave us a 10-2 record. Even with the rash of misfortunes we experienced, we came within two quarters of an undefeated season—one against Purdue and one against USC.

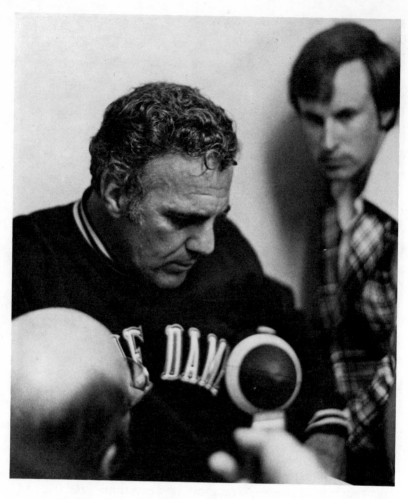

Ara conducts his final postgame press conference.

It was a festive group of men in the locker room. Ara entered with tears of joy glistening in his eyes. What he had to say to all of us wasn't important, it was just being there to hear him say anything. That high-pitched voice of his was whining like never before. He spoke in staccato phrases, trying unsuccessfully to get them out without cracking.

"I've never had a victory in my coaching career with a group of guys so dedicated," he bellowed. "I'll remember this forever. This was my last game at Notre Dame. I'm never going to forget any one of you. What a great football game! You beat an undefeated team that was ranked number one. You were the underdogs. You showed all those who were down in the mouth about us! Father Toohey, come on over here and say the prayer. We've got a lot to be thankful for."

All the coaches moved into our dressing area and surrounded Ara. He flung his arms around us collectively and promised again, "I'll never forget you guys and what you did in this game."

With that the media converged. Late in the press conference a writer asked about the internal problems during the Southern Cal game. As Ara started to refute the question a group of players assembled, kneeling in the doorway. They had quickly composed a song to the melody of "Swanee." "Ara...how we love ya, how we love ya, our dear old Ara." That gave the reporters all the answers they needed.

That ended the demands of his 243rd game and 24th season as a head coach. It was his 170th victory against 58 defeats and 6 ties, which put him among the top 30 winningest coaches of all time and second only to Knute Rockne at Notre Dame. At 50 he was young to be leaving football with such impressive credentials.

Ara showered slowly and dressed even more hesitantly. On his way out he paused to survey the players' lockers, deserted for some time now. He didn't want nostalgia to detain the team, so he turned his back on locker room memories and headed toward the bus.

Epilogue

Ara had an ice breaker he would use with me when he could see I was depressed or angry about something. However thick the atmosphere in the meeting room or on the field, he'd catch me at my least guarded moment and say, "You think you'll ever amount to much, Pagna?"

The first couple of years I'd just chuckle, but then it worked on me and I formulated an answer I liked. Thereafter, my reply was always a hearty, "Hell yes, I'm planning on it!" It was a game we played, not saying anything really, but in a way saying everything.

It was March now, slightly more than a year since Ara resigned from the Notre Dame job. A moist white snow was covering South Bend, most of which was visible from his corner office on the ninth floor of the St. Joseph Bank Building. It was after five, and the office force had already made the trek to the parking garages. Ara remained to complete some urgent matters in his upcoming television series. He was sitting in a large black leather chair, surrounded by the very few memorabilia adorning his office.

The tape deck was playing softly in the background. Ara enjoyed the unique styling of Frank Sinatra, he admired Robert Goulet's enunciation and clarity. The shelves on the walls held a selection of plaques announcing some of the countless honors he had received. There were a few prize, game balls from the

Cotton, Sugar and Orange Bowls that the team had insisted he keep.

On his desk were neatly stacked letters. One pile was from former players asking about his health and future plans, some needing his recommendation for a newly-sought position. The larger stack contained speaking requests, all urgent and special banquets. All this mail had been sorted, awaiting his reply. The speaking appearances, requests from charity organizations, television commitments and public relation ventures were more than ample to keep him busy. One weekend of travel put him four days behind in correspondence.

He put his pen down and swiveled toward the window, unaware that I was still there. He was now lost in distant thought, treating himself to an infrequent cigar—clumsy as usual with the ashes. Off toward the north of town he could easily see the shining Golden Dome of Notre Dame and the multi-colored library structure.

Perhaps Ara was mulling over his boyhood days of South Akron, and how he and his friends had to end their games if the only football they owned got kicked into the canal. Maybe he was reflecting on the 1948 team picture of the Cleveland Browns someone had just sent him that day. How young the picture made old friends and teammates appear. Otto Graham, Marion Motley, Dub Jones...and the boyish Parseghian next to his now-deceased roommate Warren Lahr.

If his thoughts flowed chronologically he would be thinking of Miami of Ohio, John Pont and Paul Shoults and Woody Hayes and Doc Urich, or the hundreds of great young men he had played with and coached there. Northwestern would follow in that line with Dick Thornton, the Cvercko Brothers, Tom Meyers and countless others. Their faces and names and maybe a flash of a great play they had made were all coming to mind now.

Notre Dame could offer many scenes and memories. Some place in the reflection of those 11 seasons, that "Era of Ara," he could easily remember the hulking frame of Pete Duranko bent in prayer at the grotto, surrounded by snow. Maybe he heard the roar of the crowd, smelled the hot dogs, peanuts and coffee of the nearly 60,000 people. Maybe the faces of each player were parading through his mind—he could never really forget any of them. Surely he was thinking of his family. There was Katie, understanding, loyal, always there for support. There were those three great kids, no longer small but now adults. He was proud of them, pleased that they had never let the acclaim and the measure of status he had earned affect them.

The media was still pressing, "Why did you quit before you broke Rockne's record?" Hell, records didn't concern Ara.

"Are you ever going to coach again? Do you think you will?"

If he had started as a head coach later in life, retirement would have been easy. Starting at 27 and coaching for another 24 years left him too young to trade the chair he was sitting in for a rocker.

"I haven't retired," he explained again to inquiries, "I've resigned from coaching." There continued to be opportunities for head jobs in the professional game, some carrying with them the role of General Manager.

All of these thoughts and others plus the present day decisions and pressures caused such a pause. I had not wanted to break into that mental picture story, but the noise I made leaving my desk broke his spell.

He looked up, somewhat startled, for he hadn't realized the office was not totally empty. At a loss for words, I said sheepishly in an effort to turn the tables on him, "Parseghian, ya think you'll ever amount to anything?"

He smiled, appreciating the joke. "Goodnight, Tom," he said softly.

"Goodnight...Coach!"

Appendix

YEAR-BY-YEAR RESULTS UNDER ARA

1964

Captain: James S. Carroll

W	Wisconsin (R)	31-7	A	c64,398
W	Purdue	34-15	H	c59,611
W	Air Force	34-7	A	c44,384
W	U.C.L.A.	24-0	H	58,335
W	Stanford	28-6	H	56,721
W	Navy	40-0	N	66,752
W	Pittsburgh	17-15	A	56,628
W	Michigan State	34-7	H	c59,265
W	Iowa	28-0	H	c59,135
L	So. Calif. (U)(1:33)	17-20	A	83,840
	(9-1-0)	287-77		609,069

at Philadelphia

1965

Captain: Philip F. Sheridan

W	California	48-6	A	53,000
L	Purdue	21-25	A	c61,291
W	Northwestern	38-7	H	c59,273
W	Army (Nt)	17-0	N	c61,000
W	So. California (R)	28-7	H	c59,235
W	Navy	29-3	H	c59,206
W	Pittsburgh	69-13	A	c57,169
W	North Carolina	17-0	H	c59,216
L	Michigan State	3-12	H	c59,291
T	Miami (Fla.) (Nt)	0-0	A	68,077
	(7-2-1)	270-73		596,758

at Shea Stadium, New York

1966

Captain: James R. Lynch

W	Purdue	26-14	H	c59,075
W	Northwestern	35-7	A	c55,356
W	Army	35-0	H	c59,075
W	North Carolina	32-0	H	c59,075
W	Oklahoma	38-0	A	c63,439
W	Navy	31-7	N	70,101
W	Pittsburgh	40-0	H	c59,075
W	Duke	64-0	H	c59,075
T	Michigan State	10-10	A	c80,011
W	So. California	51-0	A	88,520
	(9-0-1)	362-38		652,802

at Philadelphia

1967

Captain: Robert P. (Rocky) Bleier

S.23	W	California	41-8	H	c59,075
S.30	L	Purdue	21-28	A	c62,316
O.7	W	Iowa	56-6	H	c59,075
O.14	L	So. California	7-24	H	c71,227
O.21	W	Illinois	47-7	A	c59,075
O.28	W	Michigan State	24-12	H	c59,075
N.4	W	Navy	43-14	H	c59,075
N.11	W	Pittsburgh	38-0	A	54,075
N.18	W	Georgia Tech	36-3	A	c60,024
N.24	W	Miami (Fla.) (Nt)	24-22	A	c77,265
		(8-2-0)	337-124		620,282

1968

Co-captains: George J. Kunz and Robert L. Olson

S.21	W	Oklahoma	45-21	H	c59,075
S.28	L	Purdue	22-37	A	c59,075
O.5	W	Iowa	51-28	A	58,043
O.12	W	Northwestern	27-7	H	c59,075
O.19	W	Illinois	58-8	H	c59,075
O.26	L	Michigan State	17-21	A	c77,339
N.2	W	Navy	45-14	N	63,738
N.9	W	Pittsburgh	56-7	H	c59,075
N.16	W	Georgia Tech	34-6	H	c59,075
N.30	T	So. California	21-21	A	82,659
		(7-2-1)	376-170		636,229

N—at Philadelphia

1969

Co-captains: Robert L. Olson and Michael Oriard

S.20	W	Northwestern	35-10	H	c59,075
S.27	L	Purdue	14-28	A	c68,179
O.4	W	Michigan State	42-28	H	c59,075
O.11	W	Army	45-0	N1	c63,786
O.18	T	Southern California	14-14	A	c59,075
O.25	W	Tulane (Nt)	37-0	A	40,250
N.1	W	Navy	47-0	H	c59,075
N.8	W	Pittsburgh (R)	49-7	A	44,084
N.15	W	Georgia Tech (Nt)	38-20	A	41,104
N.22	W	Air Force	13-6	H	c59,075
		(8-1-1)	334-113		552,778

1970

Co-captains: Larry DiNardo and Tim Kelly

S.19	W	Northwestern	35-14	A	50,049
S.26	W	Purdue	48-0	H	c59,075
O.3	W	Michigan State	29-0	A	c76,103
O.10	W	Army	51-10	H	c59,075
O.17	W	Missouri	24-7	A	c64,200
O.31	W	Navy	56-7	N1	45,226
N.7	W	Pittsburgh	46-14	H	c59,075
N.14	W	Georgia Tech (6:28)	10-7	H	c59,075
N.21	W	Louisiana State (2:54)	3-0	H	c59,075
N.28	L	Southern Cal(R)(U)	28-38	A	64,694
		(9-1-0)	330-97		595,647

COTTON BOWL
Jan. 1 W Texas   24-11 N2 c73,000
N1 – at Philadelphia
N2 – at Dallas, Texas

1971

Co-Captains: Walter Patulski and Thomas Gatewood

S.18	W	Northwestern	50-7	H	c59,075
S.25	W	Purdue (2:58) (R)	8-7	A	c69,765
O.2	W	Michigan State	14-2	H	c59,075
O.9	W	Miami (Fla.) (Nt)	17-0	H	66,039
O.16	W	North Carolina	16-0	H	c59,075
O.23	L	So. California (U)	14-28	H	c59,075
O.30	W	Navy	21-0	H	c59,075
N.6	W	Pittsburgh	56-7	A	55,528
N.13	W	Tulane	21-7	H	c59,075
N.20	L	Louisiana State (Nt)	8-28	A	c66,936
		(8-2-0)	225-86		612,718

1972

Co-Captains: John Dampeer and Greg Marx

S.23	W	Northwestern	37-0	A	c55,155
S.30	W	Purdue	35-14	H	c59,075
O.7	W	Michigan State	16-0	A	c77,828
O.14	W	Pittsburgh	42-16	H	c59,075
O.21	L	Missouri (U) (R)	26-30	H	c59,075
O.28	W	TCU	21-0	H	c59,075
N.4	W	Navy	42-23	N1	43,089
N.11	W	Air Force	21-7	A	c48,671
N.18	W	Miami (Fla.)	20-17	H	c59,075
D.2	L	Southern Cal	23-45	A	75,243
		(8-2-0)	283-152		595,361

ORANGE BOWL
J.1 L Nebraska (Nt)   6-40 N2 c80,010
N1–at Philadelphia; N2–at Miami

1973

Tri-Captains: Dave Casper, Frank Pomarico (Off. and Mike Townsend (Def.)

S.22	W	Northwestern	44-0	H	c59,07
S.29	W	Purdue	20-7	A	c69,39
O.6	W	Michigan State	14-10	H	c59,07
O.13	W	Rice (Nt)	28-0	A	50,33
O.20	W	Army	62-3	A	c42,50
O.27	W	Southern Cal (R)	23-14	H	c59,07
N.3	W	Navy	44-7	H	c59,07
N.10	W	Pittsburgh (S)	31-10	A	c56,59
N.22TH	W	Air Force	48-15	H	57,23
D.1	W	Miami (Fla.)(Nt)	44-0	A	42,96
		(10-0-0)	358-66		555,31

SUGAR BOWL
D.31 W Alabama   24-23 N1 c85,16
(4:26) (Nt)
N1–at New Orleans

1974

Co-Captains: Tom Clements and Greg Collins

S.9	W	Georgia Tech	31-7	A	45,228
S.21	W	Northwestern	49-3	A	c55,000
S.28	L	Purdue (U) (R)	20-31	H	c59,075
O.5	W	Michigan State	19-14	A	c77,431
O.12	W	Rice (3:08)	10-3	H	c59,075
O.19	W	Army (S)	48-0	H	c59,075
O.26	W	Miami (Fla.)	38-7	H	c59,075
N.2	W	Navy	14-6	N1	48,634
N.16	W	Pitt (R) (2.49)	14-10	H	c59,075
N.23	W	Air Force (R)	38-0	H	c59,075
N.30	L	Southern Cal	24-55	A	83,522
		(9-2-0)	305-136		664,265

ORANGE BOWL
J.1 W Alabama (U)   13-11 N2 71,801
N1–at Philadelphia; N2–at Miami

ARA'S ALL-AMERICAS

1964

	AP	UPI	NEA	FC	SN	L	T	CP	FN
John Huarte, QB	1	1	2					1	1
Jack Snow, E	2	1	1	1	1	1	1	1	1
Jim Carroll, LB		2			1		1		
Tony Carey, DB			2						

1965

	AP	UPI	NEA	FC	SN	L	FN
Dick Arrington, G	1	1	1	1		1	1
Nick Rassas, DB	1	1	1		1	1	1
Tom Regner, G			2				
Jim Lynch, LB			2				

1966

	AP	UPI	NEA	FC	SN	L	T	CP	FN
†Nick Eddy, HB	1	1	1	1	2	1		1	1
†Jim Lynch, LB	1	1	1	1	1	1	1	1	1
Tom Regner, G	1	1	1	1			1	1	1
Alan Page, DE	2	2	1		1	1	1	1	
Pete Duranko, DT		1		1	2				
Kevin Hardy, DT	2	2			1		1		1
Jim Seymour, E		2	2						1
Paul Seiler, T					2				
George Goeddeke, C		2							
Tom Schoen, DB		2							
Larry Conjar, FB									1

1967

	AP	UPI	FC	SN	L	T	CP
Tom Schoen, DB	1	1	1	1	1	1	1
Kevin Hardy, DE	1	1		1		1	2
Jim Seymour, E		1					1
Mike McGill, LB				2	1		
John Pergine, LB		2					
Dick Swatland, G							2
Jim Smithberger, DB				2			

1968

	AP	UPI	NEA	FC	SN	L	T	CP	FN	WCF
George Kunz, T	2	1	1	1	1	1	1	1	1	1
Terry Hanratty, QB	1	1	2	1	1	1	1	1	1	1
Jim Seymour, E	2	1		1	1	1		2		1

1969

	AP	UPI	NEA	FC	SN	L	T	CP	FN	WCF
†Mike McCoy, DT	1	1	1	1	1	1	1	1	1	1
Jim Reilly, T			2	1	2					
Larry DiNardo, G		1						2		1
Bob Olson, LB	2							2		
Mike Oriard, C					2					

1970

	AP	UPI	NEA	FC	SN	L	CP	FN	WCF
Larry DiNardo, G	1	1	2	1	1	1	1	1	1
Tom Gatewood, E		1	1	1	2	1	1		1
Clarence Ellis, DB		1	1						
Joe Theismann, QB	1	2	2				2	1	

1971

	AP	UPI	NEA	FC	SN	L	T	FN	WCF
†Walt Patulski, DE	1	1	1	1	1	1	1	1	1
Clarence Ellis, DB	1	1	1		1		1	1	1
Tom Gatewood, E	2						1		
Mike Kadish, DT					1				

1972

	AP	UPI	NEA	FC	SN	FW	T	FN	WCF
†Greg Marx, DT	1	1	1	1	1	1	1	1	1

1973

	AP	UPI	NEA	FC	SN	FW	T	FN	WCF
Dave Casper, TE	2	1	1	1	1				1
Mike Townsend, DB	1	1	1		1	1	1	1	1

1974

	AP	UPI	NEA	FC	SN	FW	T	FN	WCF
Pete Demmerle, SE	1	1	1	1					1
Mike Fanning, DT	2		1		1		1		1
Gerry DiNardo, G		1		1				1	
Tom Clements, QB							1	2	
Greg Collins, LB	2							2	
Steve Niehaus, DT								1	

†Unanimous selection on official teams.

WINNERS OF OUTSTANDING AWARDS

Heisman Trophy
John Huarte 1964
Maxwell Trophy
Jim Lynch 1966
Vince Lombardi Trophy
Walt Patulski 1972
Academic All-Americas
Tom Regner 1966
Jim Lynch 1966
Jim Smithberger 1967
George Kunz 1968
Jim Reilly 1969
Tom Gatewood 1970
Larry DiNardo 1970
Joe Theismann 1970
Tom Gatewood 1971
Greg Marx 1971
Greg Marx 1972
Mike Creaney 1972
Dave Casper 1973
Bob Thomas 1973
Gary Potempa 1973
Pete Demmerle 1974
Reggie Barnett 1974

KEY TO ABBREVIATIONS
AA—All-America Board
AP—Associated Press
C—Walter Camp (in Collier's Magazine to 1925)
COL—Collier's Magazine (Walter Camp's selections to 1925; Grantland Rice 1925-47; American Football Coaches Association 1948-56)
CP—Central Press (1963-70 only)
FBW—Football World Magazine
FC—American Football Coaches Association (in Collier's 1948-56)
FN—Football News
FW—Football Writers' Association (in *Look* Magazine, 1946-71)
INS—International News Service (merged with United Press in 1958)
L—Look Magazine (Football Writers' Association selections from 1946)
LIB—Liberty Magazine
NA—North American Newspaper Alliance
NEA—Newspaper Enterprise Association
NW—Newsweek Magazine
SN—Sporting News (unofficial from 1965)
T—Time Magazine (unofficial)
UP—United Press (merged with INS in 1958)
UPI—United Press International (merger of INS and UP in 1958)
WCF—Walter Camp Football Foundation

POLL RANKINGS UNDER ARA

ASSOCIATED PRESS
(Selected by Sportswriters)

UNITED PRESS INTERNATIONAL
(Selected by College Coaches)

1964
1. Alabama
2. Arkansas
3. NOTRE DAME
4. Michigan
5. Texas
6. Nebraska
7. L.S.U.
8. Oregon State
9. Ohio State
10. U.S.C.

1965
1. Alabama
2. Michigan State
3. Arkansas
4. U.C.L.A.
5. Nebraska
6. Missouri
7. Tennessee
8. L.S.U.
9. NOTRE DAME
10. U.S.C.

1964
1. Alabama
2. Arkansas
3. NOTRE DAME
4. Michigan
5. Texas
6. Nebraska
7. L.S.U.
8. Oregon State
9. Ohio State
10. U.S.C.

1965
1. Michigan State
2. Arkansas
3. Nebraska
4. Alabama
5. U.C.L.A.
6. Missouri
7. Tennessee
8. NOTRE DAME
9. U.S.C.
10. Texas Tech

1966
1. NOTRE DAME
2. Michigan State
3. Alabama
4. Georgia
5. U.C.L.A.
6. Nebraska
7. Purdue
8. Georgia Tech
9. Miami, Florida
10. S.M.U.

1967
1. U.S.C.
2. Tennessee
3. Oklahoma
4. Indiana
5. NOTRE DAME
6. Wyoming
7. Oregon State
8. Alabama
9. Purdue
10. Penn State

1966
1. NOTRE DAME
2. Michigan State
3. Alabama
4. Georgia
5. U.C.L.A.
6. Purdue
7. Nebraska
8. Georgia Tech
9. S.M.U.
10. Miami, Florida

1967
1. U.S.C.
2. Tennessee
3. Oklahoma
4. NOTRE DAME
5. Wyoming
6. Indiana
7. Alabama
8. Oregon State
9. Purdue
10. U.C.L.A.

1968
1. Ohio State
2. Penn State
3. Texas
4. So. California
5. NOTRE DAME
6. Arkansas
7. Kansas
8. Georgia
9. Missouri
10. Purdue

1969
1. Texas
2. Penn State
3. U.S.C.
4. Ohio State
5. NOTRE DAME
6. Missouri
7. Arkansas
8. Mississippi
9. Michigan
10. L.S.U.

1968
1. Ohio State
2. Southern Cal
3. Penn State
4. Georgia
5. Texas
6. Kansas
7. Tennessee
8. NOTRE DAME
9. Arkansas
10. Oklahoma

1969
1. Texas
2. Penn State
3. Arkansas
4. U.S.C.
5. Ohio State
6. Missouri
7. L.S.U.
8. Michigan
9. NOTRE DAME
10. U.C.L.A.

1970
1. Nebraska
2. NOTRE DAME
3. Texas
4. Tennessee
5. Ohio State
6. Arizona State
7. L.S.U.
8. Stanford
9. Michigan
10. Auburn

1971
1. Nebraska
2. Oklahoma
3. Colorado
4. Alabama
5. Penn State
6. Michigan
7. Georgia
8. Arizona State
9. Tennessee
10. Stanford
13. NOTRE DAME

1970
1. Texas
2. Ohio State
3. Nebraska
4. Tennessee
5. NOTRE DAME
6. L.S.U.
7. Michigan
8. Arizona State
9. Auburn
10. Stanford

1971
1. Nebraska
2. Alabama
3. Oklahoma
4. Michigan
5. Auburn
6. Arizona State
7. Colorado
8. Georgia
9. Tennessee
10. L.S.U.
15. NOTRE DAME

1972
1. Southern Cal
2. Oklahoma
3. Texas
4. Nebraska
5. Auburn
6. Michigan
7. Alabama
8. Tennessee
9. Ohio State
10. Penn State
14. NOTRE DAME

1973
1. NOTRE DAME
2. Ohio State
3. Oklahoma
4. Alabama
5. Penn State
6. Michigan
7. Nebraska
8. Southern Cal
9. Arizona State
9. Houston

1972
1. Southern Cal
2. Oklahoma
3. Ohio State
4. Alabama
5. Texas
6. Michigan
7. Auburn
8. Penn State
9. Nebraska
10. L.S.U.
12. NOTRE DAME

1973
1. Alabama
2. Oklahoma
3. Ohio State
4. NOTRE DAME
5. Penn State
6. Michigan
7. Southern Cal
8. Texas
9. UCLA
10. Arizona State

1974
1. Oklahoma
2. Southern Cal
3. Michigan
4. Ohio State
5. Alabama
6. NOTRE DAME
7. Penn State
8. Auburn
9. Nebraska
10. Miami (O.)

1974
1. Southern Cal
2. Alabama
3. Ohio State
4. NOTRE DAME
5. Michigan
6. Auburn
7. Penn State
8. Nebraska
9. N. C. State
10. Miami (O.)

NOTRE DAME STATISTICAL TRENDS UNDER ARA
(Regular season only)

OFFENSE

Yr.	Record	G	TOTAL OFF. YdsPG	Rank	RUSHING YdsPG	Rank	PASSING YdsPG	Rank	SCORING PtsPG	Rank
64	9-1-0	10	401.4	2	190.0	19	210.5	5	28.7	3
65	7-2-1	10	299.5	41	214.5	15	85.0	87	27.0	9
66	9-0-1	10	391.5	3	210.6	13	180.9	17	36.2	1
67	8-2-0	10	391.1	7	217.0	16	174.1	20	33.7	4
68	7-2-1	10	504.4	2	305.9	4	198.5	22	37.6*	4
69	8-1-1	10	448.9	7	290.5	6	158.4	52	33.4	12
70	9-1-0	10	510.5*	2	257.8	14	252.7*	8	33.0	9
71	8-2-0	10	332.9	46	232.1	24	100.8	88	22.5	38
72	8-2-0	10	423.8	7	304.3	4	119.5	74	28.3	18
73	10-0-0	10	461.4	5	350.2*	6	111.2	83	35.8	8
74	9-2-0	11	434.5	4	283.5	11	150.9	29	27.7	16

*Notre Dame record.

DEFENSE

Yr.	TOTAL DEF. YdsPG	Rank	RUSHING YdsPG	Rank	PASSING YdsPG	Rank	SCORING PtsPG	Rank
64	206.3	15	68.7	2	137.6	103	7.7	11
65	194.4	6	75.4	5	119.0	53	7.3	4
66	187.6	4	79.3	9	108.3	20	3.8	2
67	220.1	13	104.3	18	115.8	22	12.4	24
68	249.0	10	79.3	4	169.7	81	17.0	33
69	218.7	4	85.1	6	133.6	31	11.3	13
70	220.7	5	96.2	5	124.5	22	9.7	6
71	198.1	4	86.4	3	111.7	23	8.6	5
72	258.3	13	143.9	26	114.4	28	15.2	29
73	201.2	2	82.4	3	118.8	38	6.6	3
74	195.2	1	102.8	1	92.4	15	12.4	14

Ara's Roster Of Players

Following are the names of the Notre Dame players who appeared in at least one varsity game under Ara. Each year listed is the season the player participated in a game.

A

Achterhoff, Jay '73, '74
Alexander, Harry '65, '66
Allan, Denny '68, '69, '70
Allocco, Frank '72, '73, '74
Allocco, Rich '74
Alvarado, Joe '71, '72, '73
Andler, Ken '74
Andreotti, Pete '64, '65
Arment, Bill '74
Arrington, Dick '64, '65
Atamian, John '64
Azzaro, Joe '65, '66, '67

B

Bake, Tom '74
Balliet, Calvin, '73, '74
Banks, Mike '73, '74
Barnett, Reggie '72, '73, '74
Barz, Bill '68, '69, '70
Bauer, Ed '72, '74
Becker, Doug '74
Belden, Bob '66, '67, '68
Best, Art '72, '73, '74
Bleier, Bob (Rocky) '65, '66, '67
Bolger, Tom '71, '72, '73
Bonder, Frank '74
Bonvechio, Sandy '64
Bossu, Frank '68, '69, '70

Bossu, Steve '74
Bradley, Luther '73
Brantley, Tony '73, '74
Brennan, Terry '67, '68, '69
Brenneman, Mark '71, '73, '7
Briick, Herb '70, '71, '72
Brown, Cliff '71, '72, '73
Brown, Ivan '73
Browner, Ross '73
Buches, Steve '68, '69, '70
Bulger, Jim '70, '71
Bullock, Wayne '72, '73, '74
Burgener, Mike '65, '66, '67
Burgmeier, Ted '74
Buth, Doug '74

C

Capers, Tony '68
Carey, Tony '64, '65
Carney, Mike '74
Carroll, Jim '64
Casper, Dave '71, '72, '73
Chauncey, Jim '74
Christensen, Ross '74
Cieszkowski, John '69, '70, '71, '72
Clements, Jack '71
Clements, Tom '72, '73, '74
Cloherty, John '69, '70, '71
Collins, Greg '72, '73, '74

Grenda, Ed '69
Gullickson, Tom '74
Gulyas, Ed '69, '70, '71
Gustafson, Phil '69
Gutowski, Denny '70, '72

H

Hagerty, Bob '66
Haggar, Joe '70, '72
Hagopian, Gary '69
Haley, Dave '66, '67
Hanratty, Terry '66, '67, '68
Hardy, Kevin '64, '65, '66, '67
Harrison, Randy '74
Harshman, Dan '65, '66, '67
Harchar, John '73
Hartman, Pete '72, '73
Hayduk, George '71, '72, '73
Heaton, Mike '65, '66, '67
Hein, Jeff '71, '72, '73
Hempel, Scott '68, '69, '70
Heneghan, Curt '66, '67, '68
Hill, Greg '71, '72, '73
Holtzapfel, Mike '66, '67, '68
Hooten, Herman '70, '71
Horney, John '64, '65, '66
Huarte, John '64
Huff, Andy '69, '71, '72
Hughes, Ernie '74
Humbert, Jim '69, '70, '71
Hunter, Al '73
Hurd, Bill '67

I

Ivan, Ken '64, '65

J

Jackson, Ernie '68

Jeziorski, Ron '64, '65, '66
Jockisch, Bob '67, '68
Johnson, Pete '74
Johnson, Ron '68, '70

K

Kadish, Mike '69, '70, '71
Kafka, Mike '74
Kantor, Joe '64
Kelleher, Dan '74
Kelly, Chuck '74
Kelly, Gerald '65, '66
Kelly, Jim '64, '66
Kelly, Tim '68, '69, '70
Kennedy, Charles '67, '68, '69
Kiliany, Dennis '67, '68
Kineally, Kevin '73
Klees, Vince '73, '74
Knott, Dan '73
Kondrk, John '70, '71, '72
Kondrla, Mike '68
Konieczny, Rudy '65, '66
Kornman, Russ '72, '73, '74
Kos, Gary '68, '69, '70
Kostelnik, Tom '64
Kucmicz, Mike '65, '66
Kuechenberg, Bob '66, '67, '68
Kunz, George '66, '67, '68

L

Lamantia, Pete '66
Lambert, Steve '68
Landolfi, Chuck '67, '68
Laney, Tom '73, '74
Lauck, Chick '66, '67, '68
Lavin, John '66, '67, '68
Lawson, Tom '67, '69

Leahy, James '68
Lewallen, Brian '68, '69
Likovich, John '74
Lium, John '66
Loboy, Alan '64
Long, Harry '64, '65
Longo, Tom '64, '65
Lopienski, Tom '72, '73, '74
Lozzi, Dennis '72, '73
Lynch, Jim '64, '65, '66

M

MacAfee, Ken '74
Maciag, Dick '70, '72
Maglicic, Ken '64
Mahalic, Drew '72, '73, '74
Malone, Mike '68
Mariani, John '70, '71, '72
Marsico, Joe '66
Martin, Dave '65, '66, '67
Martin, Mark '68
Martin, Mike '70
Marx, Greg '70, '71, '72
Maschmeier, Tom '74
Massey, Jim '69
Mattera, Vince '64
May, Paul '65, '66
McBride, Mike '72, '73
McCoy, Mike '67, '68, '69
McGill, Mike '65, '66, '67
McGinn, Dan '64, '65
McGraw, Pat '70, '71, '72
McGuire, Mike '74
McHale, John '68, '69, '70
McKinley, Tom '66, '67, '68
McLane, Mark '74
McLaughlin, Pat '74
Meeker, Bob '64, '65
Menie, Tom '70, '71

Merkle, Bob '64
Merlitti, Jim '67, '68, '69
Meyer, John '64
Minnix, Bob '69, '70, '71
Miskowitz, Lew '73
Monty, Tim '66, '67, '68
Moore, Elton '73, '74
Moriarty, Kerry '74
Morrin, Dan '71, '72, '73
Mudron, Pat '68, '70
Musuraca, Jim '70, '71, '72

N

Nash, Tom '68, '69
Naughton, Mike '71, '72, '73
Neece, Steve '73, '74
Neidert, Bob '68, '69, '70
Nicola, Norm '64
Niehaus, Steve '72, '73, '74
Nightingale, Chuck '70
Norri, Eric '66, '67, '68
Nosbusch, Kevin '72, '73, '74
Novakov, Dan '69, '70, '71
Novakov, Tony '73, '74

O

O'Brien, Coley '66, '67, '68
O'Connor, Dan '68
O'Donnell, John '72, '74
O'Leary, Tom '65, '66, '67
Olson, Bob '67, '68, '69
O'Malley, Hugh '66
O'Malley, Jim '70, '71, '72
Oriard, Mike '68, '69
O'Toole, Dan '70, '71, '72

P

Page, Alan '64, '65, '66

Papa, Bob '64
Parise, Tom '73, '74
Parker, Larry '70, '71
Parker, Mike '71, '73
Parseghian, Mike '74
Patton, Eric '69, '70, '71
Patulski, Walt '69, '70, '71
Payne, Randy '74
Penick, Eric '72, '73, '74
Pergine, John '65, '66, '67
Ploszek, Mike '74
Pohlen, Pat '73, '74
Pomarico, Frank '71, '72, '73
Pope, Al '69
Poskon, Dewey '67, '68, '69
Potempa, Gary '71, '72, '73
Pszeracki, Joe '73, '74

Q

Quehl, Steve '72, '73
Quinn, Steve '65, '66, '67
Quinn, Tom '66, '67, '68

R

Racanelli, Vito '67
Rankin, George '69, '70
Rassas, Kevin '66, '67
Rassas, Nick '64, '65
Raterman, John '69, '70, '71
Reeve, Dave '74
Regner, Tom '64, '65, '66
Reid, Don '67, '68, '69
Reilly, Jim '67, '68, '69
Reynolds, Tom '67
Rhoads, Tom '65, '66
Robinson, Tyrone '72
Rohan, Andy '73, '74
Roolf, Jim '71, '72

Rudnick, Tim '71, '72, '73
Rufo, John '74
Russell, Marv '73, '74
Rutkowski, Frank '74
Ruzicka, Jim '67, '69
Ryan, Jim '65, '66

S

Sack, Allen '64, '65, '66
Samuel, Al '72, '73, '74
Sarb, Pat '73
Sauget, Dick '64
Sawicz, Paul '73
Scales, Ed '73
Schiralli, Angelo '66
Schivarelli, Pete '69, '70
Schlezes, Ken '70, '71, '72
Schnurr, Fred '66
Schoen, Tom '65, '66, '67
Schumacher, Larry '67, '68
  '69
Seiler, Paul '64, '65, '66
Seymour, Jim '66, '67, '68
Sharkey, Ed '74
Sheahan, Jim '68
Sheridan, Phil '64, '65
Simon, Tim '73
Skoglund, Bill '66
Slager, Rick '74
Smith, Gene '73
Smith, Scott '70 '71
Smith, Sherman '72, '73, '74
Smithberger, Jim '65, '66, '67
Snowden, Jim '64
Snow, Jack '64
Snow, Paul '66, '67, '68
Standring, Jay '68, '69
Steenberge, Pat '70, '71
Stenger, Brian '66, '67, '68

298

epaniak, Ralph '69, '70, '71
ephan, Jack '74
ock, Jim '72, '73, '74
llivan, Tim '71, '72, '73
llivan, Tom '64, '65
sko, Larry '72, '73
vatland, Dick '65, '66, '67
vearingen, Tim '67, '68
veeney, Bob '73, '74
vendsen, Fred '69, '70, '71
vlvester, Steve '72, '73, '74
atko, Greg '72, '73

T

alaga, Tom '64, '65
ereschuk, John '70, '71
heismann, Joe '68, '69, '70
homann, Rick '69, '70, '71
homas, Bob '71, '72, '73
hornton, Pete '64, '65
orrado, Rene '67
ownsend, Mike '71, '72, '73
ownsend, Willie '70, '71, '72, '73
rapp, Bill '69, '70, '71
uck, Ed '66, '67, '68

V

an Huffel, Al '65, '66
asys, Arunas '64, '65

W

Vack, Steve '68
Vadsworth, Mike '64, '65
Valls, Bob '74
Vashington, Bob '71, '72, '73
Vasilevich, Max '73

Webb, Mike '70, '71, '73
Weber, Robin '73, '74
Webster, Mike '64
Weiler, Jim '73, '74
Wengierski, Tim '66
Weston, Jeff '74
Williams, Scott '69
Winegardner, Jim '66, '67, '68
Wisne, Gerald '66, '67, '68
Witchger, Jim '68, '69, '70
Wittliff, Phil '68
Woebkenberg, Harry '74
Wolski, Bill '64, '65
Wright, Jim '68, '69, '70
Wright, Tom '70
Wujciak, Al '73, '74

Y

Yoder, Jim '69, '70

Z

Zanot, Bob '72, '73
Zappala, Tony '73, '74
Ziegler, Ed '67, '68, '69
Zielony, Dick '69, '70
Zikas, Mike '69, '70, '71
Zimmerman, Jeff '67, '68
Ziznewski, Jay '68
Zloch, Bill '64, '65
Zloch, Chuck '68, '69, '70
Zloch, Jim '72, '73
Zubek, Bob '66
Zuber, Tim '70
Zurowski, Dave '64, '66

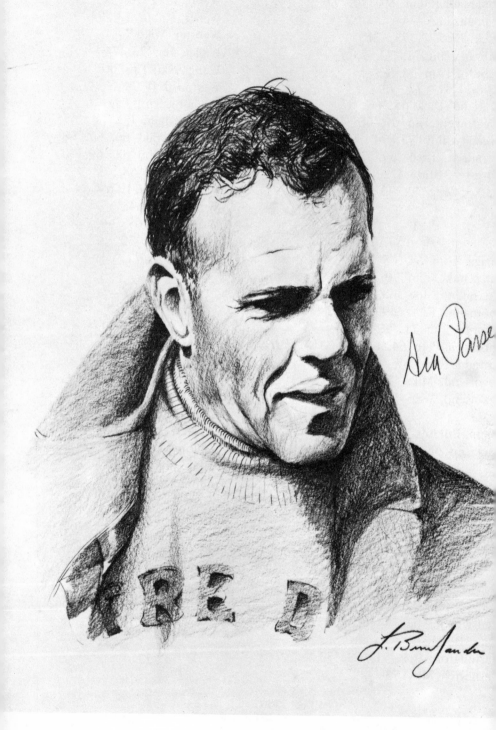

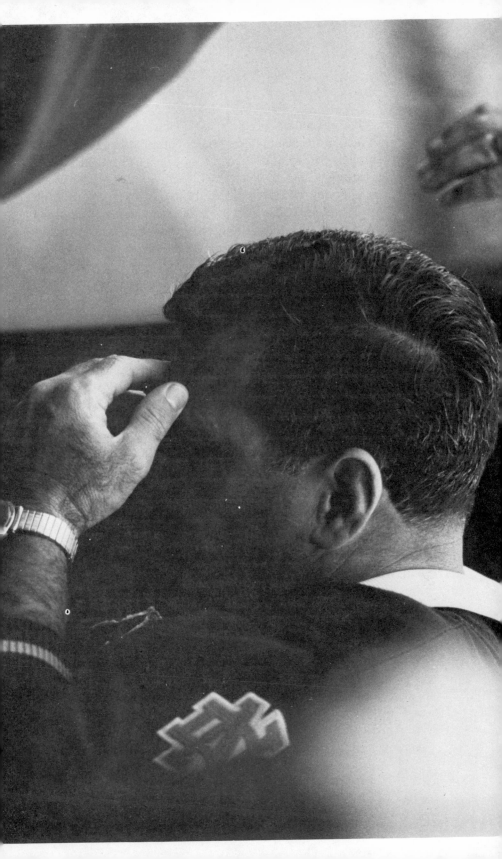

NOTE

Ara Parseghian has been a head coach since 1951. He was the head man at his alma mater, Miami University of Ohio, from 1951 through 1955, and then became head coach at Northwestern through 1956 to 1963. His Northwestern teams gained four straight victories over Notre Dame from 1959 through 1962 (30-24, 7-6, 12-10 and 35-7). Parseghian then came to Notre Dame in December, 1963, to become the school's 22nd head football coach. Ara's 24-year record shows 170 victories, 57 defeats, and 6 ties. His 100th win, a 51-0 victory over Southern Cal in 1966, clinched the National Title for the Irish.

Parseghian was born in Akron, Ohio, on May 21, 1923. After graduating from high school there, he enlisted in the Navy and while in service played football under Paul Brown at Great Lakes. Following his discharge, he entered Miami University of Ohio where he competed in football, baseball, and basketball. He won All-Ohio halfback honors and received All-America mention in 1947 when Miami played in the Sun Bowl.

Following his graduation, Parseghian played with the Cleveland Browns until an injury brought a quick end to his professional playing career. He launched his coaching career when he returned to Miami as an assistant to Woody Hayes in 1950, and moved up to the head coaching position when Hayes went to Ohio State the following year.

Parseghian has gained numerous honors. In 1964 he was named Co-coach of the Year by the American Football Coaches Association. He was also named Coach of the Year by the Football Writers of America, by the Washington Touchdown Club, the Columbus Touchdown Club, the *Football News*, and the *New York Daily News*.

Ara is married to the former Kathleen Davis, whom he met while both were students at Miami. They have two daughters, Karan and Kristan, and a son Mike.

Tom Pagna, an accomplished public speaker and writer as well as football coach, began his association with Ara Parseghian as a player at Miami of Ohio in 1950. Pagna was twice named All-American and three times chosen to the All-Ohio and Mid-American Conference teams. As the team captain in 1953 he was named most valuable player while setting school rushing records on a career and season basis. He was the only Parseghian-coached running back ever to gain more than 1,000 yards in a season. He is a member of the Miami Hall of Fame and the Summit County Hall of Fame in his hometown of Akron, Ohio.

Upon graduation he played in the National Football League for the Cleveland Browns and Green Bay Packers. He later joined Parseghian's staff at Northwestern, where he earned a master's degree in education. He continued with Ara at Notre Dame. Upon Parseghian's resignation as head coach after the 1974 season, Pagna became executive director of the Notre Dame Alumni Association. He is currently employed in the insurance field.

Pagna and Parseghian co-authored the book *Parseghian and Notre Dame Football* for Doubleday, and Pagna is in constant demand as an after-dinner speaker. He is married to the former Shirley Leib, and they have two daughters, Sandy and Susan.

Bob Best joined the Notre Dame Sports Information staff in 1973 after serving as assistant director of public relations for the Pittsburgh Pirates. Prior to that he was a sports reporter for the *Cincinnati Post and Times-Star*.

Best was graduated from Notre Dame in December 1971. While there the Cincinnati native was a student assistant in the Sports Information Department for three years and a sports announcer for WSND. He earned a master's degree in communications from Notre Dame, writing his thesis on promotions. In his current position he has edited nine award-winning sports publications. Best is married to the former Letty Marie Constantino.